The Twelve Baptist Tribes in the United States

The Twelve Baptist Tribes in the United States

A Historical and Statistical Analysis

Albert W. Wardin, Jr.

Baptist History and Heritage Society

Fields Publishing, Inc.
Nashville, Tennessee

Printed in the United States of America
Library of Congress Control Number 2007923231
ISBN: 978-1-57843-038-3

published by

Baptist History and Heritage Society
www.baptisthistory.org
151 Broadleaf Dr.
Macon, GA 31210
406-600-7433
bhhs@baptisthistory.org
and

6545 Chessington Drive • Nashville, Tennessee 37221
615-972-8402
e-mail: tfields 6545@gmail.com

Contents

Abbreviations

ABA	American Baptist Association
ABC	American Baptist Convention
ABC/USA	American Baptist Churches in the USA
BBF	Baptist Bible Fellowship
BGC	Baptist General Conference
BMA	Baptist Missionary Association of America
CBA	Conservative Baptist Association of America
CEN	Central Baptist Association
DR	Duck River and Kindred Associations
ENT	Enterprise Baptists
FBF	Fundamental Baptist Fellowship
FW	National Association of Free Will Baptists
FW-IND	Unaffiliated Independent Free Will Baptist Associations
FW-OR	Convention of Original Free Will Baptists
GARBC	General Association of Regular Baptist Churches
GEN	General Association of General Baptists
IBFI	Independent Baptist Fellowship International
IBFNA	Independent Baptist Fellowship of North America
IFA	Independent Fundamental Churches of America
IL	Unaffiliated Independent Landmark Missionary Baptist churches
IL-ASSN	Unaffiliated Independent Landmark Missionary Baptist associations
IL-SG	Independent Landmark–Sovereign Grace Baptist churches
INTER	Interstate and Foreign Landmark Missionary Baptist Association
JAS & PV	Jasper and Pleasant Valley Baptist Associations
NAB	North American Baptist Conference
NB	National Baptists
NBC	National Baptist Convention, USA, Inc.
NBCA	National Baptist Convention of America, Inc.
NH	New Hope Baptist Association
NMBC	National Missionary Baptist Convention
NPR	National Primitive Baptist Convention, Inc.
NTA	New Testament Association of Independent Baptist Churches
NTA/CAL	New Testament Association/Fellowship of Fundamental Baptists of California
NTA/IMBF	New Testament Association/Inter-Mountain Baptist Fellowship
NTA/ILL	New Testament Association/Association of Independent Baptist Churches of Illinois
NTA/IN	New Testament Association/Indiana Fundamental Baptist Fellowship of Churches
NTA/MICH	New Testament Association/Independent Fundamental Baptist Association of Michigan
NTA/MS	New Testament Association/Mountain States Baptist Fellowship
NTA/SD	New Testament Association/Dakota Baptist Association
NTA/WIS	New Testament Association/Wisconsin Fellowship of Baptist Churches
OL	Primitive Baptists–Old Line
OR	Old Regular Baptists
PNB	Progressive National Baptist Convention, Inc.

PR	Primitive Baptists–Predestinarian
PrE	Eastern District of Primitive Baptists
PRO	Progressive Primitive Baptists
REF	Reformed Baptists
REG	Regular Baptists
SBC	Southern Baptist Convention
SD	Seventh Day Baptist General Conference
SEP	Separate Baptists in Christ
SG	Sovereign Grace Baptists
SIX PR	Six Principle Baptists
ST	Strict Baptists
SWBF	Southwide Baptist Fellowship
T-S	Two-Seed-in-the-Spirit Predestinarian Baptists
UN	Primitive Baptists—Universalists
UNI	United Baptists
UNAFWB	United American Free Will Baptist Church
UNAFWB-CONF	United American Free Will Baptist Conference
WBF	World Baptist Fellowship
WT	Wayne Trail Missionary Baptist Association

Preface

From an early age I have had an interest in Baptist history. I asked my father, "Who started the Baptists in America?" He responded, "Roger Williams." At the time this satisfied me, but later I began to realize the complexity of the Baptist story. Our family, which lived in Oregon, was then a member of the German Baptist Conference in America (today the North American Baptist Conference). We were conscious of the fact that we were different from the "English" Baptists, not only in culture, but also with feelings of moral superiority.

As a young man, I saw firsthand the division in the 1940s within Northern Baptist ranks between supporters of the Convention and the Conservatives, a split that was particularly acute in Oregon. For some years, I taught in two Conservative Baptist institutions in the state—Western Seminary and Judson Baptist College. The president of Western Seminary forced my termination when I refused to sign a doctrinal statement that included an eschatological clause that I believed was unbiblical. I felt my rights as a Baptist had been infringed. In any case, I was forced to find another Baptist teaching position—this time at Belmont University, a Southern Baptist school in Nashville. I was now in a different cultural area and in a denomination that had its own special historic development.

In 1980, my interest in Baptist history led me to produce *Baptist Atlas*, which looked at Baptists worldwide but included in the section on the United States maps, diagrams, a classification of Baptist bodies, and a regional geography. In 1995, I edited *Baptists Around the World*, providing much of the text, but also including a classification of Baptist bodies, a historical diagram of Baptist bodies, and also a special feature—listing by state the various Baptist groups with statistics. At the same time, I continued to write in other areas, notably Eastern European Baptist history and a history of Baptists in Tennessee. When Deborah Van Broekhoven, executive director of the American Baptist Historical Society, raised the question, "Why so many different Baptists?," the Baptist History and Heritage Society asked me to write a pamphlet, *Doing Diversity Baptist Style: Major Variations*, which was published in 2001.

This volume is therefore the culmination of a lengthy process. I am in debt to the many different kinds of Baptists I personally contacted, who almost invariably gave me the information I sought. I greatly appreciate the fine services and resources of the Southern Baptist Historical Library and Archives in Nashville. Except for the research of such men as Howard Dorgan, Clifford A. Grammich, Jr., and Robert L. Vaughn of Mt. Enterprise, Texas, this work would be much poorer in descriptions of many smaller Baptist bodies. Dorgan and Grammich have published notable work on the smaller Baptist groups in Appalachia. Vaughn provided me with minutes and lists of associations and churches as well as sending me carefully detailed descriptions of various Baptist groups and their factions.

I also have had a fruitful tie with the *Religious Congregations and Membership* study, published every ten years, and its sponsoring organization, the Association of Statisticians of American Religious Bodies. I particularly appreciate my relationship with its Liaison for Data Collection, Richard Houseal, a member of the Church of the Nazarene. The study provided me with excellent statistical data, much of which appears in this volume. In turn, I have been able to provide the study with my own research of Baptist bodies. I greatly appreciate the contribution of Michael Thomasson, programmer analyst at the Church of the Nazarene, for the beautifully and carefully done maps, none of which were previously published, that he provided me for this volume. I also thank the Glenmary Research Center for the rights of publication.

I hope that this work will not only provide data for researchers and students of Baptist life but will bring appreciation for the contributions of each Baptist body. More knowledge perhaps will bring greater understanding, and greater understanding may bring greater forbearance, and greater forbearance should help one to see more the commonalities in the Baptist denomination rather than simply its divisions.

Introduction

Baptists in the United States, numbering 28,000,000 adherents in over 95,000 congregations, are the largest Protestant denomination in the nation. Baptist churches are not only in every state but are located in more counties or county-equivalents than any other denomination—3,036 out of 3,141. United Methodists with 3,003 and Roman Catholics with 2,987, however, are close behind. Baptists predominate in 1,287 counties, more than any other denomination.[1]

Baptists had no founding father. Lutherans claim Luther, the Reformed claim Zwingli and Calvin, and Methodists claim Wesley, but Baptists have no prime mover. John Smyth, the first Baptist in Europe, and Roger Williams, the first Baptist in America, although advocating believer's baptism, were never immersed nor remained Baptists for any length of time.

The Baptist denomination arose out of the Protestant Reformation and accepted its basic tenets—Scripture as sole authority (*sola scriptura*), justification by faith, priesthood of the believer (or soul competency), and private interpretation of Scripture. But Baptists went further, claiming they were more consistent in bringing these principles to their logical conclusion. As advocates of both Scriptural authority and soul competency, they created, however, a tension within their system of belief that has not always been successfully resolved.

Unlike most other Protestants who accepted a church-state establishment, sacramentalism, baptism of infants, and affusion or sprinkling in baptism, Baptists rejected the first three propositions and, shortly thereafter, the fourth. Baptists taught that one was not grafted by baptism into the church but by personal conversion through repentance and faith. Baptism was by immersion and for believers only. As dissenters, they became noted advocates of separation of church and state and religious liberty. Baptists were a unique amalgam. Although accepting mainline Protestant theology, at the same time they were sectarians in polity, like Anabaptists—advocating congregational church government and separation of church and state and rejecting infant baptism.

Baptists were treading treacherous ground. They shocked fellow Protestants and brought upon themselves repression from state authority as schismatic and a threat to public order. In both Europe and America, Baptists faced persecution.

However, because of their growth and success in America, Baptists have tended to look upon their development as generally onward and upward. Although recognizing their small beginnings, the jubilee volume in 1964, *Baptist Advance*, clearly epitomized this mindset. A closer look at Baptist life will detect more of an ebb and flow with periods of difficulty and serious challenge alternating with periods of significant advance.

The first century of American Baptist life, beginning in 1638 in Providence, Rhode Island, was a time of meager beginnings. By 1740, Baptists in the colonies constituted only sixty churches with a membership a bit over 3,100.[2] The next period, beginning in the mid-eighteenth century and into the first decades of the nineteenth century, was a period of boom for Baptist growth. It included the First and Second Great Awakenings for a significant forward thrust. The next era, covering the middle of the nineteenth century, even with continuing growth was filled with serious theological, political, and racial division. In the next period, from the last of the nineteenth and into the early twentieth century, Baptists demonstrated a progressive spirit, which was then followed by a period of reaction, acrimonious debate, and financial distress. A new period after the Second World War witnessed impressive expansion. Perplexity, uncertain growth, and a less inviting environment, however, have beset Baptists during the last several decades.

More than forty years ago, Ernest A. Payne, general secretary of the Baptist Union of Great Britain, wrote an article on Baptists in the United States, stating, "The bewildering disarray, which the flourishing Baptists of the United States manifest is as confusing to the average American as it is to the on-looking Englishman."[3] In his study of the development of Baptists in New England, William G. McLoughlin, professor of history at Brown University, noted, even in their early years, their great diversity. He wrote, "It is no more possible to speak of 'the Baptists' than it is to speak of 'the Indians' in seventeenth-century America because there were too many different kinds of them."[4]

At the beginning, Baptists in England appeared as twins—General or Arminian Baptists, on the one hand, and Calvinistic or Particular or Regular Baptists, on the other. Another division appeared between those who worshiped on the first day of the week and others who worshiped on the seventh. These divisions also appeared in seventeenth-century Rhode Island, the first center of Baptist life in America.

The story of division does not stop here but continues to the present. One reason is the Baptist advocacy of soul liberty or the priesthood of the believer and its corollary, congregational church government or local church autonomy. In spite of the Baptist claim that they are people of the Book, culture and environmental influences have also molded them. Baptists seemingly have a proclivity for separating even from those with whom they agree on the fundamentals of the faith but disagree on other points. The comic strip, Kudzu, in March, 2000, portrayed its pastor fervently preaching, "...and the lion shall lay down with the lamb...and one day we shall put aside our differences...black and white...catholic and protestant...Arab and Israeli...Baptist and Baptist!"

In a recent article in the *Journal of Mennonite Studies*, "Conflict and the Telling of North American Mennonite History," Fred Kniss wrote, "To quote more than one author, conflict and schism is the *Täuferkrankheit*, the Anabaptist malady."[5] He and others use the German word, *"Krankheit"* or "sickness" to describe numerous divisions among the Anabaptist descendants, who some consider are forefathers of the Baptists. The authors of the work, *Anabaptist World USA*, divide the Anabaptist groups in the United States into four tribes, with Mennonites as one tribe. Although Mennonites in the United States number around 250,000, they include thirty distinct bodies.[6]

Perhaps Baptists also have a *"Krankheit"* that one might call the "Baptist sickness." In any case, whether one feels the divisions are God-ordained or perpetrated by man, the truth is that this is the Baptist reality in the United States today. In my study, I list fifty-three distinct Baptist bodies. For organizational purposes, I also include three additional entries for independent churches and associations that are not distinctive in faith and order. My list ranges from the Southern Baptist Convention, with more than sixteen million members in over 42,000 churches, to the General Six Principle Baptists, now reduced to one church with fifteen members. In turn, I place the bodies by ideology into twelve tribes, the designation of tribe taken from the work on the Anabaptists.

Since there is no one standard list, some may argue for even more groups or may have a different list.[7] Robert G. Gardner, a student of Baptist bodies, tended to include any group with the word "Baptist" in its title.[8] I am a little more particular. In any case, it is not easy to make a list. I feel a group needs to have had a historical relationship to the Baptist movement and maintain basic Baptist theology and polity. On this basis I place some groups elsewhere, even with the Baptist name, such as the Christian Baptist Church of God in the Holiness category and the Holiness Baptist Association, the Evangelical Baptist Church, and the Pentecostal Free Will Baptist Church with the Pentecostals. German Baptist Brethren groups are clearly related to fellow Anabaptists, not Baptists.

I am also careful concerning an undue multiplication of Baptist bodies. One would have a multitude of different bodies and a list of ridiculous length if one counted each independent association as a separate entity. These independent associations must be grouped generically. Students of Baptist bodies have put associations with the same name as "Missionary Baptist," "Regular Baptist," "United Baptist," and "Free Will Baptist" into general classifications. Some associations may simply carry the name "Baptist" but are, however, placed in a category based on doctrine and perhaps also relationships. In two of the tribes, I have created "Independent" categories to include associations and churches that belong to no national body.

Another problem is the large number of ethnic conventions, associations, and fellowships that have been accelerating in recent years. Ethnic bodies that have organized as independent bodies are listed in a section of their own under the tribal designation of Conservative Evangelical (North) but exclude bodies that are part of some other larger Baptist body. Ethnics that include more than one organization, such as Slavic/Russian, which have five, and African-American Free Will Baptists, which have seven, are each counted as one although the organizations in each group are separately listed.

I do not list missionary organizations, such as the Lott Carey Baptist Foreign Mission Convention, as separate denominations. Even though described, I also do not count as separate denominations bodies that are more like parachurch or mission groups with many of their supporting churches members of another Baptist body and with no ecclesiastical and theological accountability between their supporters and the parent body. In addition, I do not list fellowships that are primarily extensions of a single church or school, such as the Liberty Baptist Fellowship of Lynchburg, Virginia.

Whatever the number of Baptist groups, the question remains—why so much diversity? Baptists have a number of principles in common—Biblical authority, baptism of believers only, immersion, soul liberty, and congregational church government. But what factors have caused division? One is *theology*. The old division between Arminian and Calvinist is not as basic as it formerly was, but it still exists. More important today is the division between liberals and fundamentalists, with various degrees of moderates in between, over biblical inerrancy, hermeneutics, confessional accountability, the character and work of Christ, the primary mission of the church, and ecumenical cooperation. A second division is *successionism*. This includes differences over Baptist origins, identifying the Kingdom with the Church, and tracing a Baptist succession to the Apostolic Age. A third is *culture and ethnicity*. Racial and ethnic differences have produced numbers of groups. Cultural dissimilarities and folkways also play a role. *Means* is a fourth category, often related to cultural differences. In this category are groups that focus on local church autonomy and reject (possibly aside from associational fellowship) various degrees of centralized authority and possibly also cooperative mission, educational, and social activity.

In time of controversy and division, bodies tend to make some aspect in their Baptist arsenal into an overriding principle, possibly even considering it redemptive. Such principles as predestination, creationism, confessionalism, separation, independence, freedom, successionism, and eschatology, valuable in themselves, become ends in themselves, destroying perspective and balance, and become denominational barriers.

Although these factors help to explain Baptist diversity, the situation is even more complex. Various combinations and overlapping of factors have produced a variety of results. To make it even more difficult, some Baptists have shifted categories. With all of this in mind, this work proposes the following twelve tribal categories:

- Ecumenical Mainline
- National (African-American)
- Conservative Evangelical (Northern)
- Fundamental (Northern)
- Conservative Evangelical (Southern)
- Fundamental (Southern)
- Landmark
- General/Free Will
- Old-Time
- Primitivists
- Progressive Primitive
- Neo-Calvinist
  - Ethnic (as a sub-category.)

The work will first describe each tribe with

its respective bodies and then will follow with a section on their numerical distribution by region and state.

A statistical analysis of Baptist groups also presents its own special problems. Although a number of bodies gather their own statistics and report to the *Religious Congregations and Membership* study, many do not. This is particularly true of National, Fundamental, Old-Time, Primitivist, and Neo-Calvinist bodies. In some cases, statistics may be obtained from printed minutes that record congregational statistics. Many times, however, one must resort to estimates, depending upon knowledgeable authorities. At times the best strategy is to use as a standard the average church membership of a body for another that is ideologically related but with no such data. Another problem is that a congregation may have two or even more affiliations. This is particularly the case with National and Fundamental congregations. One must then take particular care to ensure that Baptist statistics are thereby not unduly inflated.

With all the diversity among Baptists, are there commonalities or a substantial core that identifies all Baptists? Although acknowledging there are commonalities, Bill J. Leonard in his book, *Baptist Ways: A History*, declares that Baptist identity is best defined by diversity and an evolving identity, believing it is both impractical and fruitless to duplicate principles of a past age. Such an approach leaves the impression that, because of controversy and change, Baptist values are open-ended, dependent on changing circumstances.[9]

It is, of course, not surprising that a denomination that has existed for centuries is affected by outside circumstances and has experienced numerous variations. In fact, this work on the twelve tribes substantiates this view. On the other hand, it is important to discern the commonalities of a denomination to understand it. Variation itself does not mean basic principles are necessarily overshadowed or overcome. One should also guard against taking the views of individuals, who were exceptions in their time, or views being formulated while a denomination is defining itself as an argument that a denomination in its basics has always been in a state of flux.

Although it was born with two different centers—Arminian and Calvinist—-the mainstream of Baptist life has remarkably accommodated both Calvinist and Arminian elements throughout its history. In comparison to other major Protestant denominations in the country, Baptists, aside from a comparatively small minority of liberal and moderate elements who adopt no confessional standard, have held probably more closely to doctrine and practice and traditional values than most any mainline body. Among practically all the tribes, the great commonalities of the past, whatever the variations and tensions, continue the legacy of the forefathers. This heritage includes such items as congregationalism, anti-sacerdotalism, anti-sacramentalism, believer's baptism, immersion, biblical authority, the supernatural character of the gospel, confessional accountability, and support for religious liberty. If one takes time to notice, one should be able to see that the various tribes have probably far more in common than the elements that divide them.

Baptist Bodies by Tribe

Ecumenical Mainline
National
Conservative Evangelical (Northern)
Fundamental (Northern)
Conservative Evangelical (Southern)
Fundamental (Southern)
Landmark
General/Free Will
Old-Time
Primitive
Progressive Primitive
Neo-Calvinist

I. Ecumenical Mainline

	MEMBERSHIP	ATTENDANCE	CHURCHES
American Baptist Churches/USA (1907)	1,417,543	661,225	5,555

The American Baptist Churches, USA (ABC/USA), formerly known as the Northern Baptist Convention, is one of the major Baptist bodies in the United States. Because of its history and influence in Baptist life, it holds a preeminent position. A number of Baptist bodies have had ties with it, including Southern Baptists, various ethnic Baptist groups, and other bodies that separated from it on doctrinal grounds.

Its membership includes the first two Baptist churches in America, Providence First Baptist (1638) and Newport United (c. 1644), and the first extant church in the Middle Colonies, Pennepack in the Philadelphia area (1688). It includes the oldest extant Baptist church on the West Coast, Oregon City First Baptist (1847), as well as the oldest Baptist church in California, San Francisco First Baptist (1849). ABC/USA also incorporates the oldest regular Baptist association, Philadelphia (1707), which in turn was the first Baptist body in America to adopt a confession of faith (1742). Baptists in the North established the first Baptist college in 1764, formerly known as the College of Rhode Island, today as Brown University.

Its leaders were prime movers in forming the first national Baptist mission society (1814), which continues as the convention's Board of International Ministries. In 1832, its constituents established the American Baptist Home Mission Society, which today is the convention's Board of National Ministries. Baptists in the North also formed the Baptist General Tract Society (1824), later known as the American Baptist Publication Society. For many years, it was the foremost Baptist publishing house in the nation. Its women established woman's mission societies—foreign (1871) and home mission (1877)—that sent out their own missionaries. In 1891, it led in forming the Baptist Young People's Union.

For almost one hundred years, Northern Baptists operated through independent societies. For better coordination, they formed the Northern Baptist Convention in 1907; the societies retained their autonomy, but it began a process of greater centralization. In 1920, it established a Board of General Promotion that prepared a budget for the convention. Four years later it changed its name to The Board of Missionary Cooperation. In 1934, the convention transformed the Executive Committee into a General Council that could act for the convention except in areas that the convention reserved for itself.

The convention changed its name in 1950 to the American Baptist Convention and in 1971 to the American Baptist Churches/USA. In 1972, it established electoral districts, which elected three-fourths of the General Board of the convention; later such elected board members were also designated to represent their regions. Today regions send a limited number of delegates to the general meetings, which since 1972 have become biennial. Such changes in representation have shifted the convention toward a more Presbyterian-type polity. In 1962, American Baptists moved the headquarters of its national agencies into an impressive circular yet functional building at Valley Forge, Pennsylvania.

Its constituency formed numerous educational

institutions, establishing in time about ninety colleges and universities. Over the years many of these institutions have either ceased or continue independent of denominational ties, leaving only fifteen today related to the convention. The evangelical character of these schools and closeness to the denomination varies. The convention has a better record in theological education and currently has ties with nine seminaries or divinity schools, including three that are predominantly African American. In 1911, it organized a Board of Education, which changed its name to Board of Education Ministries, but was closed in 2003. In 1944, it established the American Baptist Assembly at Green Lake, Wisconsin.

American Baptists have produced a number of notable leaders who have had a wide influence outside their own ranks. These include Augustus H. Strong in theology; Walter Rauschenbusch, advocate of the Social Gospel; Helen Barrett Montgomery, first woman president of the convention, mission advocate, and translator of the New Testament; and Harry Emerson Fosdick, pastor at Riverside Church and champion of theological liberalism.

Denominational Characteristics

In 1971, Anthony Compolo, Jr., issued a work, *A Denomination Looks at Itself*, based on a study of Roper Research Associates, which was employed by the convention.[1] Unlike most other Baptists, the study found that the constituency was generally middle and upper middle class. Its members supported education and nurture more strongly than evangelism or revivalism and showed a strong interest in social issues. Its members expected the pastor to possess adequate academic credentials.

The study noted a decline in its traditionally strong support for foreign missions; civil rights and race relations were now of equal concern. This factor reflects at least in part the large percentage of American Baptists who today are African American, but it also indicates a reordering of priorities. In 1907, the convention supported 248 foreign missionaries, but by 1951 it only supported 136. In 2004, the *Mission Handbook* reported 149 missionaries with an income over $15,000,000, a much smaller commitment in comparison to a number of smaller Baptist bodies, but a shift reflected in other mainline denominations.[2]

American Baptists have moved away from their former, more sectarian exclusivity by accepting open communion. A significant number of churches also practice open membership, not requiring believer's baptism by immersion for membership. The denomination is notable for its leadership in the ecumenical movement. It was a charter member of the Baptist World Alliance (1905), the Federal Council of Churches (1908), the World Council of Churches (1948), and the National Council of Churches (1950). The convention, however, permits churches to list non-affiliation and non-support of the National Council of Churches; more than 600 have so registered. A lesser number are also listed for non-support of the World Council of Churches. In 1988, it became an observer body of the National Association of Evangelicals.

The Roper study found that women composed sixty-three percent of its membership, a disproportionate number in relation to the general population. Unlike many other Baptists, American Baptists have been more open to ordaining women, the first ordained in 1882. Its incorporation of the Freewill Baptist Conference of the North in 1911, incorporated a body with a tradition of women's ordinations. In 1965, the convention approved a resolution favoring ordination of women. In 2005, it included 403 women as pastors and 170 as co-pastors. The Roper study also noted that slightly more than sixty-one percent of its members were forty-five years or older with a particularly low percentage in ages eighteen to twenty-four. Only 5.5 percent of its pastors are under thirty-five, indicating an aging pastoral force, also a trend in other mainline denominations.[3]

Unlike the South, which is much more culturally homogeneous and responsive to evangelicalism, its constituency is spread over areas of much ethnic diversity and religious pluralism with Roman Catholics, Lutherans, and Mormons dominating blocks of territories in the North and West. Although it no longer appeals to the lower classes, its higher class status has not brought the appeal one might expect since other bodies, such as Methodists, Presbyterians, and Episcopalians, project a higher social standing.[4]

Although the composition of this body has changed, it still includes many small congregations located in small towns and rural areas. In 1986, the number of small churches had declined to less than fifty percent, but still about fifty-four percent of the churches were in small towns or in the open country and with 225,000 of the resident membership.[5]

Ethnic Diversity

American Baptists have had an outstanding record of reaching ethnic immigrants outside of its Anglo-Saxon core. Welsh Baptists from Europe arrived as early as the seventeenth century. American Baptists did notable work among German and Scandinavian Baptists in the nineteenth century and engaged in concerted evangelistic efforts among the newer immigrants from southern and eastern Europe who arrived in the late nineteenth and early twentieth centuries.[6] The convention still claims five "historically related organizations" with an ethnic heritage. Except for the Latvian Union, ties today with the American Baptists are generally problematic or non-existent except for some individual congregations.

In the nineteenth century, Northern Baptists worked among the freedmen in the South, including the establishment of schools for them, as well as among Native Americans, Mexicans, and Asians. Today some of the most successful work is among the Hispanic and Asiatic populations, in addition to the long-time work that has continued among Indians in Oklahoma and native peoples of Alaska.

In 1920, American Baptists claimed more than 50,000 "New Americans" in 596 churches, representing about four percent of its membership. The 1960 census of American Baptists noted 171 bilingual churches with Hispanic churches constituting the greatest number. In 1988, it claimed almost 29,000 Hispanic resident members (2.5 percent of its membership) and more than 6,000 other non-black ethnic resident members.[7]

The largest non-Anglo body within the convention is its African-American constituency. In 1920, the convention claimed more than 136,000 African Americans in 851 churches, or 10.5 percent of its membership. With its interest in issues of equality and justice, American Baptists have attracted a significant number of African-American Baptist churches since the Second World War. As a result, the convention has now become a fully national body with the creation of an ABC of the South. In 1988, a little more than 1,000 churches (17.6 percent) were African-American. Resident membership for African-Americans was 37.7 percent and 3.1 percent for other minorities.[8] In the author's study, *Baptists Around the World*, 697 African-American congregations were discovered in the 1990s with dual alignment, indicating that possibly around 70 percent of its African-American congregations are dually aligned with a National Baptist body. Since 1970, the convention has maintained an "associated relationship" with the Progressive National Baptist Convention, the most liberal and socially conscious body of black Baptists. On the down side, however, its black constituency is far from involved in the total denominational program.[9] This is in part due to the degree of participation of the pastor and also loyalty to National Baptist bodies to which many African-American churches belong.

The convention has more churches dually aligned with other denominational bodies than any other Baptist body. The 1960 census found that the convention, outside of the National Baptist Conventions, had 286 churches with dual alignments, of which fifty-one were with non-Baptist denominations. In addition, the convention has had an associated relationship with the Church of the Brethren since 1973.

Theological Diversity

Although American Baptists have been the most successful Protestant denomination in America in developing a multi-racial constituency, its theological diversity has caused conflict and has militated against gaining full support from its constituency for a unified program. Instead of the theological tension proving to be creative, it has produced division.

The capture of the old seminaries by theological liberalism and its entrenchment within the leadership caused a conservative reaction with loss of territory to Southern Baptists and the rise of separatist fundamentalist Baptist bodies. In 1907, American Baptists lost the southern third of Illinois to Southern Baptists due to liberalism in the University of Chicago. Later Southern Baptists made inroads into traditional Northern Baptist territory. The conservative forces within the convention formed new conservative seminaries and competitive mission programs. In the liberal-fundamental warfare, which began in 1920, conservatives failed to get the convention to adopt a confession of faith or limit the appointment of missionaries who conservatives felt were objectionable. As a result the convention suffered two defections—General Association of Regular Baptist Churches in 1932 and the Conservative Baptist Association in 1947, which sapped the denomination of evangelical strength. At the same time, two conservative ethnic bodies that had developed within the convention—Baptist General Conference and North American Baptist Conference—went their own way.

Believing failures in the convention were primarily systematic rather than theological, William B. Lipphard, for fifty years an American Baptist editor in missions and a liberal, wrote a biting article in 1952 in which he not only criticized the denomination's declining support for missions but also its failure to maintain unity. [10] In an article in *Christian Century*, Howard Moody, pastor of Judson Memorial Church in New York City, criticized fundamentalists for their attempts at creedal conformity but faulted liberal leadership for suppressing dissent "by political machinations." He claimed that as a result the denomination had "an open wound" with "local churches distrustful of the leaders and by leaders fearful of the local churches."[11] Although overstated, the distrust is still present.

In more recent decades, the American Baptists produced two conservative evangelical renewal groups, the American Baptist Fellowship (ABF), from 1970 to 1983, and the American Baptist Evangelicals (ABE), from 1993 to 2005.[12] At its beginning the latter group disclaimed any intention of division and sought to return the convention to a firm evangelical base.

The issue of welcoming and accepting homosexuals has now become a divisive issue, as it has among other mainline denominations. Two regions have disfellowshiped churches for their open policy. In spite of the adoption by the General Council of the convention in 1992 of a resolution declaring homosexual behavior as "incompatible with Christian teaching," it has retained these churches in the national fellowship and also accepted the Evergreen Association, an affirming body, which was organized after the Northwest Region reorganized to exclude such affirming churches.

Since the national body did not take a strong stand on the issue, another defection began. The ABC of the Pacific Southwest gave notice in 2005 that it was withdrawing from the national body. Other regions were showing dissatisfaction, and individual churches were beginning to withdraw. In 2005–2006, the ABE shifted its position from renewal to advocacy of a new organization, Cornerstone Church Network, for churches both inside and outside the convention that favor a conservative evangelical agenda. On the other hand, others in the convention have resisted any attempt by the national body to define membership. Some have decried division and insist the issue over homosexuality should be only a local church issue.

Membership

In 1910, the convention listed 10,712 congregations, which included churches in border territories. It was the leading Baptist body in all the Northern and Western states. In 1920, after losing border territory to Southern Baptists, it reported 1.2 million members in 9,150 churches. [13]

The membership at the beginning of the twenty-first century had dropped to 5,555 congregations and a membership of a little more than 1.4 million, a number that does not include the most recent defections. The average attendance of 660,000 is approximately 47 percent of the membership. The membership, which includes increasing numbers of ethnics, disguises the serious decline in the convention's Anglo population. While the black, Hispanic, and Asian constituency is between five hundred thousand and six hundred thousand, the white/Anglo constituency is only around 860,000, a net loss of 300,000, since 1920.[14] Because of this decline, coupled with the migration of both black and white Southerners and the vigorous evangelism of southern-oriented Baptists in the North and West, the convention currently is the leading Baptist body in only seven states, five of them in New England.

The decline has several causes. The drop in rural and small-town populations often results in the closing and merging of churches. As already mentioned, the loss of border territory to Southern Baptists, the independence of ethnic bodies, the division over theology, and the competition of more conservative bodies have all taken a serious toll. The convention is now particularly weak in the northern tier of states from Michigan to the Pacific Northwest and, except in West Virginia, has been almost entirely eliminated among the white population in southern-oriented territory. In the Mountain and Pacific Coast states, Southern Baptists are far in the lead, while in this area Conservative Baptists equal American Baptists in attendance. Because of the issue of homosexuality, some of the strongest calls for separation today are in West Virginia and on the Pacific Coast.

In spite of these developments, the convention still maintains a strong constituency among white Baptists in the Northeast from Maine to West Virginia, an area where it leads among the white population. It also maintains a strong band of territory in the lower Midwest from Ohio to Kansas in addition to notable numbers in Colorado and California. It also has a strong presence among African Americans in the major metropolitan areas in the North as well as an African-American constituency in the South.

A majority of its constituents would be considered moderate conservatives with the presence in some areas of a strong conservative evangelical undertow. On the other hand, the convention continues to include an entrenched and influential liberal minority that favors full religious expression and opposes any binding confession. The June, 2002 issue of the *American Baptist Quarterly* on "Crises and Confessions" indicated strong theological differences.[15]

Even though nationally the convention has not adopted a confession of faith, it nevertheless has had concern over theological issues, convening various theological conferences, beginning in Green Lake in 1954. The convention also launched a program of planting new churches. Under new leadership, the ABC of the West experienced renewal and growth,[16] which, however, is today one of the disaffected areas.

In spite of its leadership and many achievements in missions, education, social programs, and interchurch relations, the convention is facing serious problems over its demographics, finances, and unity. It is at another crossroads.

2. National Baptists

		Membership	**Churches**
National Baptist Convention, USA Inc. (1880/1895)		6,000,000	16,000
National Baptist Convention of America, Inc. (1915)		1,850,000	7,000
Progressive National Baptist Convention, Inc. (1961)		372,000	764
National Missionary Baptist Convention (1988)		200,000	701
National Primitive Baptist Convention, Inc. (1907)		53,630	547
Full Gospel Baptist Church Fellowship (1994)		n/a	995
	SUBTOTAL	8,475,630	26,007
	ADJUSTMENT	-665,000	-2,751
TOTAL		**7,810,630**	**23,256**

More than twenty-five percent of Baptists in the United States are National or African-American Baptists. While approaching eight million members, they are one of the largest segments in the denomination. The National Baptist Convention, USA, Inc., alone is the fourth largest religious body in the nation. African-American Baptists have grown significantly since 1881, when they numbered almost 800,000 in around 3,400 churches.[17]

Because of the impossibility of obtaining current numbers, statistics for the first two listed groups are based on the author's own study in the 1990s, which was based primarily on polling presidents of state convention for estimated membership and using statistics from Wardell J. Payne, ed., *Directory of African-American Religious Bodies* (1991). This study closely paralleled the statistics in *Churches and Church Membership in the United States,* 1990, where figures were extrapolated from memberships obtained in Georgia, Tennessee, and Oregon. The author obtained statistics of the National Primitive Baptist Convention primarily from the printed minutes of this group.

Because of dual and independent affiliations, adjustment is also necessary for an adequate picture. The figures includes subtracting the membership of the North and South Carolina state conventions, claimed by both National Baptist, USA, and National Baptist of America, and then adding the statistics of the General Association of Baptists in Kentucky, which is independent of all national conventions. Individual congregations may have dual alignments with other black or white Baptist bodies and are thus over reported, but no adjustment has been made for these relationships that, however, inflate the numbers. On the other hand, the lack of reporting membership for the Full Gospel Baptist Fellowship helps to balance the final figures.

The first black to join a Baptist church was simply referred to as "Jack, a colored man," who united with the church in Newport, Rhode Island, in 1652. It was not until the Great Awakening in the eighteenth century that blacks in any great number became Christians. Their African heritage and the revivalism of the day were a good match. The stress on a personal experience and believer's baptism by immersion, which signified a passing from death to life, brought many blacks to the Baptist faith. Between 1773 and 1775, a certain Palmer, probably Wait Palmer, immersed eight candidates at Silver Bluff plantation in Aiken County, South Carolina.

A leader at Silver Bluff was George Liele, who formed in December, 1777, a church at Yamacraw, near Savannah, Georgia, but who migrated to Jamaica with departing British troops at the end of the Revolutionary War. In January, 1788, Daniel Marshall, a Separate Baptist, formed the First African Baptist Church of Savannah and ordained Andrew Bryan, who had been baptized by Liele. The Savannah church is the oldest continuing African-American Baptist church in the nation.

In her study, *Trabelen' On*, Mechal Sobel documented the formation of eleven black churches before 1800, all in the South. But churches began to appear as well in the North—in New York City (1808), Philadelphia (1809), Trenton (1812), and Wood River in Illinois (1819). Before the end of the Civil War, over 200 black Baptist churches had been formed with a majority in the slave South. These congregations, however, by no means included all black Baptists since many were not in any position to organize their own congregations. Large numbers belonged to multiracial congregations controlled by whites. Others met secretly.

The first black Baptist associations appeared in the Great Lakes region in the North—Providence (1834) and Union (1836) in Ohio, Wood River (1839) in Illinois, followed by others. Black Baptists formed the American Baptist Missionary Convention in 1840 that initially included only two churches, those in New York City and Philadelphia. By 1865, it included forty-eight congregations. In Illinois and Missouri, black Baptists formed the Western Colored Baptist Convention but reorganized in 1864 as the Northwestern and Southern Baptist Convention.

After the end of the Civil War, blacks made a mass exodus from the white churches and formed numerous congregations of their own. In 1866, the Northwestern and Southern Convention united with the American Convention to form the Consolidated American Baptist Missionary Convention. In addition to new associations, state conventions appeared—Kentucky (1865), North Carolina (1867), Arkansas (1867), Virginia (1868), Alabama (1868), Mississippi (1869), Georgia (1870), Louisiana (1872), Tennessee (1872), Florida (1874), Texas (1874), South Carolina (1876), and West Virginia (1878).

Because of the district conventions and the strength of the state conventions, the Consolidated Convention weakened and ceased by 1879. But, in 1880, in Montgomery, Alabama, under the leadership of William W. Colley, a missionary from Nigeria, black Baptists organized the Baptist Foreign Mission Convention of the USA, which National Baptists consider the origin of their current cooperative work. In 1895, black Baptists established The National Baptist Convention, USA, consolidating the Baptist Foreign Mission Convention, the American National Baptist Convention (1886), and the Baptist Educational Convention (1893).

National Baptists have been unable to maintain one national body. In 1897, the Lott Carey Baptist Foreign Mission Convention separated, and the convention itself split in 1915 over control of its publishing board. Since then, the two bodies in the division of 1915 have had subsequent divisions of their own.

National Baptist organization is complex not only because of the establishment of six National bodies but also because of a multitude of state conventions and local associations. In addition, a national convention might relate to two or more state conventions in a single state. It is often confusing to determine relationships since many of the names of the bodies are very similar. Also the name of a body with a similar name to a national body may have no tie to that body. For instance, "Missionary Baptist" or "Progressive" in a state or local body does not necessarily relate that body to the National Missionary Baptist Convention or the Progressive National Baptist Convention.

Both Northern (today American) Baptists and Southern Baptists have provided assistance to black Baptist work. The American Baptist Home Mission Society and the Woman's American Baptist Home Society established twenty-seven educational institutions in the South, providing educational opportunities from common school to university and seminary. Four such schools are still related to American Baptists—Benedict College, Shaw University, Florida Memorial

College, and Virginia Union University. American Baptists also provided institutes for ministerial training. Northern Baptists have always had affiliation of black Baptist churches, which increased at the time of the Civil Rights struggle in recent years. In 1970, American Baptists formed the American Baptist Churches of the South, a regional body, which is predominately African-American.

For years Southern Baptists provided limited funds for missionaries or missionary-teachers and ministerial institutes. With The National Baptist Convention, USA, it established in 1924 the American Baptist Theological Seminary (now American Baptist College) in Nashville, Tennessee, but terminated its support for the institution in 1997. In 1959, Southern Baptists changed the name of its Department of Negro Work to Department of Work with National Baptists. In 1972, they changed the name to Cooperative Ministries with National Baptists and then again, in 1980, to Program of Black Church Relations. In 1975, it began an aggressive program to form Southern Baptist black Baptist churches.

Unlike other Baptist groups, National Baptists are a product of their struggle from slavery to freedom and from segregation to integration and social and political justice. The local Baptist church is more than a religious organization; it serves also as a social institution that provides identity and group solidarity. It is the one institution that blacks themselves control.

Worship is a celebration. The music and the preaching engage the worshiper emotionally and personally—body, soul, and spirit. In addition to congregational singing and special music by individuals, the choir, which is robed and often marches into the sanctuary singing with a rhythmic step or sway, is an important component of the service. Anthems or spirituals may be sung, but increasingly gospel hymns with contemporary sounds and syncopated rhythms have come to the forefront. The preacher generally begins softly and slowly but builds toward a climax, expecting the congregation to respond with "amens" and affirmations. He uses picturesque language, reiteration, and rhythm. Preachers relate biblical stories and themes to contemporary concerns and, by and large, are conservative on moral issues. Unlike white churches, time is not an overriding factor in the length of a service.

Although the pastor of the local church is a proclaimer of the gospel, he is also a community leader and spokesperson for social justice. The black church commingles far more the religious and the secular than the average white congregation. In the civil rights struggle in the mid-twentieth century, Baptist pastors played an important role. The most noteworthy was Martin Luther King, Jr. (1929–1968), who became the primary spokesman for social and political equality. Today a national holiday honors him.

Although National Baptists have had serious debates and divisions, their divisions have not been as divisive as among Caucasian Baptists. Many churches have dual or more relationships, and both leaders and pastors often cooperate across organizational boundaries.

Except for the National Primitive Baptist Convention, the other four National Baptist Conventions are members of the Baptist World Alliance and the Baptist Joint Committee for Religious Liberty. Because of their concern for social justice, the same four are also members of the National Council of the Churches of Christ and three of them also of the World Council of Churches. They have, however, shown very little interest in issues of "Faith and Order" in the ecumenical movement.

National Baptists are facing today serious external and internal pressures.[18] They are increasingly facing competition from Pentecostalism, black Moslems, independent megachurches, and even from white Baptists, such as the Southern Baptist Convention. As other Baptists groups, National Baptists also face such troubling trends as the dropping of the name "Baptist" and the tendency of megachurches to leave behind denominational relations. Support for black nationalism and black theology also threaten traditional Baptist theology.

Older Baptist pastors dominate the leadership, which thus excludes potential leadership from the younger generation. Women compose the great proportion of the membership and have provided much of the work with their teaching, singing, and benevolent and missionary support.

On the other hand, except in the Full Gospel Baptist Church Fellowship, the pastoral ministry is, by and large, closed to them.

Although there has been a rise in the black middle class and blacks have made some significant advances economically, socially, and politically, there are still a large number of blacks that live in poverty. The breakdown of the traditional family structure is of serious concern. Single mothers, forty percent of whom are poor, lead many black households. Two-thirds of black children are born out of wedlock. Although successful in recruiting women, black Baptists have been weak in reaching men, a crucial field when one out of three black men will experience some time in prison, often caught up in the drug culture.[19]

Black Baptists have established numerous congregations, including some megachurches, and multiple association, state, and national bodies with many official positions but yet are weak in cooperation. The cooperative work has at times been hurt by political rivalry and lack of accountability. Unlike most white churches, the black Baptist pastor controls his congregation, and his church is his own domain. The degree of cooperation the church gives to the larger Baptist work is up to him.

The conventions have had great difficulty in developing cooperative programs with each agency, more or less, on its own. Black Baptist support for educational enterprises and home and international missions has been minimal. Although the National Baptist Conventions (except for Primitive Baptists) have foreign mission programs, funds for overseas are limited. Much of the support for personnel on the fields is for non-US personnel with comparatively few American blacks serving abroad. In a study in 1998, it was discovered that only 242 African-Americans of all denominations were serving overseas.[20]

Bibliography

For popular histories written by black Baptists, see Owen D. Pelt and Ralph Lee Smith, *The Story of the National Baptists,* (New York: Vantage Press, 1960), and Leroy Fitts, *A History of Black Baptists,* (Nashville: Broadman Press, 1985). The chapter, "The Black Baptists: The First Black Churches in America," in C. Eric Lincoln and Lawrence H. Mamiya, *The Black Church in the African American Experience,* (Durham: Duke University Press, 1990), 20-46, and reprinted in Everett C. Goodwin, ed., *Baptists in the Balance,* (Valley Forge: Judson Press, 1997, 97-123, is an excellent survey of black Baptists. The works by Mechal Sobel, *Trabelin On': The Slave Journey to an Afro-Baptist Faith,* (Westport, Conn., and London: Greenwood Press, 1979), and Walter F. Pitts, Jr., *Old Ship of Zion: The Afro-Baptist Ritual in the African Diaspora,* (Oxford and New York: Oxford University Press, 1993), describe the African roots in Baptist faith and practice. For studies of black Baptists in the nineteenth century, see James Melvin Washington, *Frustrated Fellowship: Black Quest for Social Power,* (Macon: Mercer University Press, 1986), and William E. Montgomery, *Under Their Own Vine and Fig Tree: The African-American Church in the South, 1865–1900,* (Baton Rouge and London: Louisiana State University Press, 1993). For the contribution of Northern Baptists to black Baptist education, see the two issues, "Pursuit of the Promise: American Baptists and Black Higher Education," *American Baptist Quarterly,* XI/4, (December, 1992), and XII/1 (March, 1993). For blacks and missions in Africa, see Walter L. Williams, *Black Americans and the Evangelization of Africa, 1877–1900,* (Madison: University of Wisconsin Press, 1982) and Sandy D. Martin, *Black Baptists and African Missions: The Origins of a Movement, 1880–1915,* (Macon: Mercer University Press, 1989).

The National Baptist Convention, USA, Inc. (1880/1895)

The National Baptist Convention, U.S.A., Inc. (NBCUS) is the largest and most widespread African-American Baptist body in the nation. Besides a convention in the Bahamas, it includes fifty-seven state conventions. A judicial estimate of its membership is six million. It has attempted to obtain the membership of its cooperating churches but the effort was not completed.

The convention has suffered several defections. Members who objected to the removal of the Foreign Mission Board from Richmond to Louisville and wished to maintain ties with white Baptists formed in 1897 the Lott Carey Baptist Foreign Mission Convention. In 1915, it suffered a serious division upon the formation of the National Baptist Convention of America. Adherents of the new convention supported Richard Henry Boyd in his successful effort to keep the National Baptist Publishing Board, which he had founded in 1896, independent of convention control.

During the administration of J. H. Jackson in 1961, another division occurred with the formation of the Progressive National Baptist Convention because of controversy over tenure and disruptive convention sessions.[21] In the late '90s, the convention suffered scandal with the conviction of its president, Henry J. Lyons, for financial irregularities and fraud.[22] Presidents of the convention wielded immense power because of the political and religious significance of the office; also financial perquisites flowed their way with little or no accountability.

Soon after his election as president in 1999, William J. Shaw in an annual address in September 2000, "A Mirror Moment," reported that the convention faced huge debts, a mortgage of $900,000, which was past due on its headquarters, and five lawsuits. He also noted that the convention had been operating without coordination and checks and balances.[23] Shaw was able to bring stability and renewed respect for the convention. Finances were put in order and the mortgage retired in 2003. Tenure was introduced. The American Baptist College, which faced serious financial difficulties, has made significant financial progress.

The Sunday School Publishing Board of the convention is located in Nashville in a building built in 1925 for its operation. The convention also has home mission, foreign mission, and evangelism boards. It includes a number of auxiliaries—women's, laymen's, moderators', ushers and nurses', and music. It has a Prison Ministry and Criminal Justice Commission, Labor Relations Department, and a Congress of Christian Education. In 1989, it dedicated a magnificent headquarters in Nashville. Although its debt is now liquidated, the convention, however, has been unsuccessful to move all of its agencies into the building.

Contributions from the churches for foreign missions continue to go to both the Lott Carey Convention and the Foreign Mission Board of the convention. The Lott Carey Convention works in seven countries in Africa, two in the Caribbean, as well as in Guyana and India. In the *Mission Handbook, 2004–2006*, the Foreign Mission Board reported an annul income of almost $600,000 but support for only three American missionaries and seven non-Americans in ten countries.[24]

Bibliography

J. H. Jackson composed *A Story of Christian Activism: The History of the National Baptist Convention, USA, Inc.*, (Nashville: Townsend Press, 1980), which included a defense of his administration as president of this body. Three insightful accounts of the convention, written by Qinton Hosford Dixie, Aldon D. Morris and Shayne Lee, and David Emmanuel Goatley, are in David A. Rosen and James R. Nieman, eds., *Church, Identity, and Change,* (Grand Rapids and Cambridge, U.K.: William B. Eerdmans, 2005), 327-99. A helpful article is John W. Kinney, "The National Baptist Convention of the United States of America: 'Give Us Free,'" *American Baptist Quarterly*, XIX/3 (September, 2000), 232-44.

The National Baptist Convention of America, Inc. (1915)

The National Baptist Convention of America (NBCA) was formed in 1915 by those who left the National Baptist Convention, USA, in opposition to its incorporation and in support of the private ownership of the National Baptist Publishing Board. It claims, also as the parent body, the year 1880 as the date of its origin.

In 1986, the NBCA changed course and incorporated. Ironically it also entered into conflict with the National Baptist Publishing Board and its successful Sunday School and Training Union Congress over control and established its own publishing board and congress. Opponents to these measures formed in 1988 the National Missionary Baptist Convention.

The NBCA has always played a secondary role in relation to the much larger NBC/USA. It is not as well distributed with particular weakness in the Northeast. It lists thirty-six state bodies including the North Carolina and South Carolina state bodies that are also claimed by the NBC/USA. It has particularly strong support in Texas where it relates to five state bodies.

The convention has eleven boards as well as women's, brotherhood, ushers', and nurses' auxiliaries. Its foreign board has work in the Virgin Islands, Jamaica, Haiti, Panama, and Ghana. In 1998, it reported an income of $222,000 for its overseas ministry with support for eighty-seven non-U.S. mission personnel. Twenty-six U.S. personnel served short-term (less than a year).[25] The NBCA has developed CAP (Covenant Action Plan) to encourage its affiliates, churches, and individuals to give systematically to its cooperative program.

National Missionary Baptist Convention of America (1988)

At a "Restoration Meeting" in Dallas, Texas, members of the National Baptist Convention of America who supported an autonomous National Baptist Publishing Board and its National Baptist Sunday School and Baptist Training Union Congress formed a new convention—the National Missionary Baptist Convention of America (NMBCA). The new body adopted tenure for its officers. As its parent body (until 1986), it was unincorporated.

The NMBCA has five boards, including boards for home and foreign missions. Its Foreign Board has interests in Belize and Zimbabwe. As other National conventions, it also has a number of auxiliaries

The convention is closely aligned with the National Baptist Publishing Board, whose primary name since 2000 is R. H. Boyd Publishing Corporation, and its Sunday School and Training Union Congress. [26] From 1989 through 1999, the Publishing Board gave to the NMBCA around $785,000 in cash and in-kind contributions.[27] Since 1899 the Publishing Board has published the *National Baptist Union-Review*, the oldest National Baptist periodical in the nation.

The convention is limited in its geographical distribution. Only around twelve state conventions relate to it with several of them also relating to the National Baptist Convention of America. Its greatest strength is in Texas and California

Bibliography

For historical data on the National Missionary Baptist Convention, see the historical section of its *Journals*, which includes an account of the Restoration Meeting of November 15, 1988.

Progressive National Baptist Convention, Inc. (1961)

In November, 1961, in Cincinnati, thirty-three delegates, led by L. Venchael Booth, founded the Progressive National Baptist Convention (PNBC). They broke with the National Baptist Convention, USA, in a controversy with J. H. Jackson, its president, over tenure and disruption in convention sessions. The new body soon gained the support of Martin Luther King, Jr., and his supporters for a more radical program than Jackson advocated in the civil rights struggle. The new convention established tenure for all officials and a unified budget.

The Progressive Convention placed its headquarters in Washington, D.C. It includes various departments for laymen, women, young adults, youth, ushers, moderators, health ministries, and missions. Its missions department supports holistic programs in Haiti and Kenya.

As its name implies, the PNBC is a socially activist body, the most involved of any National Baptist body. Benevolence is not confined to traditional Baptist programs but includes support for such agencies as the NAACP, Urban League, Operation Push, and the Martin Luther King, Jr. Center for Non-violent Social Change.

It is difficult to ascertain the convention's membership. In 1974, it enrolled 1,130 churches, of which 718 reported a membership of 360,000 or a possible estimated membership of 550,000. In 1991, its church membership roster listed 764 churches in the USA. A number of its churches continue to relate to the National Baptist Convention, USA, and a number are also aligned with the American Baptist Churches/USA. Since 1970, the PNBC has been an "associated organization" of the latter body. In 1997, the PNBC became aligned with the District of Columbia Baptist Convention, already aligned with American and Southern Baptists.

Bibliography

William D. Booth, *A Call to Greatness: The Story of the Founding of the Progressive National Baptist Convention,* (Lawrenceville, VA: Brunswick Publishing Corporation, 2001). Booth's narrative without the appendices was published in the *American Baptist Quarterly,* XX/1 (March, 2001), 72-93. Also see Wallace C. Smith, "Progressive National Baptist Convention: The Roots of the Black Church," *American Baptist Quarterly*, XIX/3 (September, 2000), 245-59.

The National Primitive Baptist Convention, Inc. (1907)

The National Primitive Baptist Convention, USA (NPBC) has roots in the Primitive Baptist movement, but today, except for a few minor features, is much like other National Baptist bodies. In 1907, it formed a convention and has boards and auxiliaries as other National Baptists. Besides departing from its Calvinist tenets, its churches accept Sunday schools, youth organizations, musical instruments in worship, and revivals. Its pastors exchange pulpits with other National Baptists. On the other hand, its members continue to practice footwashing and use "elder" in addressing their pastors.

The convention has a Board of Evangelism and Missions that is devoted to evangelistic efforts and missions at home but not abroad. The headquarters of its Publishing Board is in Tallahassee, Florida. Its official organ is, *The New Clarion*. The convention is not a member of the Baptist World Alliance nor any ecumenical councils.

It is a comparatively small body with many churches with small memberships. It has a little over 50,000 members in 547 churches, located primarily in the South. Its greatest strength is in Florida, followed by Alabama and then Tennessee.

Some National Primitive Baptist associations do not cooperate with the national body. In addition, a number of black Primitive Baptist congregations continue as traditional Primitive Baptists in faith and practice.

Bibliography

The section, "National Primitive Baptist Convention of the United States of America" in Arthur C. Piepkorn's, *Profiles in Belief,* (New York: Harper & Row, 1978), II, 447-48, provides some limited theological and historical data. For National Primitive Baptists in Florida, see George Patterson McKinney, Sr., and Richard I. McKinney, *History of the Black Baptists of Florida, 1850–1985,* (Miami: Florida Memorial College Press, 1987), 269-72.

Full Gospel Baptist Church Fellowship (1994)

A new and dynamic black Baptist body is the Full Gospel Baptist Church Fellowship (FGBCF) founded in 1994 under the leadership of Paul S.

Morton, Sr., pastor of the Greater St. Stephen Baptist Church of New Orleans. Morton was formerly a member of the Church of God in Christ, a Pentecostal body. Its churches, although structured like National Baptist congregations, observe a Pentecostal style of worship and practice gifts of the Holy Spirit, including speaking in tongues and divine healing.

Pastors are called senior elders and include women. Over the churches is an episcopal hierarchy, which includes a Bishop's Council and a College of Bishops in addition to overseers on the general, state, and district levels. It has developed a Full Gospel Baptist Sunday school curriculum. It sponsors a Full Gospel Baptist Bible College with classes online.

Although the greater number of its churches are Baptist, the movement has attracted congregations outside Baptist ranks. Numerous churches in the National Baptist Conventions have affiliated with the movement, such as the large Mount Zion Baptist Church of Nashville, Tennessee, which has grown very rapidly to 15,000 members. The FGBCF lists around 1,000 churches in thirty-six states, but membership is undetermined. Its greatest strength is in the South and the Great Lakes region but is comparatively weak in the Northeast. Outside the USA, the FGBCF has churches in Africa, Asia, Europe, the Bahamas, and Canada with church planting in Africa and India.

Bibliography

Information on the Full Gospel Baptist Church Fellowship may be found on its web-site at www.fullgospelbaptist.org.

III. Conservative Evangelical (Northern)

	MEMBERSHIP	ATTENDANCE	CHURCHES
Baptist General Conference (1852/1879)	140,925	200,651	866
Conservative Baptist Association of America (1947)	224,306*	224,306	1,191
North American Baptist Conference (1843/1865)	47,112	49,762	290
Seventh Day Baptist General Conference (1671/1802)	4,940	2,992	81
TOTAL	**417,283**	**477,711**	**2,428**

*Membership of CBA is unavailable; thus attendance, although more than membership, is substituted.

The Baptist General Conference (1852/1879)

The Baptist General Conference (BGC) was first known as the Swedish Baptist General Conference.[28] Gustav Palmquist, who only a year before had emigrated from Sweden to America, formed in August, 1852, the first Swedish Baptist Church at Rock Island, Illinois, with only three members. Palmquist himself had only been immersed two months before and ordained a month earlier by American Baptists. Four years later nine churches or groups formed the first Swedish Baptist Conference at Rock Island. A second conference was formed in Minnesota in 1858.

In 1879, Swedish Baptists organized a General Conference, which by that time included four local conferences with about sixty-five churches and 3,000 members. In 1960, the General Conference had over 100,000 members in 534 churches. In 1985, its Canadian churches withdrew. In 2000, the Conference reached 140,000 in 866 churches.

From the very beginning, the American Baptist Home Mission Society provided significant financial support; additional funds came from the American Baptist Publication Society and American Baptist state conventions. Beginning in 1888, the American Baptist Missionary Union (later the ABFMS) provided mission assistance for Swedish Baptists who served as missionaries abroad.

Between 1871 and 1914, except from 1884 to 1888, a Swedish Baptist Seminary was located at the Baptist Union Theological Seminary of Chicago (the later Divinity School of the University of Chicago). In 1878, it began to receive some financial support from its sponsoring school, aid that terminated in 1912. The seminary then moved in 1914 to St. Paul where it was consolidated with Bethel Academy, which had been formed in 1905. Even after 1914, American aid continued for Bethel but with reductions until the '40s.[29] In 1945, the school became Bethel College and Seminary with the college becoming a four-year institution in 1947.

Beginning in May, 1874, with *Zions Wacht*, Swedish Baptists have had an unbroken chain of denominational periodicals. In 1909, the conference purchased the Swedish Department of the

ABPS and launched its own periodical, *Svenska Standaret*, which in 1918 merged with the privately owned, *Nya Weecko-Posten*. In 1931, the conference launched, *The Baptist Evangel*, a Swedish language periodical, which merged with *Svenska Standaret* in 1940, thereby producing, *The Standard*, an English language paper with an optional Swedish supplement that was terminated at the end of 1954. Its current publication is *BGC World*. Swedish Baptists also published Sunday school and youth periodicals and hymnals. They also established children's homes, homes for the aged, and even a hospital.

As with other foreign language groups, American Baptist assistance to Swedish Baptists was premised both on gaining converts and in furthering their Americanization with the belief that with assimilation they would merge completely within the larger Baptist family.[30] Thousands of Swedish Baptists joined American Baptist churches, some of whom became leaders in the Northern (American) Baptist Convention.[31] Numerous churches in the Mid-West shifted to American Baptist state conventions and the Kansas Conference dissolved in 1943. From the First World War the use of English began to accelerate until English was dominant by the '40s. In 1945, the conference changed its name to the Baptist General Conference of America (dropping "of America" in 1985). By 1945, it had been reduced to 283 churches from a high of 375 congregations in 1912.

At its first conference in 1856, in Rock Island, Swedish Baptists adopted the New Hampshire Confession of Faith, which had been translated into Swedish. Although it had several internal theological disputes, the conference with its pietistic roots remained on a steady theologically conservative course and in time accepted the premillennial return of Christ.

The conservative credentials of the conference became clearly evident in 1944 when it created its own foreign mission board, which thus indicated, among other things, its dissatisfaction with the theologically inclusive policy of the ABFMS. At this point the conference was influenced by the action of conservatives in the Northern Convention who established on doctrinal grounds the Conservative Baptist Foreign Mission Society. The conservatives were particularly influential in Minnesota, the conference's home territory. Up to this time the AFMS appointed most of the foreign missionaries of the conference. In negotiations, the ABFMS refused to give an unequivocal reply to the veracity of Christ's virgin birth, which severed the ties for cooperation.[32] In 1952, the conference adopted an affirmation of faith of twelve points.

By the 1940s, the conference no longer faced any language barrier and was financially independent. It had had a long history of collegiality and developing its own institutions. New leaders with conservative convictions had now come to the fore who in the mission spirit of the times were determined to embark on a program of advance.[33]

The BGC has been most successful on many fronts, particularly in church planting and church growth. Its average Sunday morning attendance of 200,000 with a membership of 140,000 is the best ratio of any Baptist body in the United States. Some of its most successful areas have been in its old heartland of Minnesota and Illinois and on the Pacific Coast in Washington and California. It has a home mission program extending from Alaska to the Virgin Islands. It has a significant ministry among ethnic minorities. Its foreign mission program has also flourished. In 2000, it supported 127 missionaries in sixteen different areas. For some years the conference, more than other conservative groups, has been more open to ordaining or licensing women. Today, however, although some women have been ordained who serve as associates or chaplains, the conference today has only one ordained woman as senior pastor, who at this time serves in Minneapolis. With the fading of its ethnic heritage, a new generation has now come with little or no appreciation of its heritage. Such a development produces the danger of loosening ties and the diminishing of its identity.

The BGC is a member of the Baptist World Alliance and the Baptist Joint Committee on Religious Liberty. It has also joined the National Association of Evangelicals.

Conservative Baptist Association of America (1947)

With 225,000 in average attendance in 1,200 churches, the Conservative Baptist Association of America (CBA) is a major Baptist body in the North and West.[34] As the BGC and the NABC, attendance exceeds membership. It is spread primarily across the northern and western states from Maine to California. The churches, however, are not evenly distributed. Almost sixty-five percent of its strength is in the Pacific and Mountain states, while another twenty-two percent is in New England and the Middle Atlantic. Its strength in the Mid-West is particularly weak, while the South is scarcely represented.

The Conservative Baptist movement is rooted in the fundamentalist controversy that began within American Protestantism after the First World War.[35] In 1920, Baptist fundamentalists met in a "Conference on Fundamentals of Our Baptist Faith," preceding the sessions of the Northern Baptist Convention in Buffalo, New York. From it emerged a continuing organization known in time as the Fundamentalist Fellowship of the Northern Baptist Convention. Although many of its supporters were premillennialists, premillennialism was not a test of fellowship. With its pre-convention meetings and participation in the convention itself, its members became a pressure group to maintain orthodox doctrinal standards and to contest theological liberalism in Baptist schools and then in foreign missions. Among its leaders were William Bell Riley (1861–1947), John Roach Straton (1875–1929), and J. C. Massee (1871–1965).[36]

The fundamentalist forces were defeated in the convention over the adoption of a doctrinal confession and doctrinal standards for mission appointees. In spite of defeats, the program of the Fundamentalist Fellowship continued to be that of purging the convention rather than separating from it. It was less militant than the Baptist Bible Union, formed in 1923, nor did its cooperating churches separate from the convention in the 1920s and 1930s as some of the more militant were beginning to do. In the meantime, the fundamentalist forces were maintaining if not building up their strength from graduates of Bible schools, such as the Northwestern Bible and Missionary Training School of Minneapolis, Minnesota, or from newly established conservative Baptist seminaries, such as Eastern, Northern, and Western, or from Gordon College and Seminary in New England. Conservatives were also strongly entrenched in several state conventions. In fact, moderate fundamentalist leaders felt that their cause was making progress.

In 1943, the American Baptist Foreign Mission Society (ABFMS) appointed Elmer A. Fridell as foreign secretary, which brought a storm of protests from conservatives because of his identification with the Social Gospel, which they felt overshadowed traditional evangelism. Two leaders in the protest were R. S. Beal of First Baptist Church of Tucson, Arizona, and Albert G. Johnson, pastor of Hinson Memorial Baptist Church of Portland, Oregon. The ABFMS not only refused to withdraw the appointment for the sake of denominational harmony but also rejected a directive from conservatives to appoint only missionaries who affirmed the fundamentals of the faith in respect to biblical inspiration and the supernatural character of Christ's life and mission. Thereupon the conservatives, who were already contemplating such action, formed in December, 1943, the Conservative Baptist Foreign Mission Society (CBFMS), seeking recognition as a Northern Baptist agency. But the leadership of the convention looked upon the new society as competitive and refused recognition. In 1946, the Northern Convention defeated all conservative directives as well as an alternate slate of officers and also passed a resolution that reduced the voting strength of churches contributing outside the unified budget.

As a result of being shut out of the national counsels of the convention, conservatives formed in 1947 the Conservative Baptist Association of America (CBA) and in 1948 a Conservative Baptist Home Mission Society (CBHMS) to minister in North America, the same field as the American Baptist Home Mission Society. The Northern Convention began to lose numerous churches, including the state conventions of Minnesota and Arizona. It also almost lost Oregon except for a purge of churches that supported the new movement, but in the end a pyrrhic victory as Oregon today is a predominantly Conservative Baptist state. Overtures in considering union with the Baptist General Conference (BGC) or the General Association of Regular Baptist Churches (GARBC), which militants had formed in 1932, were never consummated. A fundamental difference with the latter group was over dual affiliation of churches, a practice which the GARBC forbade.

Conservative Baptists reported in 1953 that almost 500 churches were members of the CBA and another 240 in state organizations but not in the national body. In 1958, almost 1,200 churches on both national and state levels were affiliated. Over 400 of the churches were new congregations.[37] Conservative Baptists began at a propitious time for a new evangelical movement. After the fundamentalist defeats in the '20s and the ravages of the Great Depression of the '30s, conservatives began to show increased vigor in the '40s. Evangelicals organized the National Association of Evangelicals in 1942, Youth for Christ was formed in 1945, and the Billy Graham crusades gained wide support. With the Second World War completed and an enlarged vision of evangelistic opportunity worldwide, evangelicals were energized for a post-war advance in missions at both home and abroad.

As a confessional body, Conservative Baptists were careful to insure adherence to Baptist fundamentals. The CBFMS adopted the Goodchild Confession, a minimal doctrinal statement of traditional Baptist beliefs, which the Fundamentalist Fellowship had adopted in 1921, dividing its seventh and last point in two. Although the Goodchild Confession noted a difference between confession and creed, the CBFMS omitted this statement. It also pushed the confession toward creedalism by demanding from its voting members and personnel subscription without mental reservation and by prohibiting any change in the confession except by common consent. This last provision would later prove to be most divisive when a more militant faction wished to add a premillennial article. The CBHMS adopted the same doctrinal statement, while the CBA approved a statement similar to it.

In avoiding what was perceived as the ecclesiasticism and bureaucratic control of the Northern Baptist Convention, Conservative Baptists returned to the older society method for its agencies. Each agency was independent with its own membership, board, and budget. State associations and schools were also independent.

Conservative Baptists prided themselves on their rejection of religious apostasy, but the movement was beset with internal tensions. Separation from the Northern, now American Baptist Convention (ABC), was not always clear-cut. Some congregations provided funds for the CBFMS but were still members of the ABC, while others maintained a dual affiliation. Some Conservative Baptists cooperated with the Billy Graham campaigns, but others were opposed. To complicate matters, a militant minority coalesced in the 1950s, which finally broke away in the 1960s, which like the GARBC advocated a strict separatist position. It insisted on including a premillennial amendment to the confessions of the CBFMS and CBHMS (even though the agencies declared adherence to premillennialism as a doctrinal standard), criticized Neo-Evangelicalism, and favored continuing attacks on liberalism.[38]

At the time of the separation of the "hard-core" group, as it was called, CBA numbered over 1,400 churches, but around two hundred churches withdrew. The losses were primarily in the Mid-West with some defection in the Mountain region and Northern California. The East Coast, Pacific Northwest, and Southern California remained solidly with the founding body. As a result, the major strength of Conservative Baptists is on the two coasts but weak in the heart of the nation.

Since the division of the 1960s, Conservative Baptists have not regained their peak strength in churches and membership. Although church planting is still a priority, the post-war vigor and opportunities for growth have somewhat diminished. Many of their churches are in two of the most secular areas of the nation—New England and the Pacific Northwest. On the other hand, Conservative Baptists still have had some growth in the last couple of decades. In 1982, they reported a membership of over 194,000 and in 1989 a membership of 204,000 with 195,000 in morning worship. In 2000, morning worship was 224,000, a figure which exceeded membership. Conservative Baptists have an extensive ministry among various ethnic groups, particularly on the Pacific Coast, Arizona, and the New York City area. Thirty-five percent of their churches in the Southern California Association are ethnic. In New York City in 1970 almost two-thirds of their members were Caucasian; today, less than twenty-five percent.[39]

Their commitment to missions continues as a high priority. Conservative Baptist missions are faith based; missionaries must raise their own support from the constituency. In 2004, CBMS, then called Conservative Baptist International (CBI), received an income of over $19,000,000 and supported 560 missionaries in Africa, Asia, Europe, and South America. In 2005, CBI changed its name to WorldVenture, a more generic name, although still considering itself a Conservative Baptist organization. This occurred because of the growing expansion of its base of support outside Conservative Baptist ranks (about forty-two percent of its supporting churches are not Conservative Baptist), to meet problems in recruitment, and to protect its missionaries abroad. CBHMS, now called Mission to the Americas (MTTA), in 2004 had income of $7,500,000 ($1,500,000 for foreign work) and 256 missionaries with twenty of them in Mexico, Central America, and the Caribbean.[40]

In their early days, Conservative Baptists formed numerous state associations in the North and West but a number of them soon ceased or consolidated with a stronger association. The Minnesota, Wisconsin, Illinois, Indiana, and Michigan associations were lost to the militant division and except in Indiana were then replaced by other Conservative Baptist bodies. At the beginning of the 1990s Conservative Baptists listed twenty-three state or regional associations/fellowships. Before the end of the decade, they were organized into ten regional associations, each with an executive director. Today the number has been reduced to nine.

The two mission agencies have overshadowed the associational relationship of the churches to the extent that CBA (now called CBAmerica) has played a very secondary role and at times appears almost as a fifth wheel. As an organization for fellowship and not for mission support, its financial base has been weak. Much of the associational activity is on the regional rather than national level. In fact, CBAmerica now calls itself "A Covenantal Fellowship of Regional Baptist Church Associations." The last national Conservative Baptist meeting was held in Littleton, Colorado, in 2004. On the other hand, the directors of the regions meet four times a year and the board of CBAmerica convenes twice a year.

Conservative Baptists have considered developing more unity among its agencies, but such efforts have proved to be fruitless. As a movement built primarily on cooperation in missions and opposition to ecclesiastical controls, the movement has wrestled with its identity as a corporate body. The interdenominational character of northern fundamentalism and the parachurch movement have had a notable impact, thereby weakening their Baptist roots. Conservative Baptists support numerous ministries outside their own agencies. Cooperation is based more on pragmatic means rather than denominational polity. As with other conservatives, churches, particularly newer ones, frequently do not use "Baptist" in their name even though still considering themselves baptistic.[41]

Unlike many other Baptist bodies, Conservative Baptists have no one central headquarters building, although their national agencies are in close proximity. In recent years, the three national agencies have moved from Wheaton, Illinois, to Colorado. CBAmerica has an office in Longmont. In 2000, CBI moved into a new building in Littleton. In 2003, MTTA dedicated its new ministry center in Denver. Unlike a number of other Baptist groups, Conservative Baptists have no publishing arm. Although various Conservative Baptist agencies have produced their own periodicals, they have no general publication. The CBA sponsored, *The National Voice of Conservative Baptists*, but it lasted only from 1952 to 1954.

Two of its leading and fully accredited seminaries are Denver Seminary in Denver, Colorado, and Western Seminary in Portland, Oregon. The latter maintains satellite campuses in San Jose and Sacramento, California. Both schools have dropped "Conservative Baptist" from public identification, and Denver Seminary's relationship to the movement is today only nominal. A significant majority of the students of these two schools come from outside Conservative Baptist ranks. Other Conservative Baptist schools are the Seminary of the East in Dresher, Pennsylvania; New England Bible College in South Portland, Maine; Southwestern College in Phoenix, Arizona; and International College and Graduate School in Honolulu, Hawaii. Judson Baptist College, its college in The Dalles, Oregon, closed for lack of support. Western Baptist College, a GARBC school that moved to Salem, Oregon, acquired Conservative Baptist personnel on its board and teaching staff. In 2005, this school changed its name to Corban College and has become independent.

Conservative Baptists began as opponents of theological liberalism, but the majority took the path of moderate rather than militant fundamentalism. They cooperate with other evangelicals as members of the National Association of Evangelicals and in Billy Graham campaigns. On the other hand, they are not members of any national or international Baptist bodies.

The North American Baptist Conference (1843/1865)

The North American Baptist Conference (NABC) was formerly known as the German Baptist General Conference.[42] With support from Baptists in the North, a German Baptist movement began in the 1840s. Konrad Anton Fleischmann established the first church in Philadelphia in 1843. In 1851, German Baptists formed their first conference, and in 1859 the conference separated into Eastern and Western Conferences. In 1865, at Wilmot, Ontario, Canada, a joint meeting of the two conferences formed a General Conference to meet each three years, a schedule that continues to the present.

Before the First World War, the American Baptist Home Mission Society, American Baptist Publication Society, and the Woman's American Baptist Home Mission Society provided significant support to the German work.[43] With additions from migrants from Europe, particularly German-Russians from the Russian Empire in Poland and Ukraine, German Baptists grew numerically and spread geographically. In 1880, the Western Conference divided into three conferences and in time other conferences were established in the Midwest, South, Pacific Coast, and Canada. In 1910, German Baptists numbered 30,000.

Today they include 47,000 in 298 churches in the United States and over 17,000 in Canada, for a total of 64,500 with an average morning attendance of 71,500. German Baptist work in Southern Baptist territory has generally been only outposts of the larger work. Except for scattered congregations, primarily in Texas, Oklahoma, and Florida, the conference is almost non-existent in the South, partly due to the region's much smaller German immigrant population and also the ability of Southern Baptists to integrate their foreign-language work[44] and even to gain German Conference churches. It is the only Baptist body in North America with a denominational organization incorporating both the United States and Canada.

For its size its churches are the most dispersed of any Baptist body in North America with churches from northern Canada to the Rio Grande River and from Ontario to California with concentrations in the Dakotas (its heartland), California, and Western Canada. California has been a significant area for growth, but unfortunately the Dakotas is an area of decreasing population. Nineteen associations have replaced the earlier conferences.

Although considered part of the larger Baptist work, German Baptists formed their own network of institutions for missions, publications, and education. The first two conferences each established a mission society, but in 1883 the General Conference formed a General Missionary

Society. In cooperation with American Baptists, German Baptists engaged in work among the German immigrant population and also abroad. In 1883, they began mission assistance to German Baptist work in Europe. A continuing mission interest has been in the Cameroons in Africa, beginning first in 1891 in cooperation with the Baptists of Germany. Between the First and Second World Wars German Baptists conducted a successful Danubian Mission in the Balkans.

In 1863, the Western and Eastern Conferences established their own publication societies that in 1865 led to a single society. It published the periodical, *Der Sendbote*, which had already begun in 1853, and which continued until 1971 when it became an eight-page insert. The conference issued an English-language periodical, *Baptist Herald*, from 1923 to 1995. From 1871 to 1958 the work of publication was centered in Cleveland, housed in its own building. Publications included Christian literature and in 1885 a popular hymnal, *Die Glaubensharfe*.

Rochester Theological Seminary provided ministerial training in its German Department, which for many years was headed by August Rauschenbusch. Increasingly German Baptists assumed the financial responsibility for the department, which, although still related to Rochester Seminary, developed into an independent seminary. From 1897 to 1902, August Rauschenbusch's son, Walter, taught in the German Department but then became professor of church history in Rochester Seminary where he became noted as the exponent of the Social Gospel. In 1949, the conference relocated its seminary to Sioux Falls, South Dakota, in the center of German Baptist work.

In their mission work among Germans, American Baptists undertook the twin purpose of both evangelizing and Americanizing the German population. It was assumed that the German Conference would be only temporary and that in time its adherents would be assimilated into the larger American Baptist work. As early as 1891, it was estimated that already nine thousand German Baptists had transferred to English-speaking churches.[45]

Even though German Baptists increasingly began to shift to English in the twentieth century, they continued to maintain their independence. In 1919, the conference launched a Million Dollar Offering for the next triennium, a goal which was reached. In 1920, it terminated its relationship with the American Baptist Home Mission Society. In 1940, the conference unanimously declined an invitation to become an associate member of the Northern Baptist Convention. In the midst of the Second World War in 1944, it changed its name to North American Baptist General Conference; it has since dropped "General" from its name.

A number of factors entered into the decision to continue as a separate body.[46] First, the conference was self-supporting. It not only had its own seminary, publication interests, and mission program but had established a children's home, homes for the aged, and girls' homes. As an immigrant body, it had also developed strong familial ties. In addition, numbers of its churches were outside the bounds of the Northern Convention in Canada and Texas. Unlike German Methodists and German Presbyterians who merged with their parent bodies, German Baptists with their independent polity did not face the same pressures for merger.

There was also a theological factor. Unlike many other Baptist bodies, with its pietistic heritage it avoided serious theological controversy and had followed a conservative evangelical path throughout its history. In 1868, the General Conference adopted as a standard Pendleton's *Church Manual* with its New Hampshire Confession of Faith, which was published in German.[47] In the 1940s, one of its professors was forced from his position for alleged liberal teaching. It is therefore not surprising that the theological liberalism within the Northern Convention was a deterrent.[48]

In 1946, the conference adopted in its preamble to its constitution a moderately stated list of eight tenets of faith.[49] It admires Walter Rauschenbusch, but it has never adopted the principles of the Social Gospel and continues its traditional program. Although the Conference has recognized ordination of women for various ministries, it excludes them as senior pastors.

The conference today continues to support a

strong home and foreign mission program. It engages in a church-planting ministry that includes mission work among various ethnic groups. Through the merger of one of its congregations with an independent congregation, a diverse group of independent congregations were attracted to the NABC that led in 2002 to the formation of a Florida Association that includes African-American, Haitian, Brazilian, and Anglo congregations. In 2004, it was supporting thirty-eight full-time missionaries with work in six foreign countries. In 1940, it established in Edmonton, Alberta, Canada, the Christian Training Institute, which today is Taylor University College and Seminary.

The conference is discussing with the Baptist General Conference not merger, which it had done some years before, but possibilities of partnership in ministry. The conference is a member of the Baptist Joint Committee on Religious Liberty and the Baptist World Alliance. It has fraternal ties with the Evangelical Fellowship of Mission Agencies and the Evangelical Fellowship of Canada but not the National Association of Evangelicals in the USA.

Seventh Day Baptist General Conference (1671/1802)

Seventh Day Baptists (SDB) are very similar to other Baptists in the Regular Baptist tradition except for adherence to the seventh day as the day of worship.[50] Its first adherents in America separated in 1671 from the Regular Baptist church in Newport, Rhode Island. Seventh Day Baptists moved from New England westward into the Middle Atlantic region, West Virginia, the Midwest, and finally to California.

Seventh Day Baptists have always been a small group. In 1890, they had 106 congregations (twenty-eight in New York State) with 9,143 members. In 1926, the number of congregations was sixty-seven with 7,264 members. In 2000, they had eighty-one congregations but a membership reduced to just under 5,000 with average Sabbath attendance of 3,000. Congregations were located in thirty states and the District of Columbia. New York with ten churches continues with the largest number but followed closely by California with nine.[51]

At first Seventh Day Baptists held yearly meetings between congregations. In 1802, they formed a General Conference and in the 1830s began regional associations. For their size, Seventh Day Baptists developed a surprising range of institutions, which included mission, tract, and education societies and a publishing house. They also published periodicals. In the nineteenth century they established three educational institutions of higher learning—a college and seminary at Alfred, New York, a college at Milton, Wisconsin, and a college at Salem, West Virginia. The school and seminary in Alfred closed in 1963 and the one in Milton in 1982, but the school in Salem, today the Salem International University, continues as an independent institution.

Today Seventh Day Baptists maintain a SDB Center in Janesville, Wisconsin, which includes a Center on Ministry. The SDB Missionary Society continues in Westerly, Rhode Island, and a SDB Board of Christian Education at Alfred, New York. *The Sabbath Recorder*, established in 1844, is the conference's periodical.

With the infiltration of theological liberalism in the seminary in Alfred, Seventh Day Baptists engaged in serious debate between fundamentalists and modernists in the first decades of the twentieth century. If it were not for its position on the Sabbath, its family ties, and the smallness of the conference, it may have suffered division as the American Baptists. In 1937, it adopted a new Statement of Belief, a traditional statement that recognized freedom of conscience but noted the Bible as "the inspired Word of God" and Christ's full deity, including His sacrificial death, resurrection, and Second Coming. The Statement included an article on the seventh day as the Sabbath. Over the years, the Seventh Day Baptists have ordained or licensed a limited number of women for ministry. Their 2005 Directory lists one ordained woman pastor and three licensed women, two serving as pastors and one as an associate pastor.[52]

Although Seventh Day Baptists introduced Sabbath teaching to Adventists who became the Seventh-day Adventist Church, they are far removed from the cultic characteristics of this denomination.[53] They consider themselves in the mainstream of Baptist life and are members of the Baptist World Alliance and the Baptist Joint Committee on Religious Liberty. They cooperate with other religious groups. Their pastors often have supplied the pulpits of other churches on Sunday, while lay members have served in other capacities.

At one time, they were members of the National Council of Churches and World Council of Churches. By a divided vote, they withdrew from the former in 1973 and the latter in 1976 largely over problems with theological liberalism and social activism. At one time, Seventh Day Baptists would have been considered an ecumenical mainline body, but their withdrawal from ecumenical organizations and their moderate conservative theological position place them among conservative evangelicals.

In the '60s, American Baptists and Seventh Day Baptists, on the initiative of the former, entered into conversations as to a possible merger but nothing came of the effort. In 1965, the SDB Conference with other SD conferences from abroad formed the Seventh Day Baptist World Federation. By 1989, it had grown to seventeen conferences with around 50,000 members; the largest conference was in India with 38,000.

As a small group with dispersed and static if not declining membership in a society that today has numerous social and economic barriers to a seventh-day Sabbath (from Friday evening to sundown on Saturday) and lack of concern for any type of Sabbath, Seventh Day Baptists face somewhat perilous times. Besides, the Seventh-day Adventists with whom they are at times confused have largely appropriated the Sabbath-day market. Although the decline of homogeneous farming communities has hurt the early rural base of Seventh Day Baptists, their efforts in locating in the cities have begun to produce fruit, bringing some prospect of stability if not renewed growth.

III–A. Ethnic Baptists

Baptists are the most multiracial and multilingual denomination in the United States.[54] As early as the seventeenth century, Baptists in America began to gain converts outside the white race. In 1652, the Baptist church in Newport baptized, Jack, the first black convert. In 1674, the Seventh Day Baptist Church baptized the first known American Indian converts. From about 1694 to the 1830s nine Indian Baptist churches without mission assistance appeared in New England and New York.

In 1817, Isaac McCoy under the Triennial Convention began his notable work among Indians in the West. In 1842, he led in forming the American Indian Association, which in 1855 merged with the Domestic Mission Board of the Southern Baptist Convention. Northern Baptists provided support not only for Indian work through the Triennial Convention but also its successor, the American Baptist Missionary Union, and after 1865 through the American Baptist Home Mission Society. The ABHMS did notable work among the civilized tribes in Oklahoma where in 1880 it established an Indian school, later called Bacone College. Baptists both North and South continue work among Indians but without resulting in any separate Indian convention.[55]

Black Baptists, however, did not form their first church until the 1770s, their first independent association until 1834, their first national convention until 1840. Today African-American Baptists compose the largest non-Anglo segment of the Baptist denomination in America, incorporating six national conventions. For a description of these bodies, see the section above on National Baptists. A number of African-American Baptist churches hold dual affiliation with a predominantly white body or are simply aligned with it. Membership of blacks has been augmented in more recent years with migrants from Haiti and Africa.

Hispanics

In the nineteenth century, both Northern and Southern Baptists began to engage in work among Mexicans in the Southwest. With the great upsurge of the Hispanic population in more recent years, American, Southern, northern conservative evangelicals, and fundamentalist Baptists have all found the Hispanic field most fruitful. Migrants have come from Mexico, Central America, the Caribbean (including Cuba and Puerto Rico), and South America (including also Brazilians).

In past years, Hispanics formed several Mexican or Hispanic Conventions. Three were organized among Northern Baptists—one in Southern California, in 1924, and another in Northern California, in 1934. A very small Spanish-American Baptist Convention was formed in 1928, centered in the Midwest. The ministry of the Hispanic churches in the two California regions is now conducted within the American Baptist regions themselves; the third convention is no longer listed.[56]

In Texas, a Mexican Baptist Convention existed from 1910 to 1964 until it became a department of the Texas Baptist General Convention. In 1923, Hispanic churches in New Mexico formed a convention; its churches are today integrated within the New Mexico state program. The National Fellowship of Hispanic Southern Baptist Churches is at present debating the possibility of forming a national convention.[57]

Ethnics from Asia and the Pacific

In the nineteenth century, Southern Baptists engaged in a limited Chinese work in California and the South. Northern Baptists began their Chinese work in the nineteenth century in California and New York City, besides opening work among the Japanese in Seattle in 1892.[58]

Aside from work among Chinese and Japanese, the great influx of Asiatics since the Second World War has greatly expanded opportunities for work among Asiatics. For instance, Southern Baptists, who formed their first Korean church in 1956, had by 1999 almost 600 Korean congregations. Other Asiatic Southern Baptist congregations today include Vietnamese, Laotians, Cambodians, Mien, Thai, Hmong, Filipinos, Asian Indians, Arabs, and Armenians. The various churches are distributed among various English-speaking Baptist bodies.

Compared to other Protestants, Baptist work in the Pacific has historically been weak. Baptists, however, have now increased their presence in this region and today also have work among Pacific Islanders who have migrated to the United States.

European Ethnics

The nineteenth century also experienced a great influx of Europeans, first from Northern and then from Southern and Eastern Europe. Also French-Canadians from Canada began to settle in the Northeast. The American Baptist Home Mission Society, joined by the American Baptist Publication Society and the Woman's American Baptist Home Mission Society, took the lead in the North to evangelize them with a secondary purpose of assimilating them into American culture.[59] The ABHMS first began work among the Welsh in 1836 which was soon followed by work among Germans, Scandinavians, French Canadians, and other groups.

These bodies formed their own associations and conferences, which paralleled the English-speaking bodies.[60] By 1919, thirteen such groups, including French Canadians, had organized in Northern Baptist territory. It was assumed that upon assimilation these groups would merge into the larger Baptist body. In 1940, the Northern Baptist Convention accepted seven of them as associated bodies. With emigration from the Soviet Union, three more appeared by 1950.

With lack of continuing immigration from Northern and Southern Europe and with assimilation, these sixteen bodies have diminished to eight independent bodies through transformation, merger, integration, or termination. The German and Swedish Conferences became independent English-speaking bodies, which engage in their own ethnic ministries. The Finnish Baptist Mission Union of Swedish Finns, formed in 1901, merged in 1948 with the Baptist General Conference. The Norwegian and Danish Conferences, both formed in 1910, terminated with the former merging with the American Baptist Convention in 1956 and the latter in

1958. The French-Speaking Baptist Conference of New England, formed in 1895, no longer exists. The Portuguese Baptist Convention of New England, formed in 1903, ceased functioning in the '80s. The Association of Evangelicals for Italian Missions dissolved at its centennial in 1999. Of the eight that continue as independent bodies, American Baptists today claim five of them as historically related organizations. Except for Czechoslovakian and Latvian Baptists, these ties today are practically non-existent.

With significant migration from the former USSR after World War II and the collapse of communism, many new Russian and Ukrainian churches have appeared. In recent years, three new Slavic associations have been established, bringing to eleven the number of independent ethnic bodies. With 136 churches and 23,000 members, about seventy-five percent of Baptist ethnics with European roots are today either Russian or Ukrainian. The total number would be higher if one could include the numerous independent congregations that belong to no associational body.

The division between registered and non-registered churches that existed among Baptists in the former USSR, although limited in America, exists here. One example is the existence of a large independent church in Washington State, composed of members from non-registered churches in Russia and practicing a restrictive form of close communion.

A number in the older generation of Slavic Baptists carry with them the customs and somewhat legalistic lifestyle from their homeland, but the younger generation has been quickly assimilating. In theology Slavic Baptists are conservative if not fundamentalist. The majority, however, in accord with their co-believers in the former Soviet Union, differ with the majority of Baptists in the United States over perseverance, believing in the possibility of falling from grace. Slavic Baptists practice close communion, limiting participation to those who have been immersed and are in good standing with their church. Slavic Baptists are very mission-minded, providing significant mission assistance as well as visits to believers in the former USSR. Mission support may be channeled through the Slavic Missionary Association, associational bodies, or a local church.[61]

Independent Bodies

	Membership[62]	**Churches**
Czechoslovak Baptist Convention	900	4
Hungarian Baptist Union	1,000	10
Polish Baptist Association	150	5
Romanian Baptist Association	5,200	37
Slavic/Russian Baptist Associations (5)	16,500	106
Ukrainian Evangelical Baptist Convention	6,500	30
Union of Latvian Baptists	165	6
TOTAL	**30,415**	**198**

Though numerous fellowships or associational bodies exist among ethnic Baptist groups, none of them at present, except for those of European heritage, claim to be independent conventions apart from their parent bodies. The following bodies, even though including many congregations with dual affiliation, are listed as separate entities.

Czechoslovak Baptist Convention (1912)

Czechoslovak Baptist Convention is a small body, primarily of Czech and Slovak stock, of 1,500 members in seven churches. Four are in the USA and three in Canada. All churches use English in their services except the one in Toronto, Canada; some, however, use Czech or Slovak in Sunday school. It meets annually on the campus of Alderson-Broaddus College in Philippi,

West Virginia, an American Baptist school. Its primary foreign mission program is support of outreach ministries in the Czech Republic and Slovakia. It is a member of the Baptist World Alliance.

Hungarian Baptist Union (1908)

Hungarian Baptist Union is a body of 1,500 members with ten Churches in the United States and six in Canada. Its members are originally from Hungarian communities in Transylvania in Romania. Its services and Sunday schools are in the Hungarian language.

Polish Baptist Association (1913)

Polish Baptist Association is a small body of 210 members with five churches and one mission in the United States and two churches in Canada. Services are in the Polish language. The association is associated with the Southern Baptist Convention.

Romanian Baptist Association (1913)

Romanian Baptist Association is a body of 5,500 members with thirty-seven churches in the United States from the east to west coasts and eight churches in Canada, primarily in Ontario. Its churches are Romanian-speaking. The association cooperates with the Southern Baptist Convention.

Slavic/Russian Baptist Associations

Baptists from the former USSR have established five independent associations whose services are in Russian or in some churches bilingual.

a. Russian-Ukrainian Evangelical Baptist Union (1919)

It has twenty-four churches and 1,500 members, recently reduced from 2,200 members with the exclusion in 2002 of two congregations. The major language in the services is Russian although four are bilingual and four are English-speaking. It is a member of the Baptist World Alliance.

b. Pacific Coast Slavic Baptist Association (1928)

Pacific Coast Slavic Baptist Association joined the Russian-Ukrainian Union in 1963 but because of distance operates its own program. It has twenty-one churches and 5,000 members, primarily in California. Ninety-five percent of the churches have Russian services.

c. Northwest Association of Slavic Baptist Churches (2002)

Northwest Association of Slavic Baptist Churches has 6,000 members in thirty churches—twenty-six in Washington and four in Oregon. Services are in Russian except for visiting English-speaking pastors.

d. Association of Slavic Baptist Churches, Midwest, USA (2002)

Association of Slavic Baptist Churches, Midwest, USA has 1,000 members in eight churches—three in Illinois, one in Indiana, two in Missouri, and two in Minnesota.

e. East Coast Slavic Baptist Association (2005)

East Coast Slavic Baptist Association has 3,000 members in twenty-two churches in the United States and one in Canada. The majority of its churches are in New England.

Ukrainian Evangelical Baptist Convention (1946)

Ukrainian Evangelical Baptist Convention has 7,150 members with thirty churches in the United States and sixteen in Canada. Its churches may use Ukrainian or Russian or both languages. It is a very conservative body with most of its churches in association with the Southern Baptist Convention. It has declined to consider membership in the Baptist World Alliance. It is a member of the All-Ukrainian Baptist Fellowship that includes the Baptist Union of Ukraine.

Union of Latvian Baptists (1950)

Union of Latvian Baptists is a small union of 200 members with six churches in the United States and one in Toronto, Canada. Almost all the services are in Latvian. The churches, by and large, except for one in Cleveland and one in Canada, relate to the American Baptists. It is a member of the Baptist World Alliance.

IV. Fundamental (Northern)

	Membership	Attendance	Churches
General Association of Regular Baptist Churches (1932)	188,274	205,631	1,422
Independent Baptist Fellowship of North America (1990)	6,000 (est.)		45*
Fundamental Baptist Fellowship (1920)	97,000 (est.)		606**
New Testament Association of Independent Baptist Churches/Fundamental Baptist Associations and Fellowships (1965)	106,130		649
Independent Fundamental Churches of America (Baptists only) (1930)	n/a		103***
SUBTOTAL	**397,404**		**2,825**
*Dual membership with GARBC	-800		-6
**Dual membership with NTA/Associations	-19,000		-119
***Dual membership with other Baptists	n/a		-15
TOTAL	**377,604**		**2,685**

The northern fundamentalist Baptists emerged as a separatist movement from the Northern Baptist Convention during the fundamentalist controversy. They have become a notable segment among the Baptist tribes with a membership approaching 400,000 with around 2,700 congregations. Their greatest strength is in the Midwest.

They share with conservative evangelicals similar beliefs on biblical inspiration, the supernatural character of the gospel, and a commitment to world evangelism. But they differ from them in their militant opposition to liberalism, their hostility toward Neo-Evangelicalism, and their advocacy of second-degree separation that not only counsels separation from apostasy but also from evangelicals who may have relations with those deemed apostate. For them the attack on liberalism is an ongoing battle, and separation in itself is redemptive. In eschatology they are not only premillennialists but also pretribulationist dispensationalists.[63]

Secondary issues have also marked many of them, causing at times tensions within their own ranks. For many the King James Version is authoritative. Music with styles and use of instruments from popular culture is condemned. Degrees of separation are subject to debate. Associating only with those with correct doctrine and practice and in almost total agreement with them has led to further division from those who appear more or less deviant.

Fundamentalist Baptists cherish local church independency. This is due at least in part because of their experience in breaking from former ecclesiastical relationships. They also tend to look to strong pastoral leadership. As a consequence, traditional Baptist polity of church representation has eroded among many of them with the result that many of their churches are no longer in a church association and the pastor is a member of a fellowship with no ecclesiastical jurisdiction. They major on evangelism and are strong supporters of international missions. Four of their agencies in 2004 had around 1,700 missionaries overseas with a total income of over sixty-four million.[64]

Because of independency and with few exceptions a lack of any agency to collect statistics, it is difficult to count members. Exceptions, however, include the Minnesota Baptist Association and the General Association of Regular Baptist Churches. Directories of associations/fellowships provide lists of churches but no membership for individual congregations, thus forcing one to calculate membership, often estimated, from knowledgeable individuals. The task becomes more complicated in a directory of individuals from which one then must ascertain pastors with churches. A further complication is that a church may associate with more than one association or fellowship.

The General Association of Regular Baptist Churches (1932)

The General Association of Regular Baptist Churches (GARBC) is the first independent Baptist denominational body to emerge out of the fundamentalist controversy that began in the 1920s in the Northern Baptist Convention. It has held a premier position among fundamentalist bodies not only for its pioneer efforts but also for defining fundamentalist principles and its consistency in holding to them. [65] Its roots are imbedded in the Baptist Bible Union (BBU), an organization which protested against theological liberalism not only in the Northern Convention but also in the Southern Convention and the Baptist Convention of Ontario and Quebec in Canada.[66]

Upon the defeat in 1922 by the Northern Convention in adopting a confessional statement, Ralph E. Neighbour of the First Baptist Church of Elyria, Ohio, and Oliver W. Van Osdel of the Wealthy Street Baptist Church of Grand Rapids, Michigan, led in initiating the BBU. It attracted leading fundamentalists, including T. T. Shields from Canada; W. B. Riley from Minnesota; and J. Frank Norris from Texas. An executive committee called a pre-convention meeting that met before the Southern Baptist Convention in Kansas City, Missouri, in May, 1923. It elected T. T. Shields president and adopted a confession, a revision of the New Hampshire Confession, without, however, a premillennial article as was initially contemplated.

The BBU differed on several counts from the Fundamentalist Fellowship that had existed since 1920.[67] For one thing, it included leaders from the Northern and Southern Conventions as well as Canada. Although no premillennial article was adopted (Shields himself was amillennial), premillennialism was strongly represented. While the Fellowship was bent on purging liberalism, the BBU was more militant in its attacks and more separatist in sentiment. Although denying they were separatists, Shields and Norris, due to their attacks on their respective conventions, were forced out and formed their own organizations.

In the meantime, local independent Baptist associations began to appear in the territory of the Northern Convention. As early as 1909 W. O. Van Osdel led his church out of the Grand Rapids Association that included the very liberal Fountain Street Baptist Church and with others formed Grand River Valley Association. In 1920, it took the name, Michigan Orthodox Baptist Association, but was ousted by the Michigan Baptist Convention for non-cooperation. In 1928, it changed its name to Grand Rapids Association of Regular Baptist Churches. In Ohio BBU pastors failed to get satisfaction to their complaints that included issues relating to two of the Baptist schools in the state. In addition, the Baptist state convention amended its constitution to exclude non-cooperating churches, thus helping to lead to the formation in 1928 in Columbus of the Union of Regular Baptist Churches of Ohio. In 1929, five churches in California formed an independent association. [68]

The BBU was not a mass organization but led by pastors noted for their prowess as preachers and who centered on their own personal programs. The leaders were short on cooperation and even broke ties with each other. The organization was hurt by the withdrawal of Riley, the bizarre behavior of Norris, and the debacle caused by the collapse of Des Moines University, a school that Shields headed. Shields ended his presidency in 1930. When the BBU met in the midst of the Great Depression for its last meeting in Chicago in May, 1932, aside from visitors only thirty-four delegates from eight states were present with over half from Illinois and Minnesota.

At the Chicago meeting, its members terminated the BBU and replaced it with a new organization, the General Association of Regular Baptist Churches. This was a move that the leadership had contemplated for a couple of years. The adoption of "Regular" was a name that other Separatists were using in both the United States and Canada and implied that they were not liberal but orthodox. Unlike the BBU, it was not an organization of individuals but of churches. It was strongly separatist, even rejecting the membership of conservative churches with ties to the old convention. Its confession, adopted in 1934, drew heavily on the confession of the BBU, but its final article included a declaration of Christ's premillennial return. In 1959, it approved by resolution the adding of the pretribulation rapture to its eschatological position, which later it added to its constitution. Its leadership included no national figures or "prima donnas" that had beset the BBU. [69]

It took time for many churches that opposed convention leadership to join the new organization, but it began to grow. For much of its history, at least until the 1980s, the GARBC was generally free from internal turmoil and for a number of decades experienced steady growth. [70] The association was fortunate in the leadership of Robert T. Ketcham (1889–1978), a Baptist pastor who first was the association's vice president in 1933 and then president from 1934–1938. [71] In an effort to eliminate the concept that the GARBC was under the control of one man, Ketcham proposed in 1938 to abolish the executive structure of the association, including the presidency, and replace it with a Council of Fourteen with limited terms. The GARBC adopted the measure; today there is a Council of Eighteen. Ketcham, however, continued to be very influential in the association's affairs, not only serving on the Council but also as editor of *The Baptist Bulletin,* 1938–1945, 1948–1955, as National Representative, 1948–1960, and as National Consultant, 1960–1966.

Because of its position not only on separation from apostasy but also from second-degree separation, *i. e.* from evangelicals who may have associations with liberals, the GARBC refused to cooperate in Billy Graham campaigns. Because of its hard line on separation, its overture to the Conservative Baptists for union was unsuccessful.

As with Conservative Baptists, the GARBC rejected organizing as a convention with a unified budget. It also would not establish a mission board of its own or own any educational institutions. It was nevertheless very much interested in foreign and home mission work; from its early days representatives of mission agencies spoke at its sessions. Earlier fundamentalist Baptists had begun such foreign mission agencies as Baptist Mid-Missions (1920), Association of Baptists for World Evangelism (ABWE) (1928), and Evangelical Baptist Missions (1928), and the Interstate Evangelistic Association (c. 1926). In 1933, the association's mission committee recommended for support or accreditation three missions, a procedure that in 1934 became the association's settled polity. In the early '60s, the association was endorsing the above three foreign missions as well as the Hiawatha Land Independent Baptist Mission (1942) and the Fellowship of Baptists for Home Missions (1941), which by 1950, had absorbed four other small localized home mission agencies. In 2003–2004, the GARBC listed ten missions that included the three early foreign missions and seven home missions agencies.[72]

The mission societies are faith-based with missionaries raising their own support and independent of a cooperative budget. According to the 2004–2006 *Mission Handbook*, Baptist Mid-Missions, ABWE, and Evangelical Baptist Missions had a total income of $57,500,000 and overseas personnel of 1,352. Income of these missions, however, did not come exclusively from GARBC churches; on the other hand, members of these churches also give significant sums to other faith-based missions. [73]

The GARBC also endorsed educational institutions, which in its earlier years included the Los Angeles Baptist Theological Seminary (1927), today Northwest Baptist Seminary in Tacoma, Washington; Baptist Bible College and Seminary, today in Clarks Summit, Pennsylvania (1932); Grand Rapids Baptist Seminary (1941); Cedarville College in Cedarville, Ohio; Western Baptist College in Salem, Oregon; and Faith Baptist Bible College and Theological Seminary, today in Ankeny, Iowa. In 2003–2004, except for

Grand Rapids Seminary, it continued to list the above five colleges and seminaries as well as five other schools.

Western Baptist College, located in a strongly Conservative Baptist state, came under criticism for permitting Conservative Baptists to serve on its faculty and board. In 2005, the school took the name Corban College and became independent. In 2006, the GARBC severed its connection with Cedarville College (now University) for its fraternization with Southern Baptists whose state convention in Ohio has endorsed the school. After 2003–2004 the GARBC, however, no longer lists missions or schools but allows cooperating institutions the opportunity for a display at national meetings.[74]

The 2000 Directory of the GARBC listed 190 churches with Christian day school programs, both elementary and secondary, and thirty-one camps. Regular Baptists also support several "compassion ministries," which provide services for family counseling, unwed and pregnant women, children, and the mentally disabled.

In January, 1933, the GARBC began publishing a periodical, *The Bulletin*, later called *The Baptist Bulletin*, which continues today as its organ. In 1952, it established the Regular Baptist Press, which provides materials not only for its own churches but also for many churches outside the GARBC.

In 1944, the GARBC established a home office in Chicago with an executive, who was called a National Representative (not Executive Secretary). In 1965, the offices of the GARBC moved to Des Plaines, Illinois, and in 1976 into an impressive headquarters in Schaumburg, Illinois.

In 1942, the GARBC became a member of the American Council of Christian Churches (ACCC), a militant fundamentalist organization. In 1948, it was a founding member of the International Council of Christian Churches (ICCC), the international counterpart of the earlier organization. The ACCC has not listed the GARBC as one of its members since 2002. Today it is also not a member of the ICCC, known today as the World Council of Independent Christian Churches.

In a survey of GARBC pastors in 1988, with a return of fifty-five percent, a significant majority of pastors regarded themselves as fundamentalists.[75] By a response of ninety-five percent or more, pastors opposed dancing, social drinking, gambling, use of tobacco, and membership in secret societies. While eighty-five percent disapproved attending movie theaters, only twenty-four percent outright disapproved renting movies for VCRs with fifty-five percent approving. Unlike some Baptists in the South, seventy-three percent approved mixed swimming. Ninety-six percent considered themselves to be Republican or independent but closer to Republican. Almost all opposed the ordination of women. In 1984, the GARBC approved a resolution disapproving ordination of women, although recognizing their "spiritual equality." Pastors also strongly oppose abortion, and eighty-one percent opposed granting equal rights to homosexuals.

The leadership of the GARBC has had some concerns over what it considers extreme positions on fundamentalist tests of fellowship and versions of scripture. In spite of pressure, the leaders resisted recognizing the King James Bible as the one standard version.[76] Unlike other Baptists, it has been more persistent in maintaining "Baptist" in the names of its cooperating agencies and its churches, although a struggle. Most churches continue with the name "Baptist," and the few who do not must have the name in their subtitle or as part of the official name of the church. Cooperating agencies also must have the name either in their title or subtitle. In recent years the GARBC has dropped schools, such as Grand Rapids Seminary, Cornerstone College, and Western Baptist College for eliminating their specific Baptist identity.

The beginning of the new association was small, starting with only around twenty-five churches.[77] In the 1936 census of Religious Bodies, it reported 22,345 members in eighty-four churches with fifty-five in the Midwest.[78] From this point it continued a strong steady upward increase each year until the 1970s. By 1941 it had doubled its congregations to 171 and by 1949 had tripled to 520 at a time when Conservative Baptists were also gaining congregations. By 1962, they again doubled to 1,031 congregations. A survey in the early '70s recorded 197,536 members in 1,371 churches.[79]

The GARBC recorded a top number of 1,603 churches in 1984, but it has not been able to maintain this number. It experienced a small defection with the formation in 1990 of the Independent Baptist Fellowship of North America by those who feared the GARBC was weakening its stand on second-degree separation and who opposed officials of approved agencies serving on the Council of Eighteen.

In the survey for the *Religious Congregations and Membership* study for 2000, the GARBC reported 188,274 members in 1,422 congregations. The number of congregations was a bit more than the early '70s but average membership was less. On the other hand, average attendance was 205,000.[80] The greatest losses were in the Middle Atlantic states as well as Illinois, Kansas, California, and Washington. On the other hand, significant gains were recorded in Florida, Ohio, Indiana, Arizona, and Oregon. Four states not entered in 1971 appeared in 2000—Connecticut, New Hampshire, New Mexico, and Hawaii. Seventy-five percent of the membership stretches from the Middle Atlantic states to the Old Northwest and to Iowa. From the beginning its heartland has been in the Great Lakes region and Iowa. It has some strength in California and in Washington State where pioneer mission work was begun at the very end of the 1930s in the eastern part of the state. It is extremely weak in other areas and practically non-existent in the South except in Florida.

Twenty-three state and regional associations exist as part of the GARBC but are organically separate from the national body. Thirteen of them are in the Mid-Atlantic and Midwest of the nation. A partner of the GARBC is the Fundamental Baptist Fellowship Association, a predominantly African-American body, which in 2005 included seventy-seven churches, some of which are also members of the GARBC itself. Beginning in 2005 the GARBC and the Fellowship have begun to hold joint conferences.

Independent Baptist Fellowship of North America (1990)

Dissatisfied members of the General Association of Regular Baptists formed in October, 1990, in Oshkosh, Wisconsin, the Independent Baptist Fellowship of North America (IBFNA).[81] Richard A. Harris, pastor of Bethel Baptist Church of Sellersville, Pennsylvania, initiated a reform movement called, "Regular Baptists for Revival," and edited for three years a newsletter, *Regular Baptist Review*. Soon after their defeat by a vote of 1,171 to 735 at the GARBC conference at Niagara Falls in June, 1990, of a proposed amendment to prohibit salaried officials of approved agencies (even though already limited to four) to serve on the Council of Eighteen, the dissidents formed the IBFNA. The supporters of IBFNA felt the GARBC was becoming too soft on second-degree separation, particularly evident in approved schools, and was losing its militancy in its stance against liberalism. They blamed the lack of growth of the GARBC for its departure from strict separation.

The articles of faith of the IBFNA begin with Scripture, which included an opening statement of preference for the King James Version. It declared its belief in "the Bible's infallibility and unlimited inerrancy in all areas." Its section on separation included opposition to apostasy and separation from its adherents as well as from others who themselves were not strict separationists. In eschatology it was dispensational and advocated the "pretribulational and premillennial return of Jesus Christ." Unlike the GARBC, which withdrew, the IBFNA is a member of the American Council of Christian Churches.

The membership of the IBFNA is composed primarily of individuals or couples in addition to a few supporting churches. In 1999–2000, its *Membership Directory* included 149 individuals (plus many spouses) with forty-four serving as pastors of churches. With the addition of one supporting church whose pastor was not listed, the number of churches related to the IBFNA is forty-five. Six of the churches, however, are also in fellowship with the GARBC, and the pastors of two of them are in fellowship with the Fundamental Baptist Fellowship. Based on the average membership of GARBC churches, its forty-five churches would post an estimated membership of 6,000. Pennsylvania with fourteen churches has the largest number of congregations. Other churches are scattered from New England to California.

Fundamental Baptist Fellowship (1920)

From FBF to CBF

The Fundamental Baptist Fellowship (FBF) has been a seminal body for a significant portion of the history of the conservative evangelical and fundamentalist movements among Baptists in the North.[82] It also has had a unique history of transformations. At first it was a loosely organized protest body of fundamentalists within the Northern Baptist Convention who although striving to purge it from liberalism were not separatists. Its membership helped to propel into existence the Conservative Baptist movement with first the formation of the Conservative Baptist Foreign Mission Society (CBFMS) in 1943. Beginning in 1944, with the presidency of Richard S. Beal, pastor of First Baptist Church of Tucson, Arizona, the FBF took a more militant stand. It changed its name to the Conservative Baptist Fellowship of Northern Baptists (CBF) in 1946. In 1945, Chester Tulga (1896–1976), who had pastored Northern Baptist churches, became the hard-hitting editor of *The News Letter*, the periodical of the Fellowship, and soon its research secretary. In 1946, he began the *Information Bulletin* of the CBF, and *The News Letter* was discontinued in 1948. Tulga left the CBF in 1956 and joined a GARBC church.[83] The Fellowship helped to give birth in 1947 to the Conservative Baptist Association (CBA), which was followed in 1948 with the provisional formation of the Conservative Baptist Home Mission Society (CBHMS).

From CBF to FBF

Although the Fellowship might have now expired with the establishment of the CBA, Tulga helped to keep it alive by his writing, including a very popular series of case books, which included both attacks on liberalism and support for the cardinal beliefs of orthodoxy. One of his most important works was, *The Foreign Missions Controversy in the Northern Baptist Convention*, published in 1950. In 1951, the Fellowship took simply the name, Conservative Baptist Fellowship, with no further ties with the Northern Convention. Four years later in 1955 it declared its independence even from the Conservative Baptist movement. It limited its membership to those who subscribed to both premillennialism and pretribulationism. It also prescribed an annual fee but restricted voting to those who paid a higher fee.[84]

The Conservative Baptist movement had become divided between a "soft core" and a "hard core," as they were called. The leadership of the CBF was under "hard core" leadership that advocated a continuing attack on liberalism, strict separation from apostasy, opposition to Neo-Evangelicalism, and adoption of premillennialism as a doctrinal norm. They were not only premillennialists but also favored a pretribulation rapture and the dispensationalism of the Scofield Bible. The hard core was very critical of Denver Conservative Baptist Seminary, established with a national board in 1950, for its sympathy for Neo-Evangelicalism.

The hard core was particularly influential in the CBA, particularly in its Central Region. The general director of the CBA from 1948 to 1965 was B. Myron Cedarholm (1915–1997), who favored hard core aims. Although Conservative Baptists adopted the Portland Manifesto in 1953 condemning inclusivism and in 1955 added a premillennial clause to the constitution of the CBA, the hard core was stymied constitutionally in the mission societies, which were supported by broader constituencies, to add a premillennial clause to their doctrinal statements. On the other hand, both societies adopted premillennialism as working policies and eventually added it to the purpose statements of each organization. At the same time, some in the soft core feared the eventual imposition of pretribulationism by the hard core, which they felt would narrow the theological base of Conservative Baptists.

The Conservative Baptists now faced a similar situation within their ranks from the hard core as American Baptists had faced twenty years before from them—a minority that began to organize alternative agencies, which included a new mission society, a new association, and new schools. The CBF took the lead in forming in January, 1962, the World Conservative Baptist Mission, an agency for both foreign and home missions. It adopted a doctrinal statement that included premillennialism and pretribulationism and a board that soon became self-perpetuating. The new mission never received Conservative Baptist recognition and in 1965 changed its name to Baptist World Mission. Upon failure to gain control of the CBA or the Central Region, the hard core provisionally formed in Denver in 1965 the New Testament Association of Independent Baptist Churches of America. (NTA)

The fundamentalists who now left the Conservative Baptists, however, did not coalesce into one body. First, the World Baptist Mission, although gaining some fundamentalist support, never gained the same degree of support from dissidents as did the CBFMS when it first began. Some of the hard core militants rallied around the New Testament Association with church messengers under the leadership of Richard V. Clearwaters (1900–1996) of Minneapolis. On the other hand, some were content to continue affiliation with their regional or state bodies rather than join a national association. And then numbers rallied around the Fellowship with its membership of individuals but not churches.

After helping to birth two different Baptist bodies, one more separatist than the other, one would have thought that the Fellowship would now finally terminate its career. The Fellowship nevertheless continued under G. Archer Weniger (1915–1982), pastor of the Foothill Baptist Church of Castro Valley, California, and president of the Fellowship from 1964 to 1977. In the early '50s, Weniger had already begun producing, *The Blue-Print*, known for its acerbic attacks on liberalism as well as Baptists with neo-evangelical sympathies.[85] In 1967, the Fellowship again changed its name, this time to the Fundamental Baptist Fellowship of America. Although there was tension between the NTA and the Fellowship, in 1974 the two brought about reconciliation but no merger, which in any case would have been difficult between a fellowship of individuals and a fellowship of churches.[86]

To National Status

The FBF finally experienced a fourth incarnation. Under the leadership of Rod L. Bell of the Tabernacle Baptist Church of Virginia Beach, Virginia, who was elected president in 1977, the FBF became a national organization.[87] The Fellowship established five regions—Northeast, Mid-Atlantic, Mid-South, Mid-America, and West Coast. Besides the national conference, each region had its own officers and annual conference. In the '70s, the membership fee was dropped but was reinstituted in 2000. In 2000, the Fellowship listed fifteen regional bodies including Caribbean and International regions.

A survey of the 2000–2001 *Directory* reveals 1,377 individual members with 146 outside the continental USA for a total of 1,523. The members in the United States represented 803 congregations but 197 of them were in the GARBC or a southern-oriented fundamentalist fellowship. Of the remaining 606 congregations with an estimated membership of 97,000, 119 were also in the New Testament Association or independent fundamentalist state bodies.

FBF has pastors with churches in every state except North Dakota. In the North it is well represented in the Mid-Atlantic and Great Lakes regions and in the West in Colorado and California. In the South, in part due to its alliance with Bob Jones University, it has strong representation along the eastern coast and also in West Virginia. With a bit over forty percent of its individual members in the South, it is (except for the American Baptist Churches/USA in West Virginia) the only northern-oriented body to have any significant constituency among the white population of this region.

For many years it published the *Information Bulletin*. In 1991, it began producing, *Frontline Magazine,* an attractive publication, which continues to the present. Besides Bob Jones University, FBF lists eleven other institutions, including Central Baptist Seminary and Pillsbury Baptist Bible College in Minnesota, Maranatha Baptist Bible College in Wisconsin, and Tabernacle Baptist Bible College and Theological Seminary in Virginia Beach, Virginia, founded in 1970 and led by Rod Bell, president of the FBF.

In foreign missions, it lists the Baptist World Mission (BWM) and the Gospel Fellowship Association (GFA), both founded in 1961. The BWM reported in the *Mission Handbook,* 2001–2003, an income of $6,800,000 for foreign ministry and 271 missionaries in all six continents. The GFA, a nondenominational fundamentalist agency, reported 160 missionaries from the USA serving in twenty-five countries or territories.

New Testament Association of Independent Baptist Churches of America (1965)

Individuals who were thwarted in their attempt to move the Conservative Baptist movement to accept strict fundamentalist and separatist policies formed the New Testament Association of Independent Baptist Churches of America (NTA) in 1965.[88] They included members of the hard core Conservative Baptist party, such as Richard V. Clearwaters, who established Central Baptist Seminary in Minneapolis (1956) and Pillsbury Baptist Bible College (1957), B. Myron Cedarholm, who in 1965 resigned after seventeen years as General Director of the CBA, as well as supporters of the Baptist World Mission.[89]

At pre-session meetings of the Conservative Baptist annual meeting in Denver, supporters for a new association met in the Beth Eden Baptist Church where the NTA was provisionally established. The new association forbade membership of churches with other national affiliations. In the following year at the Eagledale Baptist Church of Indianapolis, messengers from twenty-one churches adopted its constitution. In 1968, the number of churches was fifty-two.

As a national body, the NTA has always remained small. In a survey of its membership in 2000, the NTA listed 118 churches, most of which were from its original heartland of Minnesota, Wisconsin, and Illinois and the mountain states of Colorado and Montana. Almost four-fifths of the churches are also members of a state organization.

One reason for its limited size was that it was initially only a dissident faction of a much larger body. Another problem was that numbers of fundamentalists with their natural inclination toward independence found no particular appeal in joining a national association. Many of them were content with their state and regional organizations or would prefer to remain independent and associate at most with a fellowship, such as the FBF with a membership of individuals. Conflict within the ranks of the militants themselves also hurt. Cedarholm, after serving as president of Pillsbury College from 1965 to 1968, broke with Clearwaters and became the founding president of Maranatha Baptist Bible College in Watertown, Wisconsin.[90]

A logical move would have been union with the GARBC, a well-established fundamentalist body with the same ideology. *The Baptist Bulletin* of the GARBC raised the question of union. Clearwaters, however, justified, at least in part, a separate NTA for the reason that the NTA supported stronger stands than the GARBC on a twenty-four-hour day creation and opposition to ecumenical evangelism.[91] A few militant Conservative Baptists nevertheless joined the

GARBC.

The NTA insists that only the King James Version be used at its associational meetings but at the same time did not make it an issue of fellowship. The NTA produces a small bulletin, *NTA Testimonies*, and periodically prints a directory. In 1999, it established a "Land for the Lord Fund" to help churches acquire property.

Fundamental Baptist State and Regional Associations/Fellowships

Much of the associational strength of independent fundamentalists resides in state and regional associations or fellowships rather than in national bodies. Many fundamentalist churches that left the Conservative Baptist movement were already in associations that became independent of Conservative Baptists, while others, notably in California, joined a new state body. Today there are ten fundamentalist state or regional associations or fellowships, including one small one that is today not operational. These bodies are independent of each other and of any national body. On the national level, however, pastors of a number of these churches cooperate with the Fundamental Baptist Fellowship, while some churches, a minority, joined the New Testament Association.

Five of these bodies are in states that border the Great Lakes—Minnesota, Wisconsin, Illinois, Indiana, and Michigan. Additional bodies include one in South Dakota, three in the Mountain states, and one in California.

Minnesota Baptist Association (1859): 5,529 members in fifty-eight churches of which twenty-eight are also in fellowship with the NTA. The association was organized in 1859 as the Minnesota Baptist Convention and was a cooperating member of the Northern Baptist Convention until 1948. It was part of the Conservative Baptist movement until the early 1960s but began supporting the militant party that withdrew from the Conservative Baptists. In 1973, it changed its name from "Convention" to "Association." It publishes a quarterly, *The North Star Baptist*, and publishes an *Annual* of its sessions and reports from its churches. The association lists two camps—Camp Shiloh in the south and Camp Jim in the north. In 1964, leaders loyal to the Conservative Baptists formed the Fellowship of Minnesota Conservative Baptists.

Wisconsin Fellowship of Baptist Churches (1950): 12,750 members in 112 churches, including churches whose pastor, but not the church, is in membership. Eleven churches also relate to the NTA, ten to the FBF, and two to both NTA and FBF. The Fellowship was formerly the CBA of Wisconsin, organized in 1950, but separated from the Conservative Baptists and in 1968 adopted its present name. A minority continued as a CBA of Wisconsin. The Fellowship publishes a paper, *The Baptist Badger*. In its 1999 *Directory* the Fellowship lists Maranatha Baptist Bible College in Watertown, Northland Baptist Bible College in Dunbar, and three Bible camps.

Association of Independent Baptist Churches of Illinois (1948): 20,000 members in 86 churches, including non-member but supporting churches. Fifteen churches associate with the FBF, three with the NTA, and five with both FBF and NTA. It was formerly known as the CBA of Illinois, but in 1971 it changed to its present name. At the division in the '60s the Conservative Baptist minority formed the Fellowship of Illinois Conservative Baptists.

Indiana Fundamental Baptist Fellowship of Churches (1955): 25,200 members in 126 churches. Fifty-five are member churches and seventy-one are fellowshipping congregations. Fifteen associate with the FBF, thirty with the BBF, eight with both the FBF and BBF, and nine with the GARBC. Its *Directory* lists eight institutions of higher learning, including Pillsbury, Maranatha, and Bob Jones. The Fellowship was formed as the CBA of Indiana in 1955, but in 1967 it left the Conservative Baptist movement and adopted its present name. Conservative Baptists were left with no continuing state association.

Independent Fundamental Baptist Association

of Michigan (1948): 16,502 members in 58 churches. Sixteen of them also hold membership in the FBF. The association supports a camp, CoBeAc, at Prudenville. The association was formerly the CBA of Michigan. In 1979, after some years of alienation from the Conservative Baptist movement, it formally separated by adopting its current name. The Conservative Baptist minority withdrew and formed the Fellowship of Michigan Conservative Baptists.[92]

Dakota Baptist Association: 275 members in five churches in South Dakota. They no longer meet as an association.

Mountain States Baptist Fellowship (1962): 6,300 members in fifty-nine churches. Fifty-six churches are in Colorado, two in New Mexico, and one in Kansas. Thirty churches are members, six are associate members, and twenty-three only in fellowship. Ten churches relate to the FBF, twelve to the NTA, four to the GARBC, and eleven to the BBF. An additional five churches in Colorado are not members of the Mountain States Baptist Fellowship but are members of the NTA.

The CBA of Colorado, formed in 1948, broke apart in the '60s between a hard core, which condemned the neo-evangelical orientation of Denver Seminary, and a soft core, causing it to dissolve in 1962.[93] The hard core formed the Mountain States Baptist Fellowship, while the soft core formed the Rocky Mountain CBA. The hard core supported the Denver Baptist Bible College and Seminary, which Sam Bradford, pastor of the Beth Eden Baptist Church of Denver, began in 1962 as Baptist Bible College. At first, it was located at the Beth Eden Church. In 1972, the school expanded its graduate program, forming a graduate school of theology, which in 1974 became known as the Denver Baptist Theological Seminary. In 1975, it moved to Broomfield, a suburb of Denver. In 1977, the GARBC approved it as one of its schools, but because of financial difficulties it merged in 1986 with Faith Baptist Bible College in Ankeny, Iowa, a GARBC school.[94]

Inter-Mountain Baptist Fellowship (IMBF) (1949): 960 members in thirteen churches. All churches are in Montana except for one in Wyoming with seventy-five members. Six churches associate with the FBF, while five with the NTA. It has operated more like an association of churches rather than as a fellowship of pastors. The Fellowship began in 1949 in northern Wyoming as the Big Horn Baptist Fellowship but in 1952 changed its name to the Inter-Mountain Conservative Baptist Fellowship. During the '60s a majority supported the hard core party, and in 1967 the IMBF dropped "Conservative" from its name. About a third, numbering eventually thirteen congregations, withdrew, which greatly reduced the Fellowship's Wyoming base. Beginning in 1950, the IMBF has produced a bulletin, under various names, but today it appears only very sporadically.

Because of factional differences between two groups in the Fellowship, it voted in 1992 to divide its assets between the two parties. One group kept the name, IMBF, and Castle Rock Baptist Camp at Gallatin Gateway, Montana. The second group formed the Grace Baptist Fellowship.[95]

Grace Baptist Fellowship (1992): 1,210 members in twelve churches. All churches are in Montana except two in Wyoming with a membership of 250. It was formed in 1992 in Billings, Montana, by churches that left the Inter-Mountain Baptist Fellowship. It claims to continue the original position of the IMBF and is less legalistic on such issues as ecclesiastical separation, the use of the King James Version, and contemporary music.

Fellowship of Fundamental Baptists of California (1969): 14,710 members in ninety-five churches, including churches whose pastors are only in fellowship. Thirty-eight relate to the FBF and twenty-nine to the BBF. The hard core Conservative Baptist party in Northern California left the Conservative Baptists in the '60s and in 1969 organized the Fellowship as the Association of Fundamental Baptist Churches of Northern California. Today, its *Directory* lists pastors, and its name no longer includes the words "Association" or "Churches." It now includes the entire state of California, but most of its churches are still in the northern part of the state. Two of its leaders were brothers: G. Archer Weniger and Arno Q. Weniger. G. Archer Weniger (d. 1982) was pastor of the Foothill Baptist Church of Castro Valley from 1942 to 1982 and for many years president of the FBF and editor of *The Blue Print*, which aggressively attacked liberalism and neo-evangelicalism. Arno Q. Weniger (d. 1995) became pastor of the Hamilton Square Baptist Church of San Francisco in 1941. With support of the San Francisco Bay Area Conservative Baptist Ministers Fellowship, the San Francisco Conservative Baptist Theological Seminary was founded in 1950 and met on the premises of the Hamilton Square Church. In 1961, Arno Q. Weinger became the second president of the school. The seminary dropped "Conservative" from its title but about 1992 ceased to exist.

Independent Fundamental Churches of America (1930)

The Independent Fundamental Churches of America (IFCA) is an association of individuals and churches, formed in 1930 by individuals from different denominations but united on the fundamentals of the faith. Its *Directory* for 1999-2000 listed among its churches 103 Baptist congregations, primarily in the Middle Atlantic area and states bordering the Great Lakes with smaller numbers in other regions. Many of the churches, however, are non-members but relate to the IFCA through their pastors. Fifteen of the churches relate also to other Baptists, including nine to the BBF and three to the GARBC.

V. Conservative Evangelical (Southern)

	Membership	Attendance	Churches
Southern Baptist Convention	16,244,258	535,891	42,723

Southern Baptist Convention (1845)

The Southern Baptist Convention is the largest Baptist body in the world. Its membership is the most distributed Baptist body in the United States and includes over half of all Baptists in the country. In ranking with other American denominations, it is second only to the Roman Catholic Church and is the nation's largest Protestant body. As its name implies, its constituency, although nationwide, is concentrated in the South, a region where it is dominant except for certain Roman Catholic enclaves primarily of French and Hispanic origin.

The roots of this body are in the colonial period with the first church in the South. First Baptist of Charleston, South Carolina, was established by 1696 with the settlement from Maine of its first pastor, William Screven. It was Regular Baptist. Two of its later pastors, Oliver Hart from Pennsylvania, serving from 1749 to 1780, and Richard Furman, who served from 1787 to 1825, were statesmen of the highest order. Hart founded the first Baptist association in the South, the Charleston in 1751. Furman was the first president of the South Carolina Baptist Convention, organized in 1821, and the first president of the Triennial Convention.

Shubal Stearns, originally from Connecticut but settling in the Piedmont of North Carolina in 1755, led in establishing a Separate Baptist movement. He formed in 1758 the Sandy Creek Association. With a strong emphasis on revivalism, Separate Baptists multiplied, spreading their churches northward to Virginia and southward into South Carolina and other adjoining areas. Between 1787 and 1801, most Regular and Separate Baptists in the South amalgamated into one body, becoming known as United Baptists.

In its earliest years, Baptists in the South were dependent for much of their leadership from the North. They were influenced by the outreach of the Philadelphia Association and adopted its confession of faith. The Philadelphia Association provided a framework of church order, including associational organization and confessional standards, while the Separate Baptists provided evangelistic zeal.

Baptists in the South were in a very fruitful mission field and faced, except for Methodists and the Stone-Campbell Christian Church movement, an almost open field unlike the experience of Baptists in the North who faced more strongly entrenched denominations and a foreign immigrant tide. The South also produced a multitude of farmer preachers. Although many of them were poorly educated and lacked the educational opportunities found in much of the North, they nevertheless identified with the common folk from whom they gained many converts. Baptists also gained numerous adherents from the African-American population, most of whom were slaves.

In 1790, the South had 540 Baptist congregations with 41,679 members as compared to the North with 431 congregations and 25,367 members. With the explosion of Baptist growth during the second Great Awakening, Baptists in the slave states by 1851 numbered almost 500,000 in over 5,700 congregations. Baptists in the North, although also showing significant growth, numbered a bit over 300,000 in almost 3,800 congregations.[96]

In spite of indifference if not outright opposition to educational institutions, including pastoral training, progressive leaders began to establish in the 1820s institutions of higher education. Although limited in number, some Southerners supported the Triennial Convention, formed in 1814 for cooperative work in foreign missions, and the American Baptist Home Mission Society, founded in 1832.

Division and War

Because of slavery, the country experienced a growing sectional divide between North and South. Although only a fourth of Southern white families owned slaves, the greater majority supported the institution not only for its economic benefits but also as a social good for both whites and blacks, fearing social disruption if slaves were emancipated. Religious leaders cited the Bible as recognizing the legitimacy of slavery. When under pressure from abolitionist forces in the North the Triennial Convention and American Baptist Home Mission Society declared that they would not appoint slaveholders as missionaries, Southern Baptists felt they had been unconstitutionally disfranchised. As a consequence, Southern delegates met in 1845 in Augusta, Georgia, and formed the Southern Baptist Convention with two boards—one for foreign missions and one for home missions. Before the division, some Southerners had wanted a more consolidated organization in missions, and some felt the North was sadly neglecting the South as a mission field, but such concerns were not significant factors in the division.[97]

Under the influence of William B. Johnson of South Carolina, presiding officer, who favored a consolidated approach, the new constitution placed the two boards under the convention. Although seeds of consolidation were now planted, the operation of the convention was like the society method with each board an independent agency with its own headquarters, trustees, and budget and membership on a monetary basis.[98]

The delegates issued a Public Address that stressed the division was not doctrinal as Baptists in North and South were of one faith. The Address, reflecting Johnson's views, also declared that the convention has not adopted any creed, recognizing only the Bible as the standard. This did not mean, of course, as some have asserted, that the convention began without a confessional basis. In those days, mission organizations did not set confessional standards, a matter left to associations and the churches. With the general adoption of the Philadelphia Confession and local confessions, confessional standards were in place.[99]

The sectional division in the country not only led to ecclesiastical division of Baptists and other denominations, such as Methodists and Presbyterians, but also led to outbreak of the Civil War in 1861. With the secession of Southern states and the establishment of the Confederate States of America, the South experienced invasion from Union forces. Although some Baptists, particularly in the mountain areas, opposed secession, Southern Baptists, as a whole, endorsed the Confederacy with Baptists providing a significant proportion of its soldiers.[100]

The war brought disruption and devastation. Many soldiers died from combat or disease. Church property was destroyed, church services and associational meetings were disrupted, and educational institutions were forced to close. Numbers of churches lacked pastoral care, and denominational programs in missions and publication suffered financially. The South as a whole suffered great economic loss and was prostrate at the end of the war. In addition, the slaves were now freed but faced serious problems in social and economic adjustment.[101]

After the end of the war in 1865, Southern

Baptists faced a daunting number of critical problems: first, the need of rehabilitation of church and denominational life; secondly, the need for reconciliation among Baptists themselves, such as in Tennessee where strong political differences had existed over the war; and thirdly, the need for new social and religious relations with African Americans now freed from slavery. Blacks began to leave the white churches, where they had been treated as second-class members. They formed their own churches and denominational organizations.

A fourth area was the question of reunion with Northern Baptists. The American Baptist Home Mission Society re-entered the South, claiming North America as its mission field. The U.S. government gave its mission forces permission to occupy Baptist properties, and it worked among both African Americans and Whites. Several Southern Baptist state organizations entered into cooperative relations with it, and its Church Edifice Fund provided gifts and loans. At the same time, the Home Mission Board of the SBC was struggling to survive.

Although there was discussion of reunion, it was not to be. Sectional feelings were too high. The South was unrepentant, and it glorified and sanctified its war-time experiences in "The Lost Cause." The South was also not ready to recognize the equal status of African Americans, which the North was demanding. In addition, Landmarkism, which began in the 1850s, further distanced Baptists in the South from those in the North. Landmarkism not only placed a premium on the local church but also regarded Baptist churches as the only true churches in succession from Apostolic times and rejected all baptism of other denominations and any pulpit affiliation.[102]

Renewal

When the American Baptist Home Mission Society celebrated its fiftieth anniversary in 1882 and was at the peak of its strength, Southern Baptists took in that year two strategic steps in its home mission work. It moved the headquarters of its Home Mission Board from Marion, Alabama, to the rising city of Atlanta, Georgia, and gained the services of an aggressive secretary, Isaac T. Tichenor, who served until his retirement in 1899. Through his energetic efforts the home mission forces multiplied. By 1887, all state conventions in the South were related to the Home Mission Board as well as all missionaries to the white population. The Home Mission Board began a church loan fund in 1884 and entered Cuba in 1886.

In 1888, women formed the Woman's Missionary Union, an auxiliary of the SBC. It provided mission funds and education for both foreign and home missions but did not appoint its own missionaries as did Baptist women in the North. In 1891, Southern Baptists organized their own publishing agency in Nashville, the Baptist Sunday School Board. In a comparatively short time it captured the Southern Baptist market from the American Baptist Publication Society.

In 1891, Southern Baptists cooperated in the formation of a national Baptist Young People's Union but in 1895 formed their own B.Y.P.U. as an auxiliary of the convention. After beginning in 1929 to provide materiel for adults, the B.Y.P.U. Department became in 1934 the Baptist Training Union (today Discipleship Training), a program for all ages, unique to Southern Baptists.

In the traditional Southern states, Southern Baptists continued to support numerous colleges and junior colleges. In 1970, they were supporting forty-three senior colleges, twelve junior colleges, seven academies, and four Bible schools.[103] In the nineteenth century Southern Baptists began to establish mountain mission schools; forty-seven of them received some support from the Home Mission Board between 1891 and 1931.[104]

In 1859, Southern Baptists established their first seminary, Southern Baptist Theological Seminary, in Greeneville, South Carolina, but later moved to Louisville, Kentucky. In 1904, Baptists in Texas formed Baylor Theological Seminary, which in 1908 became Southwestern Theological Baptist Seminary. By 1958, the convention had come to support four additional seminaries. In providing support and retirement for denominational workers, the convention in 1918 formed a Relief and Annuity Board.

In 1894, at Fortress Monroe, Virginia, Northern and Southern Baptists agreed to operate on a basis of comity, not entering areas already occupied by the other party. This led to a general understanding of a geographical line between the two parties, particularly enhanced with the formation in 1907 of the Northern Baptist Convention that drew together the various Northern Baptist agencies. But conflict arose in New Mexico, and after meetings in 1911 and 1912 the difficulty was resolved with the formation of a new state convention aligned with the SBC. Also in 1912, the two conventions affirmed mutual respect and cooperation and to refrain inflicting injury on another Baptist body, recognizing as an ideal only one state body in a state.

The boundary did not remain static and Southern Baptists made other advances in addition to New Mexico. Even earlier, the Illinois Baptist State Association, which broke away from Northern Baptists in 1907, joined Southern Baptists in 1910. The Oklahoma Convention, which in 1906 united various state bodies, voted in 1914 for single alignment with the SBC as did Missouri in 1919.[105] In 1920, Southern Baptists claimed, including separatist Landmark associations, 3,100,000 members in almost 27,000 churches.[106]

A revolution in convention organization, highlighting efficiency and coordination, surged in the first years of the twentieth century. The financial appeals of numerous national and state agencies were costly in time and effort. States began to form executive committees or state mission boards to coordinate all state mission work. States also began to purchase their respective state papers. After the First World War with its high-powered example of enlistment and the plans of other denominations for fundraising for the post-war period, Southern Baptists launched in 1919 a five-year cooperative effort, the Seventy-Five Million Campaign, to fund agencies of the denomination. Although it never reached its goal, it nevertheless set the stage for the establishment in 1925 of the Cooperative Program, a cooperative arrangement of fundraising between the SBC and the state conventions with set allocations for national and state programs.

In spite of the high expectation and record giving to mission and benevolent causes, the convention began to face serious financial problems from falling revenues produced by the coming of an agricultural depression in the South in the '20s, serious defalcations of mission funds in the late '20s, and the serious economic depression of the '30s. Heroic efforts were made to save convention agencies from bankruptcy. Only in 1943 did the convention become free of debt. The return of prosperity in the Second World War and the post-war years brought each year a continuing ascent, although fueled in part by inflated currency, in both mission gifts and total church expenditures.[107]

EXPANSION

Territorial

Even with solidifying its control of border territory in the early years of the twentieth century, the Southern Convention felt confined if not feeling somewhat cornered to traditional Southern territory, extending from Maryland to Texas with some overlapping. Southern Baptists, however, began to migrate outside the South, particularly westward to New Mexico and then to Arizona and California. Migration to California was particularly heavy during the Great Depression in the '30s and during the Second World War in the '40s. During the war years, Southern migrants undertook a second major thrust outside the South by moving to the industrial cities of the Mid-West.[108]

The adjustment with Northern Baptists in 1912 that ceded New Mexico to the Southern Baptist Convention did not end Northern-Southern conflict. Churches with Southern members began to form outside the South without the initiative of the SBC. The New Mexico Convention in 1925 recognized a new Southern Baptist association in Arizona, and in 1929 the Southern Baptist Convention accepted a new Arizona Convention, formed the year before. In 1942, the SBC accepted a Southern Baptist General Convention of California, formed in 1940. These developments brought complaints from Northern Baptist officials who felt this was a Southern Baptist invasion of their territory.

In 1947, Northern Baptists approached the Executive Committee of the SBC to support the appointment of a comity committee to work with a like committee from the Northern Convention. The committee, later called a Committee on Relations with Other Religious Bodies, failed to resolve the problem of boundaries. In responding to the committee's report in 1951, the SBC noted the adoption by Northern Baptists of a continental name (*i. e.* American Baptist Convention) and declared that all SBC agencies were free to operate anywhere in the USA.[109] In the meantime, the SBC had accepted new Southern Baptist state conventions in Kansas in 1948 and Oregon-Washington (now Northwest) in 1949. In 1948, the SBC authorized the Home Mission Board to assist the weak Alaska Convention. With an energetic evangelistic thrust, new conventions later appeared in the Mountain states and Mid-West.

The third Southern Baptist thrust was to the Northeast, which had a much smaller Southern Baptist presence than other areas. The Home Mission Board took the initiative, beginning in 1957, to establish a base in New York City. Mission work spread throughout the Northeast. In 1962, Vermont was the last state to gain a Southern Baptist congregation. Conventions were established in New York (1969), Pennsylvania-South Jersey (1970), and New England (1983). At the beginning of 2004, Southern Baptists covered the entire USA with a state convention by the transformation of the Dakotas Fellowship, formed in 1983, into a state convention.[110]

A number of factors propelled the emergence of Southern Baptist churches and conventions outside the South. First, cultural differences played a significant role.[111] Numbers of transplanted Southern Baptists wished to maintain their own church practices including evangelistic/revivalistic preaching and denominational programs. Many Southerners felt more at home with fellow Southerners.

Some Southerners, particularly in the West and Mid-West, often came from Landmark areas and felt they did not find the same Baptist exclusivism and consciousness in Northern churches. To distance themselves from Northern Baptists and to justify Southern Baptist entry into northern territory, Southern spokesmen pointed out what they considered were objectionable practices of Northern Baptists: ties with the Federal Council of Churches, comity agreements, tolerance of liberalism, open communion, and accepting immersions from non-Baptist churches. Some, including the first executive secretary of the California Southern Baptist Convention, even opposed accepting baptisms from Northern Baptist churches because of their alleged loose practices.

Southern Baptist leaders were also motivated to spread the gospel. Southern Baptist missionaries, supported by the Home Mission Board and Sunday School Board, looked with post-war confidence upon the territory outside the South as a vast untapped mission field.[112]

Urban

Southern Baptist expansion has not only witnessed the transformation of the convention from a regional body to a national body but also has included urban and multi-ethnic expansion. Until the Second World War, the Southern Convention, even with leading churches in cities and county seats, was still predominantly rural, reflecting the economic status of the South itself. Many rural churches faced poverty, possessed poor facilities, enjoyed only part-time preaching, and were served by untrained pastors.[113] In more recent decades, the rural churches that have survived, by and large, now have greatly improved facilities, weekly preaching, a fuller church program, and better trained pastors.

As late as 1949, only sixteen percent of the churches were in urban areas, but as Southerners moved to the city the percentage by the early sixties reached twenty-eight percent.[114] The urban church, including churches in the growing suburbs, has become an increasingly important segment of Southern Baptist life. Southern Baptists have also witnessed the coming of the megachurch, a phenomenon particularly seen in the South and West. Megachuches draw 2,000 or more in weekly attendance and possess large campuses, extended staff supported by numerous volunteers, greatly expanded programs and services, numerous fellowship groups, and provide contemporary worship. The largest number of megachuches are independent, yet Southern Baptists claim nineteen percent of them.[115]

Ethnic[116]

Before the Civil War Southern Baptist churches included a significant number of African-American members and also engaged in Indian missions but, in comparison to Baptists in the North, for years their outreach to ethnics was otherwise limited. After the war, its African-American membership left, and its home mission program to ethnics was weak. In addition, the South did not attract the multitudes of ethnic populations as in the North.

Under I. T. Tichenor, who became executive secretary of the Home Mission Board in 1882, Southern Baptists increased their support for ethnic work. Such efforts continued to be modest, including their work among Indians, Hispanics, and Chinese, until the Second World War. A decided shift occurred in 1940 with the inauguration of a city mission program that included a significant increase in foreign-language missions. The expansion of the convention to the Pacific Coast, which helped to open the door to national expansion, also opened a door to a national commitment of ethnic ministries.

The great increase of immigrants from around the globe also greatly expanded the mission field for ethnic work. Besides 500,000 African Americans in over 2,100 churches and missions, in 1999 the SBC claimed 300,000 additional ethnics in over 4,200 churches and missions.[117] The largest non-African-American groups were Hispanics with 122,485 members in 2,074 congregations; 38,205 Native Americans in 326 congregations; 34,959 Koreans in 593 congregations; 24,559 Haitians in 238 congregations; 22,090 Chinese in 189 congregations; 7,658 Filipinos in 133 congregations, and 7,379 Vietnamese in 108 congregations.

New mission starts continue apace; in four years from 2000 through 2003 Southern Baptists established over 4,000. A total of twenty-two ethnic fellowships, with their own presidents, cooperate with Southern Baptists. Southern Baptists probably worship in over one hundred different languages.

Southern Baptists have always had a special relationship with African Americans. Between the end of slavery in the 1860s and the Civil Rights Revolution of the 1960s, Southern Baptists accepted segregation of blacks as the norm and rejected any suggestion of social equality. On the other hand, Southern Baptists retained a paternalistic interest in the black race and provided assistance in a number of areas, including mission aid, education, scholarships, and conferences. With National Baptists, they opened in 1924 the American Baptist Theological Seminary in Nashville for the training of black pastors.

The Civil Rights movement of the '60s helped to change racial attitudes. Convention and mission leaders, in spite of opposition, helped to lead the convention in acquiescing to desegregation, and a new era of cooperation began to dawn. Even earlier in the '50s a few black Baptist churches sought affiliation with Southern Baptists. By 1975, the number had grown to about 400 with many of them dually aligned with a National Baptist body. In its reorganization in 1959, the Home Mission Board established a Program of Work with National Baptists and with convention approval in 1973 changed its name to Cooperative Ministries with National Baptists to emphasize a fraternal rather than a paternal relationship. In 1975, the Home Mission Board took a significant step in its mission strategy to begin establishing Southern Baptist African-American congregations. In 1991, black Southern Baptists formed an African American Southern Baptist Fellowship.[118]

The SBC has today a significant number of African-American churches. African-American personnel have been incorporated in staff positions and some have been elected as denominational officers. The churches themselves, however, remain largely segregated. Although almost twenty-five percent of Southern Baptist churches have some black members, few fully integrated congregations exist.

In recent years, the convention has attempted to shed its image of past support of slavery and segregation and insensitivity toward racial issues. In 1968, the convention, upon the assassinations of Martin Luther King, Jr., and Robert Kennedy, although opposed by a minority of the messengers, adopted "A Statement Concerning The Crisis in Our Nation," which condemned violence and racism. In 1995, the convention publicly apologized for its past acceptance of slavery and racism.

ECCLESIOLOGY

Southern Culture

In a map projecting religious patterns of dominant groups, except for Roman Catholic enclaves, Southern Baptists dominate where Southern culture dominates. To a remarkable degree Southern Baptists have helped to mold Southern culture and in turn has been molded by it, reflecting to a significant degree the South's conservative ethos and folkways. Critics have called Southern Baptist religious expression a folk religion, a faith of the common people who major on fraternal identity, religious feeling, and personal fellowship with intellectual concerns and societal problems playing minor roles. In its expansion into non-Southern areas, much of its early work there was primarily establishing Southern outposts.

In spite of changes in the names of its agencies and its national constituency, the convention has resisted eliminating "Southern" from its name. In 1974, the convention authorized a committee to study the issue but in 2004 even rejected the authorization of any committee. In spite of the handicap of the name in non-Southern areas, the name provides for many both a regional and a theological identity.

Some academicians, such as Rufus B. Spain and John Lee Eighmy, have noted the close affinity of Southern Baptists to Southern social views, beginning with slavery and majoring on personal rather than social morality. Spain accused them of being "at ease" in their social environment, and Eighmy, although noting an opening to more moderate social views, suggested their churches were in "cultural captivity."[119]

In any case, even if wedded to Southern culture and conservative values, Southern Baptists have nevertheless made positive social contributions, particularly in their establishment of numerous benevolent and educational institutions and their support of personal morality. From their revivalist heritage, the majority of Southern Baptists have tended to stress individual conversion and personal ethics as over against social reconstruction or reforming the structures of society.

Centralization

For a denominational body rooted in a section fighting for states' rights and with Landmark roots that upheld the independence of the local church, it is somewhat ironic that Southern Baptists developed the most coordinated Baptist body in the USA.[120] An additional irony comes from Landmarkism itself. Its identification of the totality of Baptist churches with the Kingdom of God and its view of Baptist successionism helped to create the consciousness of a corporate body.

In the face of the growing fundamentalist conflict in the '20s, the Southern Convention, in contrast to the Northern Convention, adopted a confessional standard, *The Baptist Faith and Message*, a revision of the New Hampshire Confession of Faith. As a body rooted in a socially conservative region of the nation, wary of liberal developments outside its area, and even with some diversity a rather doctrinally homogeneous constituency, it was much easier for it to take this step than for Northern Baptists. Unlike in the North, its seminaries, all with doctrinal standards, were controlled by the convention. The convention had already earlier approved statements on its identity, and in 1920 its foreign board adopted a doctrinal standard for new appointees.

In his study of Southern Baptist ecclesiastical development, William Barnes, professor of church history at Southwestern Baptist Theological Seminary, pointed out that the convention simply began as a body for missions, controlled by its financial contributors as any mission society. Almost a century later he noted that the convention had become a centralized body engaged in a multitude of causes with voting members limited to the churches, some of which gave just minimal support. The convention also now recorded its constituency as encompassing all churches, whether contributing, which were in associations of the cooperating state conventions.

Barnes noted, besides Landmarkism, a number of other contributing agents to centralization. He pointed out the development of state conventions with combined programs, the establishment of an Executive Committee, the Seventy-five Million Campaign that led to the

Cooperative Program, the ownership of religious papers by the denomination, and the adoption of a doctrinal statement, which he called a creed. He felt that in the future the convention might impose the doctrinal statement upon the churches.

A former Southern Baptist professor, LeRoy Moore, wrote a critical article in the '70s on the Southern Baptist Convention in which he charged it with majoring on efficiency, financial growth, and statistical increase and being run like a business corporation. He noted the convention's control of its seminaries and conformational Sunday school program. He nevertheless admitted, however, that seminary professors, if circumspect in their publishing efforts, were comparatively free in the classroom.[121]

THEOLOGY

The Question of a Theological Center

In his work, in 1983, on Baptists polity, James L. Sullivan, the head for many years of the Baptist Sunday School Board, placed Southern Baptists in the center of a continuum from left to right, eschewing liberalism, on the one hand, but also ultraconservatism, on the other hand.[122] He contended that Southern Baptists were conservative without a capital "C". Sullivan denounced J. Frank Norris, a rabid fundamentalist of an earlier time, for his extremism and disruptive activity. Sullivan wrote as a denominational official who with other leaders for years had been able to maintain a generally acceptable somewhat right-of-center consensus.

Wayne Flynt, professor at Auburn University, developed the thesis that, although no Southern Baptist ever became an advanced liberal, nevertheless Southern Baptists included an influential minority that was more open to motifs of the social gospel, liberal theology, and ecumenism than the mainstream of Southern Baptist life.[123] One such figure was W. O. Carver (1868–1954), for many years professor of comparative religion and missions at Southern Baptist Theological Seminary.[124] In his work, *A Genealogy of Dissent*, David Stricklin describes the work of a small group of progressives but who, he claimed, were not adequately supported by the then moderate leadership of the convention.[125]

A debate between James Leo Garrett, Jr., professor of theology at Southwestern Baptist Seminary, and E. Glenn Hinson, professor of church history at Southern Baptist Seminary, was published in 1982 on the question whether Southern Baptists were evangelicals. Garrett argued in the affirmative, pointing to Southern Baptist allegiance to Biblical authority and passion for missions. Hinson answered in the negative, pointing out their dissenting origins and advocacy of voluntarism that made them anti-creedal, anti-sacerdotal, anti-sacramental, and anti-establishmentarian.[126]

Foy Dan Valentine, at the time executive secretary of the convention's Christian Life Commission, denied that Southern Baptists were evangelicals by denouncing northern evangelicals for their politics, fastidiousness in their fundamentalist formulations, and theological attacks.[127] For Hinson and Valentine, as moderates, they were above all ready to deny identification of Southern Baptists with northern evangelicals whom they regarded as fundamentalists.

Timothy Weber, who after teaching for years among northern evangelicals, joined the faculty of Southern Baptist Seminary in 1991. In a discerning article in 1995, comparing evangelicalism North and South, he noted that in contrast to the rest of the nation that evangelicals in the South appeared to own the culture. In addition, Southerners differed from northern evangelicals historically and culturally and were more exclusively denominational. On the other hand, in contrast to Valentine, he found far more in common and even convergence between evangelicals North and South.[128]

Even if one accepts Garrett and Weber's views that Southern Baptists are in the mainstream of evangelicalism, differences between the SBC and evangelicals in the North are nevertheless evident. Joel A. Carpenter's essay, "Is 'Evangelical' a Yankee Word? Relations Between Northern Evangelicals & the Southern Baptist Convention in the Twentieth Century," points out not only the cultural and organizational differences but also doctrinal tensions, including the ironic observation that many northern evangelicals would find the ascendant conservatives in the SBC as too fundamentalist.[129]

For northern evangelicals, eschatology has played a more defining role while ecclesiology a much lesser role; the reverse is true for Southern Baptists. Unlike northern evangelicals, many of whom were struggling minorities, Southern Baptists until more recent years have had a feeling of regional and cultural security and a sense of Christian progress and were thus less attracted to premillennial and dispensational views. Their denominational control of theological education also limited far more the impact of the premillennial teachings of independent Bible schools and seminaries than among Baptists in the North. In ecclesiology with their Landmark heritage, Southern Baptists had developed a successful denominational system, while northern evangelicals almost as a necessity looked for allies across denominational lines for intellectual and fraternal support. But times change—for Southern Baptists premilllennialism has become more important and ecclesiology much less.

Doctrinal Conflict

In the early '60s, the convention engaged in heated controversy over *The Message of Genesis*, a book with higher critical views, written by Ralph H. Elliott, professor at Midwestern Baptist Seminary. The furor led to Elliott's dismissal in 1962 and a revision of the *Baptist Faith and Message* in 1963. In a criticism of Genesis in volume one of the *Broadman Bible Commentary*, the convention in 1970 voted for the volume to be rewritten and in the following year for the replacement of the original writer.

Even with these victories, conservatives still continued to be wary of the infiltration into the seminaries and colleges of historical-critical views of the Bible. Judge Paul Pressler of Houston and Paige Patterson of Dallas spearheaded a movement to elect conservative presidents of the convention who, in turn, with their power to appoint the Committee on Committees would ensure the nomination of conservative trustees of the agencies and seminaries of the convention.

The plan began to work with the election in 1979 of Adrian Rogers of Memphis, Tennessee, as president of the convention. With the subsequent election of conservative presidents, by 1990 the conservatives had full control of the convention. As a result moderates lost their positions as heads of agencies, and in the seminaries moderate officials and many professors either left or were forced to resign.[130]

Both conservatives and moderates used code words or shibboleths. For the former, it was "biblical inerrancy;" for the latter it was "freedom."[131] Both appealed to Baptist history. The conservatives pointed to Baptist allegiance to biblical authority and the confessional heritage that stated the Bible was infallible and "without any mixture of error." The moderates pointed to Baptist support for soul liberty and the right of private interpretation.

The interpretation and use of Scripture was fundamental since both sides claimed allegiance to scriptural authority. Conservatives were more literal in biblical interpretation, highlighted the Bible's supernatural character, defended it against alleged inconsistencies and errors, and strongly criticized more liberal options. Although not denying the divine inspiration and authority of Scripture, moderates included those who either accepted or tolerated views more open to higher criticism and the possibility of scientific and historical error. Moderates were also more sympathetic toward cultural trends in academia and modern life.

With their conservative view of Scripture and opposition to liberal trends in society, conservatives also had an impact on the SBC in moral and social issues. In an article in 1982, entitled, "The New Religious Right and Its Implications for Southern Baptists," James E. Wood, Jr., former executive of the Baptist Joint Committee on Public Affairs and a moderate, noted the growing ties between Southern Baptist leaders and the Religious Right. He criticized the Religious Right for simplistic answers to complex issues, its sanctification of American nationalism, its transforming political issues into moral absolutes, and a lack of a social conscience.[132] In fact, the emergence in 1979 of the Religious Right coincided in the same year with the Southern Baptist shift. Nevertheless, Wood pointed out that Southern Convention resolutions up to his writing in the early '80s, by and large, did not follow the agenda of the Religious Right and possibly the

Religious Right had reached the peak of its influence. But with the continuing success of the conservative forces in the convention in the '80s, his hope for moderates proved illusory. Moderates no longer set the agenda.

After reducing its funding, the convention withdrew from the Baptist Joint Committee on Public Affairs in 1991, an agency that advocated strict separation of church and state. The convention also condemned abortion and homosexuality (which included the disbarring of churches that accepted gay members) and advocated prayer in the public schools. Although beginning in the '50s, some churches began to ordain women as deacons and by 1979 may have ordained as many as sixty-five women (the first in 1964) as pastors, conservatives have resisted this development. With amendments to the Baptist Faith and Message in 1998 and 2000, the convention upheld traditional views of the role of women, including an article on the family that supported male headship and limited the pastoral office to men. Today the amended confession has become a statement of accountability for SBC agencies. In 1995–1997, the conservatives restructured the convention, eliminating four of its agencies—historical, stewardship, Brotherhood, and education.[133]

For conservatives their resurgence proved to be a resounding success but also left scars and produced division. The controversy politicized the convention into two warring parties. With the winner taking all, a number of moderates, theologically evangelical, were forced out or left the convention for competing organizations. Some no longer cooperated with Southern Baptists on the national level and confined themselves to the state level or left completely. Although in time most of the state conventions have fallen in line with the conservative trends, in Virginia and Texas, however, moderates maintained control of their respective state conventions with the result that in these states conservatives have formed their own state conventions. In Missouri the opposite occurred with moderates forming in 2002 a second convention—Baptist General Convention of Missouri—but not recognized as a cooperating convention by the SBC.

Many in the conventions tried to be neutral or were critical of both sides. One such person in the latter group was Kenneth Mahanes of Ohio, who in a message entitled, "Caught in The Cross Fire," at a pastor's conference decried the turmoil and disunity. He said he would join the conservatives if they would permit free expression of interpretation and practice or join the moderates if they would recognize that "freedom has legitimate limits."

Beginning in the '60s, Southern Baptists with other Southerners have shifted from their traditional allegiance from the Democratic Party to the more conservative Republican Party. Because of its alignment with views of the Religious Right, the Republican Party with Southern Baptist support has today unparalleled predominance in the South, helping to propel Republicans to victory in national elections.[134]

The convention has witnessed a revived interest in Calvinism in some circles. The current president of the Southern Baptist Seminary, Albert Mohler, is a committed evangelical Calvinist. Since 1983 the Southern Baptist Founders Conference, which promotes Calvinism, has met in annual session.[135]

While doctrinally and on moral issues the convention has shifted more towards the fundamentalist right, its ecclesiology, however, has been shifting away from exclusive Landmark Baptist tenets. In 1970, a Baptist Viewpoll recorded that about twenty percent of the pastors would accept alien immersion, *i.e.* believers immersed in non-Baptists congregations. Twenty years later, a Baptist Viewpoll in 1990 exhibited even greater openness—half would not require rebaptism if the immersed believer was in agreement with Baptist doctrine and another eight percent would receive any immersed believer. The same poll revealed a wide acceptance of open communion with seventy-six accepting any believer at the Lord's Table or leaving it up to the individual. Only fifteen percent would invite only individuals "of like faith and order" and five percent would restrict the Table to members of the local church. On the other hand, unlike many American Baptist churches in the North, most Southern Baptists practice close membership, requiring believer's baptism by immersion for membership.

As Samuel S. Hill, Jr., has pointed out, Southern Baptists are both sect-type and church-type; acting like a sect outside the South but like a church-type denominational body in the South in its identification with Southern culture.[136] Southern Baptists are probably both church and sect and be best described as "denominational sectarians."[137] The SBC is sectarian in its exclusivism, its magnification of distinct characteristics, its priority on personal morality, and opposition to the dominant culture. It is church-like in its identification with the culture of its home region, its concerns with national policy, the increasing identification of its membership with the general population due to the lack of church discipline, the inclusion of a large non-resident membership, and the widespread practice of baptizing children before the age of accountability.

DENOMINATIONAL RELATIONS

Its very size and financial strength have forced the SBC, even in spite of itself, to play a role—positively or negatively—in its relations to other denominations.[138] By refusing to join the Home Mission Council and Federal Council of Churches, both formed in 1908, the World Council of Churches in 1948, and the National Council of Churches in 1950, Southern Baptists, unlike the mainline denominations in the USA, have, by and large, remained outside the ecumenical movement.[139]

Because of their conservative doctrinal and social concerns, many Southern Baptists have felt their positions to be incompatible with the theological liberal and social priorities of ecumenists. Baptists have also used the argument that the convention cannot commit its independent churches to any other agency, although such an argument was no hindrance to their joining the Baptist World Alliance. In addition, the Southern Convention did not seek to join the National Association of Evangelicals when it was formed in 1942. In this period, Southern Baptists, as Great Britain felt at the turn of the twentieth century, that it could follow a policy of "splendid isolation," rejecting blandishments from both the ecumenists on the left and evangelicals on the right.

On the other hand, Southern Baptists have not been complete isolationists. For instance, on the basis of practicality if not expediency, they have been more amenable to consultation if it involves cooperation in foreign missions. Representatives of the Foreign Mission Board were present at the London Mission Conference in 1888, although refusing to accept comity. The Foreign Mission Board became a founding member of the Foreign Missions Conference of North American in 1893. They continued as a member to 1919 and then again from 1938 to 1950, leaving when the Conference joined the National Council. The Foreign Board, now called the International Mission Board, in 1995 became a member of the Evangelical Fellowship of Mission Agencies (EFMA).

Southern Baptists have been supporters of the American Bible Society, the Billy Graham evangelistic campaigns, and have cooperated with other groups in opposing gambling and liquor interests. Various Southern Baptist educational institutions and individuals have engaged from time to time in a number of consultations

Up until recently, Southern Baptists have devoted most of their ecumenical energies in relationships with fellow Baptists. It gave the denomination a sense of reaching out beyond its own boundaries. It was a founding member of the Baptist World Alliance (BWA) in 1905 and for years its strongest financial supporter. The BWA allowed Southern Baptists to be a major player on the world stage and a means of helping to solidify Baptist identity; the BWA was also a natural tie to their own international mission interests. In 1965, after some hesitation, it joined the North American Baptist Fellowship, a regional body of the Alliance.

Today, however, the SBC is no longer a member of the BWA. In questions over the full commitment of the BWA to conservative evangelical tenets and the acceptance by the BWA of the Cooperative Baptist Fellowship (CBF), a moderate dissident body coming out of Southern Baptist ranks, the SBC withdrew in 2004. Although it has withdrawn from the BWA, it does not seek to isolate itself from other world Baptists but is seeking fraternal ties abroad, such as in Eastern Europe.

In 1938, the Southern and Northern Baptist committees on public relations held a joint conference that resulted in the following year in the formation of a joint committee on public relations, later calling itself the Baptist Joint Committee on Public Affairs. Other Baptist bodies also joined. In opposition to the position of the Joint Committee on issues of church and state, the SBC withdrew in 1991 from the organization, today called the Baptist Joint Committee for Religious Liberty.

While the Southern Baptist leadership has shifted away from cooperation with groups that include moderates and liberals, at the same time it finds itself opening to fraternal relations with Baptist fundamentalists who years before had separated from the convention. Southern Baptist leaders have spoken at conferences sponsored by Jerry Falwell, a leader in fundamentalist circles, who died in May of 2007. They have served on the board of his Liberty University. Falwell's large independent Thomas Road Baptist Church of Lynchburg, Virginia, is a member of the Southern Convention and has joined the conservative Southern Baptist state convention in Virginia.

In addition, the SBC leadership has shown an interest in associating with the International Baptist Network (IBN), a fellowship of fundamentalist Baptists, formed in 2003. At a joint meeting of three fundamentalist fellowships in the Network, held in September, 2004, at the Highland Park Baptist Church in Chattanooga, Southern Baptists participated. They again participated at the public meeting of IBN in Dallas in February, 2005. The director of IBN is Gene Mims, former president of LifeWay Christian Resources, who is stationed in Atlanta.[140]

Southern Baptists have also shifted somewhat toward northern conservative evangelicals not only with its International Board joining the EFMA but also engaging evangelical scholars to teach in their seminaries and to write for their *New American Commentary*. In early 2005, *Time* magazine noted twenty-five most influential evangelicals in the United States among whom were Southern Baptists. The list included not only Billy Graham but also Rick Warren of Saddleback Church, called "America's New People's Pastor," and Richard Land of the Ethics and Religious Liberty Commission of the SBC.[141]

DANGERS

Because of its size and expansion, the convention has been more successful than others to disguise its weaknesses and potential threats. Today the South is less homogeneous than in the past. With migration from the North, the increase of ethnic populations, the growth of a more sophisticated and secular population, and a generation devoted to consumerism, it has become a less congenial mission field. The large families of the past are no longer the potential source of converts as before. Southern Baptist observers have noted a slowing down of the rapid increases in the years after the Second World War. The convention is experiencing a decline in the ratio of baptisms to membership and an increase in declining churches and an aging membership. Today there are 400,000 less children in Sunday school than in 1971.

The departure of certain moderate elements, however, is more problematic. A number of churches now contribute to agencies outside the SBC and declare they are no longer Southern Baptists. Such division lessens membership and also a progressive element that helps to develop a creative tension that keeps a denomination from ossifying; on the other hand, it may remove elements that dilute a denomination's character and fractures a united mission. In addition,, the oldest and most prestigious schools in Virginia, North Carolina, Georgia, Florida, Kentucky, and Texas have severed their relations with state Baptist conventions over such issues as academic freedom, student behavior, and control. Some of them have left their Baptist identity but others still seek to retain it.

Although the denomination has sought to protect its denominational identity, it faces, however, the threat of loss of identity from across-the-board evangelicalism. In an effort to be more effective in evangelism, some Southern Baptists have begun to settle for a generic evangelicalism in theology and worship, thereby losing denominational distinctives and even a willingness to give up the name "Baptist" in a church's name. In addition, strong parachurch organizations also beckon for the talents and support of potential denominational leaders. Even the megachurches that add significant numbers to membership and average attendance can also be a weakening factor as they become sufficient unto themselves, feeling little or no need of a denominational tie.

Much of the dangers are within. With the decline of church discipline and its requirement of living a disciplined lifestyle, the membership itself has become inclusive, numbering many on church rolls who have become inactive or nonresident. The *Religious Congregations and Membership* study in 2000 reported that the average attendance in Southern Baptist churches was just under thirty-five percent of membership. On the other hand, a recent Gallup Poll reported Southern Baptists claiming sixty percent for weekly or almost weekly attendance, higher than any mainline denomination. Although infant baptism is rejected, numbers are now baptized at very young ages, introducing what some would consider not believer's but child baptism.

In a recent article, Bill J. Leonard, dean of the Wake Forest University Divinity School, critical of the recent shifts in Southern Baptist policies and programs, suggested that the SBC is "a crumbling empire" that no longer has its former regional dominance.[142] Although including a number of valid observations, such as pointing out the rise of agencies outside the SBC orbit, the article fails to balance his views with anything positive, including the convention's financial health, its resiliency, a strong theological center, and its ability to keep the vast majority of its constituency united on moral issues, unlike the case in a number of other denominations.

Unlike other major Protestant denominations, the Southern Baptist Convention has generally posted an annual increase, reaching over 16,000,000 by 2002. It includes a significant number of megachurches. It also has some of the largest accredited theological seminaries in the country with Southwestern (3,000 students), New Orleans (2,800), and Southern (2,250) respectively holding second, third, and fourth place in 2004. With 5,400 missionaries and 34,000 short-term volunteers in 2004, the International Mission Board is the largest Protestant agency for overseas work, reporting an income of around $200,000,000. Along with the Red Cross and Salvation Army, the SBC is in the top three agencies for disaster relief.[143]

The Alliance of Baptists and the Cooperative Baptist Fellowship

The conservative resurgence within the Southern Baptist Convention produced dissident groups, the Alliance of Baptists, formed first in 1987 as the Southern Baptist Alliance, and the Cooperative Baptist Fellowship (CBF), which after an initial meeting in 1990 was formally organized in 1991. Their supporters claimed that such organizations were needed to uphold the historic principles of Baptist freedom and to give a forum to critics of the new conservative leadership. Both give equity for women in pastoral roles, although in both groups men predominate.

The more radical of the two, the Alliance of Baptists, claims the affiliation of 121 churches in twenty-five states. Its largest number of churches—twenty-one—is in North Carolina. Although the Alliance has severed all ties with the convention, a number of its churches continue to have ties with Southern Baptist state conventions. With its role as a support group for moderates, the Alliance has engaged in a number of special projects. It formed the Baptist Theological Seminary at Richmond, helped to establish the CBF, and developed the "Formations" Sunday school curriculum.

The Alliance and CBF considered merger in 1991–1992, but because of the Alliance's promotion at the time of women in pastoral ministry and its acceptance of homosexuals the merger was not consummated. In 2002, it was reported that over eighty percent of the churches of the Alliance also support the CBF. The Alliance has become a member of the National Council of Churches and has engaged in conversations with the United Church of Christ and the Disciples of Christ.[144]

Like the Alliance, the CBF is an advocate of ecclesiastical freedom, gender equality, and ecumenical dialog. Its primary focus, however, has been missions. Over sixty percent of its budget goes for missions, while other moneys are spent for theological education and other objects. The CBF also includes eighteen state or regional fellowships, most of which employ full-time coordinators. The CBF is also an endorsing agency for chaplains in the United States armed forces and correctional institutions.[145]

In 1991, the CBF received $4,500,000 from almost 400 churches. In 2002, it had a budget of $18,000,000 and 130 missionaries with 1,774 churches providing some degree of support. Seventy-seven percent of the support of the CBF comes from six states as follows in descending order: Texas, Virginia, North Carolina, Georgia, Kentucky, and South Carolina. A majority of the supporting churches of the CBF have not withdrawn entirely from the Southern Convention or at least still maintain ties on the state level. Numbers of supporting churches do not identity themselves as CBF churches or provide funds for it from their budgets but permit their members to designate to it. On the other hand, a total of 115 churches have declared themselves in partnership with the CBF and have left the SBC.[146]

For years the CBF has struggled with problems of identity and its future. If it is not a traditional denomination in a so-called post-denominational age, as its spokespersons aver, what is it?[147] Many of its constituency would prefer just to recreate the Southern Baptist consensus and program of the past, while others are open to more advanced views on women in ministry, homosexuality, ecumenical ties, and open membership.

Both the Alliance and the CBF act more like parachurch groups with special interests—the Alliance as an advocacy group for moderate Baptist principles and programs, while the CBF is primarily a mission organization. Neither claims to be a denomination with the CBF rejecting in 1995 to establish a new convention. Even attempts in the CBF to align churches as members of the CBF have been met with strong resistance.[148] Unlike almost all other Baptist bodies, they have no doctrinal statements or formal ecclesiastical ties with their supporting churches.

On the other hand, the development of a cluster of moderate organizations and moderate educational institutions has for all practical purposes created a quasi-denominational structure. These organizations, each independent, include Associated Baptist Press (1990), Baptist Center for Ethics (1991), Smyth & Helwys Publishing (1991), the periodical, *Baptists Today* (1983), Baptist Women in Ministry (1983), and the William H. Whitsitt Baptist Heritage Society.[149]

The CBF also partners with organizations from which the Southern Baptist Convention has severed its ties such as the Baptist Joint Committee for Religious Liberty and the Baptist World Alliance. The CBF joined the latter in 2003, which helped to precipitate the full withdrawal of the SBC from this organization in the following year. The CBF also partners with fourteen theological schools and seminaries with four given a privileged status.

The time may come when the CBF becomes a full-fledged denominational body with formal ecclesiastical ties and with a majority of its churches fully separated from the SBC with numbers possibly maintaining a dual affiliation. In part this may come from either the actions of state conventions in Virginia and Texas, controlled by moderates, or by the action of the SBC itself as to affiliation. But this time has as yet not come.

Some moderates both inside and outside the CBF also support the Mainstream Baptist Network, an organization formed nationally in 2000 to combat fundamentalism within the state conventions of the SBC. With Texas Baptists Committed, an organization within the Baptist General Convention of Texas, serving as a model, about fifteen state mainstream organizations have appeared with very loose ties.[150]

The question is whether moderates, now fragmented, would be able to unite and on what basis. Cecil Sherman, the first coordinator of the CBF, declared in 2002 that moderates need to unite in one encompassing denomination, a suggestion that was met by strong opposition from within the CBF itself.[151]

VI. FUNDAMENTAL (SOUTHERN)

	MEMBERSHIP	CHURCHES
World Baptist Fellowship (1932)	158,500	998
Baptist Bible Fellowship (1950)	525,165	3,294
Independent Baptist Fellowship International (1984)	103,300	650
Southwide Baptist Fellowship (1956)	80,500	507
SUBTOTAL	867,465	5,449
Multiple memberships	-173,465	-1,091
TOTAL	**694,000**	**4,358**

Southern fundamentalists, also known as Independents, belong to four national fellowships.[152] An estimate of their membership is around 700,00 members in over 4,300 churches. Many churches relate to more than one fundamentalist body, thereby creating a large number of multiple memberships. They are well represented throughout the South but with particular strength in the Trans-Mississippi South where around twenty-five percent of their membership is located. They have a strong representation in the Great Lakes region where twenty-two percent of their membership resides.

Southern fundamentalists are strong adherents of the fundamentals of the faith as well as firm advocates of premillennialism and pretribulationism. They are militant opponents of theological liberalism. They have been more outspoken than most other Baptists in upholding traditional values and denouncing personal worldliness and immorality. With roots in the South and former association with the Southern Baptist Convention, they often come with a southern accent, not only in cultural traits but also for some affinity for Baptist successionism and rejection of cooperation with non-Baptists.[153]

They are strong advocates of local church independency with the pastor playing a dominant role in church affairs. They favor "fellowships" rather than "conventions" for their general bodies, regarding the latter as bureaucratic and controlling the local church. In some cases churches may send messengers to an annual assembly for electing officers and boards for the national body but are not members of any local associations. Pastors, who are all male, meet in state or regional fellowships for inspiration and discussion of mutual concerns.

The national fellowships use a three-pronged strategy—a missions office or missions program, support of one or more educational institutions, and the publication of a paper.[154] Both the World Baptist Fellowship and the Baptist Bible Fellowship International adopted the revision of the New Hampshire Confession of Faith as adopted by the Baptist Bible Union. Except for the Southwide Fellowship that lists membership by individuals, the other three fellowships list membership by churches.

Southern Fundamentalists continue the southern tradition of revivalism and evangelism. At the same time they have been very adept in adopting modern media, such as radio and television, to proclaim their message. With the Southern migration during and after the Second World War, they, along with Southern Baptists, have planted churches throughout the North and West. Along with northern fundamentalists, they are strong supporters of international missions. In 2004, four of their mission agencies raised about seventy million dollars to support over 2,000 missionaries on foreign fields.[155]

J. Frank Norris (1877–1952), pastor of First Baptist Church of Fort Worth, Texas, from 1909 until his death, was the founding father of Southern Fundamentalism. He established the first Southern fundamentalist fellowship that set the pattern for later fellowships. He was a dynamic pulpiteer and radio preacher and at the height of his career was pastor simultaneously of two huge congregations, 1,200 miles apart, claiming 25,000 members—First Baptist of Fort Worth, Texas, and Temple Baptist of Detroit, Michigan. He was also a founder of a training school, an editor, and crusader for religious and moral causes.

At the same time, Norris became America's most controversial pastor. He was noted for his egoism, sensationalism, judicial indictments, dictatorial control of his churches, fellowship, and educational agencies, and attacks against religious, social, and political foes, including fellow fundamentalists. One of his biographers denominated him "Violent Fundamentalist," while another called him "God's Rascal."[156]

He thrived on controversy. He was successful not only because of his gifts of persuasion and organization but also due to the times in which he lived. His career coincided with a time in the South when crusades against Darwinism, the Roman Catholic Church, communism, the gambling and liquor interests, and theological liberalism received widespread popular support.

Norris left his heirs a mixed legacy. On the positive side, he began a movement that today numbers over 4,000 independent Baptist churches across the nation with a strong commitment to personal evangelism. He was a master in reaching the masses with the gospel. Norris supported training for both preachers and laypersons. Fundamentalist Baptists admire him for maintaining biblical orthodoxy, premillennial eschatology, evangelistic zeal, the ability to grow churches, and upholding the independence of the local church free from denominational control.

On the other hand, Southern Fundamentalists today repudiate Norris's excesses and bizarre behavior. Even before Norris's death, many of his adherents broke with him because of his dictatorial behavior. Norris's legacy has left the Southern Fundamentalist movement with certain weaknesses within its ranks such as an inordinate stress on church independence, autocratic pastoral leadership, an excessive attachment to numbers, use of sensationalism, and a type of church planting and evangelism irrespective of the cultural context. Because of its loose organization and local church independence, the movement is particularly vulnerable to organizational division with the rise of charismatic leaders with their own fellowships, institutions, and agendas.

Some Southern Fundamentalists have begun to show a tempering attitude toward other conservative evangelicals and even a critical reexamination of fundamentalism itself. As a result, two parties have arisen—"neo-fundamentalists" and the "hyper-fundamentalists." The former party condemns second-degree separatism, extreme legalism, and adherence only to the King James Version, while the latter part takes an opposite position. A leading neo-fundamentalist was Jerry Falwell (1933-2007), pastor of Thomas Road Baptist Church of Lynchburg, Virginia, and moral crusader, who developed strong ties with Southern Baptists, which has included his church joining the Southern Baptist Convention. Southern Baptist leaders serve on the board of his school, Liberty University, and spoke at his conferences. But spokespersons for the "hyper-fundamentalists" emphatically oppose any rapprochement with Southern Baptists, faulting them for their bureaucratic structure, theological diversity, and lack of militant separationism.[157]

Southern Fundamentalists have begun to develop closer ties, although not merger, among themselves. Independent leaders met in April, 2003, in Atlanta to form the International Baptist Network (IBN). In the following year, its members also updated the New Hampshire Confession, naming it the Georgia Confession. IBN held a joint meeting of cooperating fellowships—the Baptist Bible Fellowship, World Baptist Fellowship, and Southwide Baptist

Fellowship—in the Highland Park Baptist Church of Chattanooga, Tennessee, in September, 2004. Southern Baptists were also present with a message by Jerry Vines, former president of the Southern Baptist Convention, and a display.[158]

With the departure of the SBC from the Baptist World Alliance, in 2004, and its leadership reaching out to Fundamentalist Baptists, the IBN is not only a means of cooperation between Independents and some Southern Baptists but also a vehicle of worldwide cooperation among like-minded Baptists. IBN has an office in Atlanta with Gene Mims, formerly president of LifeWay Christian Resources of the SBC, as executive director, as well as offices in Philadelphia and Europe.[159]

World Baptist Fellowship (1932)

The beginning of World Baptist Fellowship (WBF) is rooted in the ministry of J. Frank Norris, pastor of First Baptist Church of Fort Worth from 1909 to 1952.[160] Norris was a strong critic of the Seventy-Five Million Campaign inaugurated by Southern Baptists in 1919. He attacked Baylor University, alleging its teaching of evolution. Because of his intemperate attacks on Southern Baptist leaders and programs, he and his church were forced out of the local Tarrant County Baptist Association in 1922 and the Texas Baptist General Convention in 1924.[161]

Although Norris was a member for a time of the Baptist Bible Union, he generally did not cooperate with any group not his own. A role in the Southern Baptist Convention, where he aspired to its leadership, was closed, and for years he harassed its leadership. Soon after he became pastor of Temple Baptist Church in Detroit in 1935, he withdrew it from the Northern Baptist Convention. In the meantime, young ministers under Norris's influence began to form independent Baptist congregations in Texas as well as outside the state. By 1932, there were nineteen of them. Many of these churches built large but cheaply constructed tabernacles.[162]

It was customary for Norris to hold training schools and conferences at his church. In November, 1931, he held for the first time what was called a Premillennial Bible School. At the third semi-annual Premillennial Bible School in November, 1932, the assembly approved the establishment of a Premillennial Baptist Missionary Fellowship with C. P. Stealey as secretary-treasurer to send financial assistance to three mission stations in China. The Fellowship would transmit funds directly from the churches to the mission.[163]

In 1938, Norris removed Robert White, the president of the Fellowship, and moved the Fellowship to Chicago, then in 1948 to Springfield, Missouri, and then in 1950 to Fort Worth. He renamed it the North American Fundamental Baptist Missionary Fellowship (1938), then the World Fundamental Baptist Missionary Fellowship (1944), and then simply World Baptist Fellowship (1950). In 1950, it had the support of about 300 congregations.[164]

Norris continued in the '30s his semi-annual Bible schools, which were more like Bible conferences of one or two weeks rather than an educational agency. In 1939, with Louis Entzminger, he founded the Fundamental Baptist Bible Institute, located at Norris's First Baptist Church. It began with sixteen students. Entzminger was the first president and at first the only full-time professor. The school was chartered in 1945 as Bible Baptist Seminary. After moving from First Baptist Church in the '50s and renting property for two years, it purchased in 1956 its present campus in Arlington, Texas.[165]

In 1917, Norris began publishing *The Fence Rail*, which he soon changed to *The Searchlight*, and then in 1927 to *The Fundamentalist*. After Norris's death, his son, George, gave the paper to the WBF, which continues to publish it as its official organ.[166]

Because of his autocratic control and arbitrary behavior, Norris faced revolt in his own ranks with the establishment in 1950 of a new fellowship, the Baptist Bible Fellowship International, and a rival school. About 150 of the 300 churches in his fellowship left; he also lost his entire foreign mission force. With

Norris's death two years later, the WBF faced a serious problem of leadership.

Although the major thrust of Southern fundamentalism now passed to the BBFI, the WBF managed to survive. It suffered, however, another defection with the founding in 1984 of the Independent Baptist Fellowship International. In its 2000–2001 *Directory*, the WBF listed 998 congregations in forty-seven states. Sixty percent of the churches, however, related to some other fundamentalist body. Its greatest strength is in Texas, Ohio, and Florida. It supports 145 missionaries with the greater majority in Mexico and South America.

Baptist Bible Fellowship International (1950)

Individuals who revolted against J. Frank Norris over his domineering and erratic behavior founded in 1950 a new fellowship, Baptist Bible Fellowship International (BBFI); a new school, Baptist Bible College; and a new paper, *Baptist Bible Tribune*.[167] The new fellowship was very similar to its parent body, following a three-pronged approach in its ministry and adopting the same doctrinal basis.

The foremost leader in the formation of the BBFI and guiding spirit for its first quarter of a century was G. Beauchamp Vick (1901–1975).[168] Soon after moving to Fort Worth in 1920, Vick and his wife participated in the ministry of Norris's First Baptist Church. After a period of evangelistic work with others, Vick became Norris's very able assistant at the Temple Baptist Church in Detroit in 1936, which led to his becoming its co-pastor in 1948 and on Norris's insistence also president of the Bible Institute in Fort Worth. In 1950, Norris ousted Vick from the presidency of the school that led to the founding of the new fellowship. In return, the Temple Baptist Church, where Vick continued as pastor until his death, severed all ties with Norris.

Much of the early strength of the BBFI came through the development of the Baptist Bible College in Springfield, Missouri, under the leadership of Vick, its first president. The school opened in the fall of 1950 and at first had only a dormitory and four army-type barracks, but other buildings soon followed. Enrollment climbed from 107 in its first year to over 2,000 by 1971; during its first twenty-five years it graduated 4,502 students.[169] The graduates of the school provided much of the backbone of the movement.

Vick's Temple Baptist Church also thrived, claiming in 1961 17,000 members and 4,299 in average attendance with a staff of ten full-time ministers. Vick spent a week each month at the college. Through his control of the school and the financial contributions of his church, which could help make or break the financial goals of the Fellowship, Vick played a dominant role until his death in 1975.[170]

The world mission program of the BBFI under F. S. Donnelson, former missionary in China, also expanded. The Fellowship, gaining all the missionaries of the WBF, began with nineteen missionaries in four fields. By 1956, excluding the Chinese field that closed, the Fellowship had ninety missionaries on thirteen fields, primarily in the Far East, the Indian subcontinent, and Latin America. It also had two fields among Indians in the USA.[171] By 1995, the number of missionaries had risen to 806 on ninety-five fields with contributions of over twenty-four million dollars.[172] In 2004, it reported 819 missionaries and an income for foreign missions of thirty-six million dollars.[173]

The Fellowship began with 142 churches, most of which were small with only four of them with over 500 in attendance in Sunday school. But its numbers soon expanded. By 1958, the BBFI had 600 churches with an estimated membership of 220,000.[174] Although many of its churches continue to be small, at the same time the Fellowship has included some of the largest Baptist congregations in the nation, such as Akron Baptist Temple in Akron, Ohio; Landmark Baptist Temple in Cincinnati, Ohio; and Thomas Road Baptist Church in Lynchburg, Virginia. Its growth has been due to a number of factors, including the evangelistic fervor of its pastors, its church planting, the growth of the Baptist Bible

College, its extensive bus ministries, and its ability to grow large Sunday schools, some of the largest in the nation. In 1991, it was reported that five of the thirty largest Sunday schools in the country were in churches related in some way to the BBFI.[175] The migration of Southerners also helped to provide ready mission fields.

In a survey of membership in 2000, the BBFI had 3,294 congregations in every state with 525,000 members. Even with a number of megachuches, the average membership per congregation was only around 159 persons. Almost a thousand of its congregations are also members of other groups—781 with other Southern Fundamentalists and 186 with Northern Fundamentalists. Three of its largest states are Texas (75,000 members), Ohio (63,200 members), and Florida (34,100 members). Due in part to its mass appeal and mission strategy, a significant number of its churches are in cities in contrast to many other Baptist groups. It has surprising strength in New England with 12,000 members. Members of the BBFI established a school in New York State in 1976, which in 1981 moved to Boston where it became known as Boston Baptist College, an institution that has helped the pioneer efforts of the Fellowship in this region.[176]

The BBFI has a very modest administrative staff. In 1991, it was reported that its Mission Office had a staff of less than twenty-five.[177] Missionaries must raise their support in deputation from the churches and not receive it from the Mission Office. The *Baptist Bible Tribune*, the organ of the BBFI since its inception, has been an important instrument for unity and promotion. Its first editor was Noel Smith (1900–1974), who ably served over twenty-three years until his death. He was also a professor at the Baptist Bible College.[178]

Even with its achievements, the BBFI has had its share of internal problems. Because of the independency of its churches, financial accountability has at times been lacking and ordination standards improperly maintained. With limited denominational help, churches also have often found it difficult in their search for a new pastor. Untried men have often with more zeal than practical sense failed to establish lasting work in difficult mission areas.[179]

Although the BBFI lists fellowshipping churches, the pastor is the key in its fellowship. First, the pastor exercises pastoral authority in his own church. A pastor of a fellowshipping church casts the church's one vote at the annual meeting of the Fellowship. Pastors compose the regional and state fellowships, and pastors are the state representatives of the national fellowship. Because so much depends on the cooperation of its pastors, its ties as a church-related body are particularly weak. In fact, pastors of many churches listed in the directory of the BBFI are not active participants in either national or state work. Such pastors and their churches are listed because of their desire for a listing and for their support of one or more BBFI missionaries.

Some pastors develop such large congregations with their own schools and mission work that they themselves become a mini-denomination. A prime example is Jerry Falwell, founder of the Thomas Road Baptist Church of Lynchburg, which reported 22,000 members in 1996. Falwell was founder of Liberty University, a televangelist, and moral crusader. He also established in 1978 Liberty Baptist Mission and in 1980 a Liberty Baptist Fellowship, composed primarily of pastors who were alumni of his school, which plants churches and endorsees chaplains.[180] Another example is Jack Hyles (1926–2001), pastor of First Baptist Church of Hammond, Indiana, whose church in 2000 was listed with both the BBFI and WBF. Hyles served the church from 1959 until his death. In 2001, the church claimed 75,000 members and Sunday school attendance of 18,500. Hyles founded Hyles-Anderson College and conducted an annual Pastor's School that attracted thousands.[181]

Beginning around 1998, the BBFI has been facing dissension that has brought in recent years a drop in cooperating congregations. Dissidents have formed a Church Planters Fellowship that is centered on Heartland Baptist College of Oklahoma City. Supporters of the new fellowship are hyper-fundamentalist, insisting on using only the King James Version, opposing rock in contemporary worship, disapproving women wearing slacks, and insisting on second-degree separation to the extent of condemning fraternization with Southern Baptists.[182]

Independent Baptist Fellowship International (1984)

Raymond W. Barber (b. 1932), pastor of Worth Baptist Church of Fort Worth, Texas, founded Independent Baptist Fellowship International (IBFI) in 1984. Barber was a former president of the World Baptist Fellowship and taught at Arlington Baptist College. He founded the new fellowship after a serious controversy at the school.[183]

At the same time, Barber founded Norris Baptist Bible Institute, which was dedicated to the memory of J. Frank Norris; a missions office; and began publishing *The Searchlight*, named after Norris's earlier paper. In 1998, the Fellowship listed 650 churches with 408 of them related to other fundamentalist organizations. Many of its churches are in Texas with Barber's own church claiming in the mid-'80s over 2,000 members and an average Sunday school attendance of 800.[184] The IBFI has some strength in Ohio and Florida and a scattering of churches in other regions.

In 2005, the IBFI *Directory* listed fifty-two active missionaries with contributions reported in 1998 of almost one million dollars.[185] Most of the missionaries were in Mexico, Central America, and Brazil. Six missionaries worked among American Indians and two in radio. The IBFI has declined to join the International Baptist Network with other fundamentalist Baptists.

Southwide Baptist Fellowship (1956)

The foremost leader in forming the Southwide Baptist Fellowship (SBF) was Lee Roberson (b. 1909), pastor of the Highland Park Baptist Church of Chattanooga, Tennessee, from 1942 to 1983.[186] Under his leadership, the church grew to be one of the largest in the nation. In 1982, it claimed membership of over 57,000 with 9,000 in attendance in Sunday school. Membership and attendance included sixty satellite chapels, which were as far as seventy miles distant. The church's ministry embraced a camp, rescue missions, and bus, radio, and tract ministries. In 1948, Robertson also established World Wide Faith Mission, an agency for support of foreign missionaries.

Roberson also founded a series of educational institutions that became known as Tennessee Temple Schools. The first was Tennessee Temple Bible School in 1946, then a seminary in 1948, and a college (now Tennessee Temple University) in 1950. He also added an elementary school and a high school. These institutions were clustered in numerous buildings near the church. Students from the Tennessee Temple Schools were instrumental in sustaining the church's chapel program.

Because of Roberson's development of his own educational and mission program with only token support for the Southern Baptist program, the Executive Committee of the Hamilton County Baptist Association criticized him and his church for non-cooperation. Upon the Association's sustaining its Executive Committee, Roberson and his church withdrew from the Association in November, 1955. He soon also withdrew from the Southern Baptist Convention.

As early as 1948, Roberson helped to form a Premillennial Fellowship but was now prepared to form a fellowship that would become independent of Southern Baptists. In August, 1955, he was guest speaker at the Carolina Baptist Fellowship (formed in 1954), meeting in Aiken, South Carolina, and hosted by John R. Waters. Its participants discussed the need for a new fellowship. With support from the Carolina Fellowship, Roberson hosted in his church in November a pre-organizational meeting. In March, 1956, again in Roberson's church, the Southern Baptist Fellowship was launched and elected Roberson its president. In November, at its first annual meeting, members adopted a premillennial statement of faith, written by George W. Dollar, fundamentalist educator and historian. In 1963, the Fellowship changed its name to Southwide Baptist Fellowship.[187]

Unlike other Southern fundamentalist fellowships, the SBF lists not churches but pastors and laypersons as members but at the same time noting church affiliation. Members must subscribe to the doctrinal statement and pay an annual fee. At the organizational meeting 147 ministers and laypersons joined as charter members, a number that increased to 423 at the first annual meeting. In the early '70s, the SBF estimated its membership at 130,000 with about 750 churches or 173 members per church.[188] In 2000, the SBF *Directory* listed 1,149 individual members. These members were related to 507 churches with a possible membership of 80,500 of which 227 or almost half were also related to some other fundamentalist body.

Unlike other fellowships, the SBF has no missions office. On the other hand, Baptist International Missions, Inc. (BIMI) with headquarters in Chattanooga is an important mission arm for the SBF as well as other independent Baptists.[189] Tom Freeney, while a pastor and a student at Tennessee Temple College in the '50s, began thinking of the need for another fundamentalist mission agency. Through his promotion, an organizational meeting for BIMI was held in June, 1960, at Tennessee Temple College during its Preacher's School. Roberson was one of the supporting pastors. BIMI is an agency for both foreign and home missions. In 2004, it reported income of $26,400,000 for overseas work and over 1,000 missionaries serving abroad.[190]

VII. Landmark Missionary Baptists

	Membership	Churches
American Baptist Association (1905/1924)	225,479	1,867
Baptist Missionary Association of America (1950)	235,345	1,322
Independent and Foreign Landmark Missionary Association (1951)	12,737	121
Unaffiliated Landmark Missionary Baptist associations	3,636	30
Unaffiliated Landmark Missionary Baptist churches	26,500	663
Sovereign Grace Landmark churches	5,840	396
TOTAL	**509,537**	**4,399**

Landmark Missionary Baptists are another fundamentalist tribe. With its emphasis on the fundamentals of the faith, premillennialism, church independency, anti-conventionism, and roots in the Southern Baptist Convention and Southern culture, it shares many of the attributes of Southern fundamentalist bodies. On the other hand, Landmark Baptists portray their own distinctives. First, they are more concerned about proper ecclesiology than fundamentalist bodies and will criticize them for unionist activities with non-Baptists. As adherents of a high-church Baptist ecclesiology that recognizes only Baptists in a line of apostolic succession, they reject other churches as human organizations, the concept of an invisible church, and the contention that Baptists are Protestants.

Secondly, Landmarkers are also much more wedded to the traditional South of small towns and rural areas, while the fundamentalists are oriented more toward the masses in the cities. Their churches generally include "Missionary Baptist" in their names, an older designation that, except for African American Baptists, is not now generally used by other Baptists. While fundamentalists emerged during the period of the fundamentalist controversy with liberalism between the First and Second World Wars, Landmarkism has had a much longer period of gestation, emerging as a distinct party in the nineteenth century in a time of intense inter-denominational battles.

Landmark Baptists are heirs of the Landmark system as propounded by James R. Graves (1820–1893), editor and polemicist of Tennessee, and his co-workers, James M. Pendleton (1811–1901), and Amos Dayton (1813–1865).[191] Although some of its principles were already present among Baptists, Graves formed it into a tightly held logical system and a standard of orthodoxy. He believed in church succession or perpetuity of Baptists and sought to justify it on both biblical and historical grounds. He maintained that Baptist congregations alone had the authority to perform "Gospel acts," and rejected as "alien" baptism performed by non-Baptists, even if proper by design and mode. Graves and his co-workers also rejected pulpit affiliation with non-Baptists.

Graves's influence extended into other areas. He magnified the independence of the local church, which helped to cast doubt on organizations beyond the local church. Although not rejecting associational ties, his equivocal support of mission boards led some Landmarkers to reject conventions and boards. Numbers of Landmarkers also accepted his view of later years that only members of a local church may participate in the Lord's Supper. He also made a mark in eschatology by advocating premillennialism and a system of dispensationalism.

The impact of Landmarkism was particularly strong among Baptist bodies in the South, including the Southern Baptist Convention and bodies that broke from it. Landmark Missionary Baptists who reject conventionism number today around 500,000 with major strength in the Trans-Mississippi South. In Arkansas, they are the leading tribe in eleven counties. Although rejecting conventionism and unified budgets, Landmark Missionary Baptists, however, differ among themselves as to cooperative efforts, ranging from national bodies that have much of the characteristics of organized denominations to independent churches with no associational ties.

American Baptist Association (1905/1924)

With a growing centralization of denominational organization and paid officials, some Landmarkers within the Southern Baptist Convention began to attack the policies and methods of their respective state conventions.[192] In 1900, dissidents formed the East Texas Baptist Convention (soon named the Baptist Missionary Association of Texas). The State Association of Missionary Baptist Churches of Arkansas was formed in 1902, and the Baptist State Association of Oklahoma was organized in 1903.

In March, 1905, the dissenting Landmarkers met in Texarkana, Arkansas, and formed the General Association of Baptists in the United States (later named the Missionary Baptist General Association). In an attempt to avoid a final division, the General Association appointed a committee to memorialize the Southern Baptist Convention that demanded the removal of the financial and associational basis in church representation and deny authority to mission boards to appoint and remove missionaries. Ben M. Bogard presented the memorial, but with its rejection the schism was complete. In November, 1905, the General Association held its first annual meeting. The General Association established committees, not boards, for its work. Among the most important were the Missionary and the Religious Literature Committees. In the meantime, the Baptist Missionary Association of Texas continued its own mission program.

To attain national unity, the General Association and the Baptist Missionary Association of Texas united in 1924 as the American Baptist Association (ABA). No one man controlled the General Association or American Baptist Association as did J. Frank Norris his fellowship. Landmark Missionary Baptist organization rested on traditional Baptist associational relationships; the messengers from the churches composed the associational membership.

Among the early leaders of the Landmark Missionary Baptist movement, the most influential was Ben M. Bogard (1868–1951), a disciple of James R. Graves.[193] He was a leading preacher, publicist, and polemicist of the movement. He was a friend of J. Frank Norris. Although some resented his undue influence, he was never the authoritarian master.

Bogard was pastor of the Antioch Missionary Baptist Church of Little Rock, Arkansas, from 1920 to 1947 and began a radio ministry in 1929. Bogard wrote twenty-nine books, including two in collaboration with others. He had editorial responsibilities for a number of Baptist periodicals, including from time to time from 1901 to 1937 the *Baptist and Commoner* and from 1937 until his death the *Orthodox Baptist Searchlight*, changing its name in 1949 to *Missionary Baptist Searchlight*. Bogard was a noted debater, engaging in 213 of them; the first in 1904 and the last, when he was eighty years old, in 1948. In 1928, he was instrumental in the passage of an anti-evolution bill in Arkansas. In 1927, he became president of the board of the Missionary Baptist College in Sheridan, Arkansas (founded in 1919). After the school's demise in 1933, he led with others in establishing in 1934 the Missionary Baptist Seminary at his church. The school continues today. He with others also began to publish Sunday school material, a responsibility later taken over by the General Association and then the American Baptist Association.

In 1926, the American Baptist Association reported 1,431 churches and around 118,000 members.[194] Most were in the Trans-Mississippi South with 42,000 in Arkansas and almost 54,000 in Texas. Almost ninety-five percent were in rural territory. In 1949, the ABA reported 245,000 members in almost 2,300 churches.[195]

From its very beginning in 1905, the General Association indicated its interest in foreign missions by endorsing two missionaries in the Moslem world—one in Lebanon (then part of Syria) and the other in Persia. Before the Second World War, the ABA was engaged in mission efforts in Brazil and for a short time in Portugal. The ABA also supported interstate missionaries in the United States.

Two factions began to appear in the ABA, one headed by Bogard and the other by D. N. Jackson. At the annual meeting in Lakeland, Florida, in 1950, the Bogard faction prevailed in the acceptance of messengers from churches of which they were not members. But issues were far deeper, involving a contest for control. Conflict had developed earlier when the Bogard faction charged financial mismanagement in the publications. A second conflict occurred over the charge of financial irregularities at Jacksonville Baptist College. In both cases, the Jackson faction was the defendant. In addition, Jackson and his followers resented the establishment by Bogard of the Missionary Baptist Seminary that was under the sole authority of Bogard and his church.[196]

The division touched almost everywhere with separations in state and local associations and in some churches. The ABA lost about 1,300 churches, about half its strength, and such large associations as Texas, Missouri, and Mississippi. In spite of the heavy losses, the ABA was able to recoup. Today it claims 225,000 members in 1,867 churches. A survey of its churches and associations in 1996 revealed twenty state associations and seventy-three local associations. A bit over forty percent of its membership is in Arkansas.[197]

One of the most important committees of the ABA is the Missionary Committee. In 1999, the ABA reported support for twenty-five American missionaries serving abroad and seventy-five national missionaries with a concentration of mission work in Latin America and the Orient, particularly in the Philippines. In 2005, the ABA received $2,100,000 for its missions at home and abroad. The Sunday School Committee is responsible for Sunday school material and other publications. The ABA also has a History and Archives Committee, Chaplaincy Commission, National Women's Auxiliary, National Youth Fellowship, and National Fellowship of Music Directors.

Within the United States, ABA churches sponsor twenty institutes and seminaries (with some of the latter also maintaining institutes), besides colleges in Ohio and Florida. The state association of Arkansas operates an orphanage at Texarkana, Arkansas.

Baptist Missionary Association of America (1950)

The Baptist Missionary Association of America (BMA) was established in Little Rock, Arkansas, in 1950 as the North American Baptist Association by seceders from the American Baptist Association. In 1969, it took its present name.[198] The BMA and the ABA are alike in ideology and very similar in operation. Unlike the ABA, the BMA requires church messengers to be a member of the church the messenger represents and supports both local church and associational control of educational institutions. Both have mission and publication programs. The BMA established its permanent offices in Little Rock.

Much of the efforts of the BMA have been expended in its mission program including both interstate and foreign fields. For 2005 it had a mission goal of a bit over $4,700,000.[199] A present it supports twenty-three missionaries for work abroad and also gives assistance to over 1,000 native missionaries, church planters, and support workers. It lists work in forty-eight countries, including Puerto Rico. It shows particular interest toward Latin America, including Mexico, Central America, and Brazil. Support for native workers include such disparate areas as Cape Verde (off the coast of Africa) and church planters in the former Soviet Union. It also supports a national and international radio ministry.

The BMA also formed a Publications Department and established in 1965 a Baptist Publishing House in Texarkana, Texas. Jacksonville College in Jacksonville, Texas, became associated with the new association. In 1955, the BMA opened a theological seminary in Jacksonville. Other BMA schools are in Arkansas, Mississippi, and California. The BMA also has a woman's auxiliary, state brotherhoods, an encampment, three children's homes in Arkansas, Mississippi, and Texas, an Armed Forces Chaplaincy, and several music fellowships.

For the year 2000, the BMA reported 235,000 members in 1,322 churches. It is about the same size as the ABA and parallels its growth. A bit over forty percent of its constituency is in Texas. In a survey in 1996, the BMA had fifteen state associations and eighty-one local associations.[200]

Interstate and Foreign Landmark Missionary Baptist Association (1951)

The Interstate and Foreign Landmark Missionary Baptist Association (IFLMBA), formed in 1951, is a body independent of the two major Landmark Missionary Baptist bodies. This group is also known as Faithway Landmark Baptists. In the Landmark division of 1950, it went its separate way, holding to its own distinctives. First, it believes that missionaries are supported by contributions by faith and not on a set salary. Secondly, unlike other Landmark Baptists, its churches observe footwashing. Thirdly, it is unnecessary for a candidate for ordination to have earned a theological degree for ordination. Ministers are generally called "elder" or "brother."

Today the IFLMBA provides support for native workers in Quebec, Mexico, Philippines, and Korea. At present no American missionaries from this group serve abroad, although ministers from America periodically undertake short-term visits. The IFLMBA in 2000 reported 12,737 members in 121 churches. Most of the constituency is in Mississippi (8,178 members) and Louisiana (3,408 members).[201]

Unaffiliated Landmark Baptist Associations/Churches

Unaffiliated Associations

Independent landmark Missionary Baptist associations that exist apart from the national Landmark bodies are present in several areas. A survey for the *Religious Congregations and Membership* study for 2000 records at least four such independent associations including: Old California State Association; Central Missionary Baptist Association (Texas); Landmark Missionary Baptist Association (Arkansas); and Mt. Pisgah Missionary Baptist Association (Mississippi) for a total of thirty-nine churches and 3,636 members.

Unaffiliated Churches

In recent research, Robert L. Vaughn of Mt. Enterprise, Texas, recorded, excluding missions, 663 independent Landmark Baptist congregations unaffiliated with any national or local association. In addition, Vaughn developed a number of categories in describing differences among them.[202] One category was composed of unaffiliated Landmarkers who argue for direct missions, that is, mission support from the church to the missionary independent of any mission agency. Vaughn discovered sixty-two direct-mission churches, particularly in Oregon, California, and the Trans-Mississippi South.

Vaughn designated "Independent Fundamental Baptist" for another category. This group included unaffiliated Landmark churches, often with strong pastoral leadership, which have much affinity with fundamentalism that may overshadow their Landmarkism. Vaughn located 354 such churches, found in every section of the nation except New England with special strength in the Trans-Mississippi South. Vaughn found a subsection of thirty-one churches that were, by and large, fundamentalist but opposed to church incorporation.

A third category included Covenant Landmark Baptists in twenty-seven churches, primarily in the Pacific region. This group believes that only members in a local New Testament church are in the New Covenant. A fourth category of 189 congregations includes unaffiliated Landmark churches without distinguishing characteristics or unclassified for lack of information.

Sovereign Grace Landmark Churches

Sovereign Grace Landmark churches are not only Landmark in polity but are also neo-Calvinists, accepting the Calvinist doctrine of God's sovereign grace. While most Landmark Baptists follow the general amalgam of Calvinism and Arminianism in today's Baptist theology, these congregations have returned to the doctrinal roots of Regular Baptists of the seventeenth century. Neo-Calvinism is a rather recent phenomenon, creating its own bodies but also impacting other Baptists.

In his research, Robert L Vaughn located 396 Landmark Sovereign Grace churches. Their areas of greatest strength are in the Upper and Lower South and the Great Lakes. They are nonexistent in New England and have only two churches in the Middle Atlantic.

VIII. General/Free Will Baptists

	MEMBERSHIP	CHURCHES
General Six Principle Baptists (1652/1692)	15	1
General Association of General Baptists (1823/1870)	74,284	787
National Association of Free Will Baptists (1727/1780/1935)	205,617	2,466
Convention of Original Free Will Baptists (1727/1961)	37,198	237
Unaffiliated Free Will Baptist Associations	19,946	264
United American Free Will Baptist Church (1867/1901)	75,000	500
United American Free Will Baptist Conference (1968)	11,250	75
Separate Baptists in Christ (1803/1912)	8,716	94
TOTAL	**432,026**	**4,424**

The General Baptist and Free Will Baptist bodies differ from other Baptists in their acceptance of the free operation of the will in salvation and in falling from grace. Unlike Particular or Regular Baptists, who originally believed in the limited atonement of Christ, they have always been advocates of Christ's general atonement. On the other hand, they reject the Wesleyan Arminianism of a second blessing and with Reformed adherents accept the substitutionary atonement of Christ.

General/Free Will Baptists and most other Baptists are much closer theologically today than in the past since most Baptists accept some degree of free will in salvation and a general atonement. The big divide between the two groups is over perseverance or eternal security of the believer. The majority of Baptists accept it while General/Free Will Baptists reject it. General/Free Will Baptists have historically observed open communion, while Regular Baptists historically practiced close communion. Although open communion has become more acceptable among many Regular Baptists, numbers still observe some form of it. Churches in the General/Free Will tradition, by and large, observe the rite of footwashing.

General/Free Will Baptists, although practicing congregational church government, include elements of connectionalism not present among Regular Baptists. Among Regular Baptists, the church, usually with the assistance of an advisory council, ordains a candidate. On the other hand, General/Free Will Baptists maintain presbyteries or standing committees on the associational level that approve candidates for ordination. The General Association of General Baptists, Free Will Baptists, and Separate Baptists also determine a minister's standing. The Original Free Will Baptists and the United American Free Will Baptist Church even go further in their connectionalism by permitting the association or conference to take disciplinary action in cases of congregational conflict.

History has not been kind to General/Free Will Baptists. For one thing, their constituencies have been rooted in rural areas; they have either failed or been slow in adapting to urban life. For another, they have been prone to be absorbed by the much larger and more aggressive Regular Baptists or lose members to other movements. The General Six Principle Baptists, once the largest Baptist group in New England but letting the Great Awakening pass them by, is today reduced to one church. In the eighteenth century, Regular Baptists almost completely absorbed the General Baptist movement in North Carolina. Free Will Baptists in the South suffered defections to Alexander Campbell's movement in the nineteenth century and to Pentecostalism in the twentieth century. At the beginning of the twentieth century, Northern (American) Baptists absorbed the Freewill Baptist Conference of the North, leaving only a remnant who remained Free Will Baptists from this body. Except for some strength in the Great Lakes area and California, their churches are, by and large, confined to the South with an average membership of a little less than one hundred per church.

General Six Principle Baptists (1652/1692)

The oldest General/Free Will Baptist body, but today the smallest, is the General Six Principle Baptists. The Providence Church, the oldest Baptist church in America, formed in 1638, included both Regular and General Baptist members but in 1652 suffered division with the exodus of the Regular Baptist party. The General Baptists not only believed in Christ's general atonement but observed the six principles as outlined in Hebrews 6:1-2. This included the laying on of hands on all newly baptized for the reception of the gifts of the Holy Spirit. Many Baptists in the American colonies and in England, both General and Regular, observed the laying on of hands but finally dropped the practice. This body, however, continued to maintain it and made it a test of fellowship. Other Baptists today observe the rite only for the ordination of pastors and deacons.

In the eighteenth century, up to 1770, General Six Principle Baptists were the strongest Baptist body in New England. By 1692, if not earlier, they had organized a yearly meeting, the first associational Baptist body in America. They moved westward into New York, forming their first church there in 1724. Their first church in Pennsylvania was not established until 1817.

The Six Principle Baptists did not adopt the revivalism of the Great Awakening. They lost the Providence Church when James Manning, a Calvinist, became pastor in 1771. Manning dropped the laying on of hands and also introduced congregational singing. With their concentration in rural areas with untrained pastors, their growth was limited and began to decline in the nineteenth century. Except for feeble attempts, they never engaged in cooperative mission or publication work.

In 1813, they formed a Yearly Meeting in New York and in 1836 they extended it to Pennsylvania. With the demise of the last New York church in 1865, this body became simply the General Six Principle Baptist Association of Pennsylvania. From 1869 to 1879, Six Principle Baptists, in what was then called the Rhode Island and Massachusetts General Baptist Conference, suffered division. In 1895, the Rhode Island body incorporated as the General Six Principle Baptist Conference of Rhode Island. Over time numbers of churches dissolved or joined other groups, such as Free Will Baptists or American Baptists. In 1954, the Rhode Island Conference lifted its ban on communion with other Christians.

In 1955, General Six Principle Baptists numbered only 254 members in three churches in Rhode Island and two churches in Pennsylvania. In 1984, the Maple Root Church in Coventry suspended its association in the Rhode Island Conference, which left only the Wood River Church in Richmond and the Stony Lane Church in North Kingston to hold the last meeting of the Rhode Island Conference (claiming to be the 314th). All three Rhode Island churches, which today total over 300 members, have given up their Six Principle identity. The Maple Root Church has joined the Conservative Baptist Association of America, and the Wood River Church associates with this body. Only one Six Principle church is left, the Pine Grove Church in Susquehanna County, Pennsylvania, with a membership of fifteen.

Bibliography

An old-fashioned study is the work by Richard Knight, *History of the General Six Principle Baptists, in Europe and America* (Providence:

Smith and Parmenter, 1827; reprint, New York: Arno Press, 1980), which included churches which practiced laying on of hands but were not Six Principle. A valuable study with statistical data is the work by Nelson Robert Elliott, *A History of Six Principle Baptists in America,* (Th.D. dissertation, Southwestern Baptist Theological Seminary, 1958). Two helpful articles are W. T. Whitley, "The Six Principle Baptists in America," *The Chronicle*, III/1 (January, 1940), 3-9, and James E. Taulman, "The Origins of the (General) Six Principle Baptists," *Quarterly Review*, XXXIII/1, (October–December, 1972), 37-42. The work by J. Stanley Lemons, *First: The First Baptist Church in America* (Providence: The Charitable Baptist Society, 2001), 13-18, provides valuable information on the Providence Church as a Six Principle congregation.

General Association of General Baptists (1823/1870)

The origins of the General Association of General Baptists begin with Benoni Stinson (1789–1869), a Baptist minister in Kentucky and then in Indiana, who rejected the Calvinism of many of his contemporaries and preached that "Jesus tasted death for every man" (Hebrews 2:9). He left the Regular Baptists after failing to get the association he was planning to join to adopt his views. This association, then in formation, was under the influence of the hyper-Calvinistic views of Daniel Parker. He became pastor of the newly organized Liberty Baptist Church in Howell, Indiana, (now in metropolitan Evansville) in 1823, whose articles contained the doctrine of the general atonement. Stinson soon established three other churches of the same faith. In 1824, the four churches formed the Liberty Association of General Baptists.

The break with Regular Baptists was not as decisive as it later became. At first, General Baptists observed close communion and did not oppose the doctrine of the perseverance of the saints; only later did they adopt open communion and formally adopt apostasy as a doctrinal tenet. General Baptists have practiced footwashing, a rite which at times has been divisive, but it is not mandatory nor a bar to fellowship. As a rule, this body does not ordain women with the exception of its White River Association that may ordain women as deacons. As a southern rural movement, its churches spread in the border area of the Ohio, Tennessee, and Mississippi Rivers, with churches particularly in southern Indiana, Kentucky, Tennessee, southern Illinois, southern Missouri, and Arkansas.

In 1870, delegates from three associations formed the General Association of General Baptists. In time, it created a number of boards, including a home mission board in 1871 and a foreign board in 1903. Before the Second World War it had a limited work on Guam where during the war its missionary was captured by the Japanese. Since the war, it has greatly extended its mission outreach to Saipan in the Northern Mariana Islands, establishing there the largest Protestant church on the island, as well as to India, Philippine Islands, Jamaica, and Honduras. Today, its foreign mission program is in a Department of International Missions, which reported in 2004 around $300,000 with fifteen full-time overseas personnel.[203]

Its denominational offices are in Poplar Bluff, Missouri, which includes Stinson Press and a Christian Book Center. In 1886, it began publishing, *The General Baptist Messenger*, which continues as the denomination's chief organ. In 1942, General Baptists began printing their own Sunday school literature. In 1891, it opened Oakland City College in Oakland City, Indiana, a liberal arts school. Because of financial difficulties, the denomination almost lost the school, but under new leadership it survived and gained accreditation in 1977. In 1983, the school began a Graduate School of Theology and in 1995 changed its name to Oakland City University. It has shown notable progress with new buildings and an enrollment today of 2,000. General Baptists also have nursing homes at Campbell, Missouri, and Mt. Carmel, Illinois.

In 1971, General Baptists reported in the *Churches and Church Membership* study 66,435 members in 789 churches; today they have about the same number of churches with 75,000 members in around sixty-five associations. Although they have increased in urban areas, much of the constituency is rural or in small-town areas which has suffered loss in population. The denomination also has had problems in retaining its young people. The constituency includes a limited number of ethnic congregations, notably Hmong refugees from Southeast Asia, members of the Lao Evangelical Church, which joined as an association in 1990.

The attempt of General Baptists to associate with the Freewill Baptists of the North was a fiasco because of the latter's strong abolitionist views. General Baptists discussed developing working relations with the Churches of God of North America (founded by John Winebrenner) and the Original Free Will Baptists of North Carolina, but such relationships were never consummated, although there was some limited cooperation with the latter group. They have no ties with the National Association of Free Will Baptists. Located within the strong institutional presence of Southern Baptists, they are more prone to be open to Calvinistic influences than other similar bodies. The General Baptists are the only Arminian Baptist body in the United States to join the Baptist World Alliance. It also joined the National Association of Evangelicals.

Bibliography

The standard history of General Baptists has been the work by Ollie Latch, *History of the General Baptists,* (Poplar Bluff, MO: General Baptist Press, 1954). For a later account by Latch, see "The General Association of General Baptists," *The Baptist Program*, February, 1971, 15-7, 21. For General Baptist developments since 1950, see Leland Duncan and Edwin Runyon, *The Journey with General Baptists* (Poplar Bluff: Stinson Press, 2005). The work by Randy Mills, *Christ Tasted Death For Every Man: The Story of America's Frontier General Baptists,* (Poplar Bluff: Stinson Press, 2000), is a careful investigation of General Baptist beginnings. For foreign missions work, see Charles L. Carr, *Seed, Soil and Seasons,* (Poplar Bluff: General Baptist Foreign Mission Society, 1988).

National Association of Free Will Baptists (1727/1780/1935)

Although the National Association of Free Will Baptists was not organized until 1935, the roots of this body are in the eighteenth century in the General Baptist movement in eastern North Carolina and the Freewill Baptist movement in New England. Paul Palmer formed in North Carolina the first General Baptist church in Chowan County in 1727, followed in the state by a second in 1729 and then a third in 1742. In 1755, twenty General Baptist churches were in existence but, with the penetration of Regular Baptist teaching and mission work from representatives of the Philadelphia Association between 1755 and 1761, twelve churches were reorganized as Regular Baptist. The Meherrin Church followed suit in 1794. Unlike General Baptists of the time, Regular Baptists demanded more than a simple statement of faith but a recital of an experience of grace.

Although the General Baptist movement was near extinction, it survived largely because of the ministry of Joseph and William Parker, cousins. In 1812, the General Baptists, now calling themselves Free Will Baptists, adopted a revision of the General Baptist confession of 1660, which had been adopted in England. Free Will Baptists gained adherents from sources outside eastern North Carolina. One such area was Tennessee that by 1850 had four Free Will associations, including the Cumberland Association, which came out of Separate Baptists.

Another source will later come from the Free Will movement (but using "Freewill" as its name) that appeared in 1780 in New England under the ministry of Benjamin Randall (1749–1808). The major strength of the Randall movement was in northern New England; by 1805 it had already spread to nine states. It developed Quarterly and Yearly Meetings and in 1827 established a General Conference. It was strongly anti-slavery, ordained women to the ministry, and unlike other Baptists in the North practiced open communion. This body established a number of educational institutions and engaged in work among the Freedmen, establishing for them Storer College at Harpers Ferry.

According to the Federal census of 1890, this body had around 88,000 members in almost 1,600 churches in thirty-three states. In spite of decline in its home territory, it sustained its membership because of accessions in Quarterly Meetings among the Freedmen in the South. With decline in its own ranks, on the one hand, and a shift among Northern Baptists in modifying their views of election and close communion, on the other, a merger with Northern Baptists was consummated in 1911. Although the Freewill Baptists of the North and Free Will Baptists in the South had had some limited correspondence, because of regional differences no merger of the two groups was ever contemplated.

Some remnants of the northern group, however, resisted the merger, particularly in Nebraska, Missouri, and Indiana. In December, 1916, Freewill representatives of the Randall movement from the Great Plains and Trans-Mississippi South formed the General Co-operative Association of Freewill Baptists.

In the meantime, the Free Will Baptists in the South formed in 1896 a Triennial General Conference, which even included churches in Ohio, and which lasted to 1910. Then, in 1920, Free Will Baptists in the Southeast reestablished the General Conference. Finally in 1935 in Nashville, the General Conference merged with the General Co-operative Association to form the National Association of Free Will Baptists, which at the time included most Free Will Baptists in the nation.

The Religious Census of 1936 recorded 920 congregations and around 76,000 members with over ninety percent in rural territory. Aside from churches in Ohio and Missouri, practically all churches were in the South. In spite of a division in North Carolina in 1961, the National Association has continued to grow with 205,000 members in almost 2,500 churches in the year 2000. Most of its churches are small and average less than eighty-five members per church. A bit over eighty percent of its membership is in the South with a strong concentration in Appalachia but with additional strength in the Great Lakes region, Missouri, Oklahoma, and California. It still has a strong rural base but has increased its numbers in urban areas. Many of its churches, but not all, observe footwashing.

The National Association established its headquarters in Nashville in 1953. In 1965, it moved to more commodious quarters in the city and then moved once more in 1991 to a new building in the Antioch area. The National Association has a number of departments, including Home, International, Sunday School and Training Union, as well as a woman's auxiliary. In 2004, its International Department recorded an annual income of $4,500,000 and seventy-eight personnel serving overseas in ten countries in Africa, Asia, Europe, South America, and Central America.[204] With eleven other Free Will Baptist bodies, the National Association is a member in the International Fellowship of Free Will Baptist Churches, which was formed in 1995.

In 1942, the National Association opened the Free Will Baptist Bible College in Nashville, its major school. Free Will Baptists also have regional colleges in California, Oklahoma, North Carolina, and Virginia. In 1962, it established in Nashville, Randall House Publications, its publishing arm.

Free Will Baptists have always been a conservative evangelical denomination with its adherents following a traditional moral code. Their churches do not ordain women.

Denominationally they have become more isolationist and, like the fundamentalist bodies, have adopted second-degree separationism. In 1967, it terminated its relations with the American Bible Society and in 1972 withdrew from the National Association of Evangelicals. It has never been a member of the Baptist World Alliance.

Bibliography

The standard history of the National Association of Free will Baptists and its antecedents is the work by William F. Davidson, *The Free Will Baptists in America, 1727–1984,* (Nashville: Randall House Publications, 1985). For a careful study of early General Baptist and Free Will Baptist beginnings in the South, see Davidson, *An Early History of Free Will Baptists,*

(Nashville: Randall House Publications, 1974), which was a dissertation written at New Orleans Baptist Theological Seminary. Davidson has also written, "The National Association of Free Will Baptists," a very helpful survey in Jonas, *The Baptist River*, 129-57. For a popular history, see Damon C. Dodd, *The Free Will Baptist Story* (Nashville: Executive Department, National Association of Free Will Baptists, 1956). An excellent history of the Freewill Baptists of the North (the Randall movement) is the work by Norman A. Baxter, *History of the Freewill Baptists* (Rochester, NY: American Baptist Historical Society, 1957). Another fine volume on the Freewill Baptists of the North is the publication on their centenary, *The Centennial Record of the Freewill Baptists, 1780–1880* (Dover, NH, 1881).

Convention of Original Free Will Baptists (1727/1961)

As other Free Will Baptists, the Original Free Will Baptists trace their heritage to Paul Palmer and the first General Baptist church in North Carolina in 1727. In 1912, Free Will Baptists in North Carolina formed the "North Carolina State Convention of the Original Free Will Baptist Church of Jesus Christ." In 1935, the convention joined the National Association of Free Will Baptists as a charter member, dropping "Original" from its name.

In 1961, the North Carolina Convention withdrew from the National Association in a dispute over polity. The North Carolina Convention insisted that an annual convention had the right to discipline a local church. But there were deeper differences in temperament and educational philosophy. The North Carolina Convention supported Mount Olive College, opened in 1952, a liberal arts school, while the National Association maintained the Bible college in Nashville. In addition, the North Carolina Convention wished to continue controlling its own press and publication of Sunday school materials.

In the separation, the North Carolina Convention, although losing a number of churches, retained, however, a majority of them. In 1947, it again added "Original" to its name. In addition to Mount Olive College and Free Will Baptist Press, Original Free Will Baptists maintain retirement homes, a children's home, and an assembly. Its foreign board, now called OFWB International, has an annual budget of $600,000. It began a foreign mission work in Mexico in 1962 and now has missions as well in the Philippines, India, Nepal, Bangla Desh, and Bulgaria. All support for personnel, except for one couple, is for nationals on the field.

It has a bit over 37,000 members in 237 churches. Except for three churches in South Carolina, all are in North Carolina, primarily in the eastern section of the state. Its churches practice footwashing but with voluntary participation by members. Only one of its conferences include any ordained women.

Bibliography

Floyd B. Cherry, *An Introduction to Original Free Will Baptists* (Ayden, NC: Free Will Baptist Press Foundation, c. 1974). Michael R. Pelt, *A History of Original Free Will Baptists* (Mount Olive, NC: Mount Olive College Press, 1996).

Unaffiliated Free Will Baptist Associations

A number of Free Will Baptist associations remain unaffiliated with either the National Association of Free Will Baptists or the Conference of Original Free Will Baptists. They are concentrated primarily in Appalachia, the Cumberland Plateau in Tennessee, and the Ozarks in Missouri but also with some limited strength in southwestern Middle Tennessee and Indiana. They total around 20,000 members in 264 churches with the largest number in Tennessee with almost 9,800 members in 110 congregations.

The John-Thomas Yearly Meeting with 6,100 members and eighty-eight churches has five conferences in Kentucky, Virginia, Ohio, and Indiana. The Mt. Mitchell Association is located in North Carolina. In addition, North Carolina shares with Tennessee the French Broad, Jack's Creek, and Toe River Associations. Toe River also has a church in South Carolina. Tennessee also includes the Original Stone Association of the Free Will Christian Baptist Church of Christ, the Eastern Division of the Stone Association, and Muscle Shoals Stateline Association, which also has three churches in Alabama.

Indiana includes the Stone Association of Central Indiana. Missouri has two associations, Union and Ozark, with the latter practically extinct. Oklahoma has one, the Original Grand River, which has only two churches. There are also independent Free Will churches in West Virginia.

Bibliography

For information on the independent associations, see two works by Robert E. Picirilli, *History of Free Will Baptist State Associations,* (Nashville: Randall House Publications, 1976), and *The History of Tennessee Free Will Baptists,* ([Nashville]: Historical Commission of the Tennessee State Association of Free Will Baptists, 1985). For a description of Free Will Baptists in Appalachia, including the John Thomas Quarterly Meeting, and their differences with the National Association of Free Will Baptists, see John Sparks, *The Roots of Appalachian Christianity,* (Lexington: University Press of Kentucky, 2001), 264-78.

National Convention of Free Will Baptists

Seven African-American Free Will Baptist bodies, independent of each other and headed by their respective bishops, are members of the National Convention of Free Will Baptists. Two of the major ones are the United American Free Will Baptist Church and the United American Free Will Baptist Conference, which are described below. A third body is the Western Division General Conference of Free Will Baptists, located in the Mississippi Valley with 125 churches. A fourth body is the Original Free Will Baptist General Conference, which extends from New Jersey to Alabama. Other conferences are the Old Original in North Carolina, Unified in New York and Pennsylvania, and United in the northeast. Unlike most other Free Will Baptists, these bodies ordain women for ministry.[205]

United American Free Will Baptist Church (1867/1901)

The United American Free Will Baptist Church arose from African-American Free Will Baptists who separated after the Civil war from their white brethren. The first church, Shady Grove in Green County, North Carolina, was formed about 1867. This body formed quarterly and annual conferences. Before the end of the nineteenth century, it began an annual general conference, which was incorporated in 1901. A senior bishop is the presiding head. The general conference published a book of discipline in 1903, which has been revised from time to time.

Officers of the local church include a pastor, deacons, and ruler elders who are to deal with controversies among members. The ordinances include baptism, the Lord's Supper, and footwashing.

This body formed Kinston College in Kinston, North Carolina in 1902, which ceased in 1931 because of financial difficulties. In 1966, it established permanent headquarters in Kinston. In 1981, a tabernacle was built and used for conferences. In 1991, it finished constructing a new headquarters building, which also houses a Bible college, which opened in the same year. Around 1930, it began publishing the *Free Will Baptist Advocate*, which, however, is no longer published because of losing its materials in a flood.

The census of religious bodies in 1936 recorded this body as having 19,616 members in 226 churches. In 1968, it suffered a small division, losing primarily its churches in Florida. A fair estimate of membership today is possibly 75,000 in around 500 churches, although it has been estimated higher. Its greatest strength has always been in North Carolina.

Bibliography

For a chronology of historic events, see the program, *Centennial Convocation 1867–1967*. The United States census, *Religious Bodies: 1936*, II, part one, 176-89, includes statistical data and limited information on the history and organization of this body. For some current material, see L .H. Williams, "United American Free Will Baptist Church," *Dictionary of Baptists in America*, 273.

United American Free Will Baptist Conference (1968)

In 1968, the United American Free Will Baptist Conference was formed under the leadership of O. L. Williams of Lakeland, Florida, who had failed in his bid for election as general moderator of the United American Free Will Baptist Church. All of the churches in Florida left the parent body. Today the conference has seventy-five churches with an estimated membership of 11,250. Sixty-one of the churches are in Florida.

A headquarters building is in Lakeland. It has a general conference, headed by a general bishop, and four divisions, meeting in annual conferences. This body also includes additional bishops with supervisory functions and pastors who are called elders. It has no periodical but has a book of discipline.

Bibliography

George Patterson McKinney and Richard I. McKinney, *History of Black Baptists in Florida, 1850–1985,* (Miami: Florida Memorial College, 1987), 274-76. Telephone interview with Henry J. Rodmon, general bishop, June 9, 2004. Its web-site, www.uafwbc.org, lists its churches.

Separate Baptists in Christ (1803/1912)

In 1801, Regular Baptists and most Separate Baptists in Kentucky merged as United Baptists. In 1803, however, Kentucky Baptists refused to recognize the majority party in the South District Association as the true association for its refusing a corresponding letter from another association. The unrecognized South District Association continued independently and in 1806 took the name, the South Kentucky Association of Separate Baptists.

Other Separate Baptist associations were formed—Nolynn (1819) in central Kentucky; Northern Indiana (1854); Central Indiana (1870); Ambraw (1870) in Illinois; and Mt. Olive (1892) in Tennessee. Separate Baptists began to correspond with the Christian Unity Baptist Association of North Carolina and Virginia, formed in 1935.

As in the General/Free Will tradition, these Separate Baptists accepted Christ's general atonement and the possibility of falling from grace. With baptism and the Lord's Supper, footwashing was also an ordinance of the church. In the nineteenth century they shifted from close to open communion. At first Separate Baptists simply wrote descriptions of their faith but later adopted confessional statements that have come to define strictly their doctrinal standards.

In their services, worshippers participate emotionally; pastors speak with rising emotion and generally without manuscript or outline. Pastors are generally bivocational without formal theological training, although today some have received some college training. In the associations, presbytery boards give final approval for ordination of ministers and deacons and also determine ministerial credentials. Although supporting Sunday schools and youth camps, Separate Baptists have established no educational institutions.

In 1877, Separate Baptists formed their first General Association, but it dissolved and was reestablished in 1912. At first they were opposed to the organized missions movement but later accepted associational home mission boards and also began to provide some support for foreign missions. In 1969, they formed Separate Baptist Missions, Inc., to promote both home and foreign missions. It has a mission field in northern Ivory Coast in Africa, where an association has been organized, which consists today of fourteen churches.

With one exception, the churches are small and serve primarily a rural constituency. In 1969, Separate Baptists numbered 7,734 in eighty-seven churches. This number included the six associations formed in the nineteenth century as well as the Christian Unity Association, which after a split, joined in 1965. In 2000, they numbered 8,716 in ninety-four churches, which included one church in West Virginia and one in Florida.

The General Association, however, has only 6,746 members in seventy-nine churches because of the withdrawal of two associations—Ambraw in 1991 and Northern Indiana in 1992—upon the adoption by the General Association of an article that denied a literal millennium after Christ's second coming. In 2000, the two independent associations totaled 1,970 members in fifteen churches, including the large Union Oakford Separate Baptist Church (now called Crossroads Community Church) of Kokomo, Indiana, with 1,300 in average attendance. Neither of these two associations today practices footwashing, a rite, however, continued by other Separate Baptists.

Bibliography

For a helpful study of the faith and practice of Separate Baptists, see James Owen Renault, "The Changing Patterns of Separate Baptist Life," *Baptist History and Heritage,* XIV/4, (October, 1979), 16-25, 36. For an old history of the movement, see Morgan Scott, *History of the Separate Baptist Church,* (Indianapolis: Hollenbeck Press, c. 1900). For a description of the Baptist divisions in Kentucky out of which the Separate Baptists in Christ developed, see John Sparks, *The Roots of Appalachian Christianity,* (Lexington: University Press of Kentucky, 2001), 199-210. For a history of the Christian Unity Association, see the U.S. census, *Religious Bodies: 1936,* II, part one, 252-53.

IX. Old-Time Baptists

	MEMBERSHIP	CHURCHES
Duck River and Kindred Associations (1826/1939)	10,188	99
Old Missionary Baptists	60,423	444
Enterprise Baptists (1894)	4,310	65
United Baptists	100,000	800
TOTAL	**174,921**	**1,408**

Old-time Baptist bodies are wedded to a Southern rural culture. They rank between Primitivists and Baptists with integrated organizations. They never evolved, as most other Baptists, in accepting integrated structures with boards and denominational programs. Their major organizational standard is the traditional association for inspiration and fellowship. Pastors are generally bivocational and preach extemporaneously. Although they may accept some limited training for pastors, they see no need, however, for a seminary-trained clergy.

Unlike Primitivists, however, they generally accept musical instruments in worship, Sunday schools, and revivalism. In theology, they reject the predestinarianism of the Primitivists, accept a general atonement, and recognize the believer's will in salvation. Some of them have an interest in missions, while others are non-missionary but not anti-missionary.

They tend to perpetuate older practices, such as the mourner's bench. Although many do not practice footwashing, numbers do. In preaching, pastors use exclusively the King James Version, which is considered God's inerrant Word. With some limited exception, they observe close communion. Like Landmark Baptists, they tend to be successionists, looking upon Baptists as apostolic, but it is not a major issue as with Landmarkers. Unlike Landmarkers, who are premillennial, they tend to be amillennial.[206]

Duck River and Kindred Associations (General Association of Baptists) (1826/1939)

The General Association of Baptists are often called Duck River and Kindred Associations, named after the Duck River Association, its initial body, and to associations with which it corresponds. In 1826, the founders of the Duck River Association, located in Middle Tennessee, separated from the Elk River Association in opposition to the latter's strong Calvinism and associational presbytery. The Duck River Association split in 1843, with one party continuing as a Separate Baptist body and refusing to cooperate with the United Baptists and their agencies. It entered into correspondence with associations of like mind.

They are exclusive and presumptuously call themselves, "The Baptists." They are moderately Calvinistic, maintain the mourner's bench, where a seeker is expected to pray through until experiencing God's grace, and observe footwashing. The Lord's Supper is observed once or twice a year, generally using homemade crackers and homemade wine or grape juice. They have Sunday schools but no mission programs or benevolent institutions. Pastors are bivocational and often addressed as "elder." The Duck River Association maintains an educational program for pastors, but seminary training is considered unnecessary.

They are a comparatively small rural group of ten thousand members with around 100 churches. For years, their membership has been static. They have five associations in Tennessee and two in Alabama and one church in Kentucky with membership primarily in lower Middle Tennessee and northern Alabama. In 1939, they formed a general body called the General Association of Baptists, which meets annually.

Bibliography

Forrest Shelton Clark, *A History of the Duck River Baptists,* (Term paper, Southern Baptist Theological Seminary, 1969). Clifford A. Grammich, Jr., "Duck River and Kindred Baptists," in *Local Baptists, Local Politics,* (Knoxville: University of Tennessee Press, 1999), 65-71. Albert W. Wardin, Jr., "Duck River and Kindred Associations, (General Association of Baptists)," *Tennessee Baptist History*, IV/1 (Fall, 2002), 23-5.

Old Missionary Baptists

Old Missionary Baptists is a designation given to a number of associations that consider themselves in lineage with the Missionary Baptist movement that separated from the non-missionary Primitive Baptists in the nineteenth century. Their associations or churches carry the name "Missionary Baptist" or simply "Baptist," except for Regular Baptists in Arkansas and Oklahoma. Unlike Missionary Baptists that formed conventions and boards, their organizational level is the local association that includes the option of correspondence with other associations. Although at one time some of the Old Missionary Baptist associations were in a state convention, they either dropped away or were themselves dropped by the convention for refusing to participate in a unified program of missions and benevolence.

Old Missionary Baptists hold a modified Calvinistic position much like Southern Baptists. Most of them are amillennial although a minority is premillennial. They consider baptism from other Baptist groups "alien" if not performed by proper order and authority. A distinguishing feature of Old Missionary Baptists is the mourner's bench. Salvation is far more than a verbal declaration of faith; one needs to express repentance and undergo an emotional experience. Footwashing is not widespread, although it is observed in some churches, such as in the Southwestern District Association in Tennessee, Edmonson Association in Kentucky, and among Regular Baptists in Arkansas and Oklahoma.

Pastors, who may be addressed "elder," are often bivocational. They preach either extemporaneously or from notes. The Old Missionary Baptist Church in Bowling Green, Kentucky, conducts a short-term training session for pastors each year. Old Missionary Baptists have Sunday schools. A number of them receive their literature from Missionary Baptist Literature (MBL), located in Tennessee. It has been publishing since 1978.

Old Missionary Baptists oppose the cooperative programs of Baptist conventions. Some in Kentucky and Tennessee support direct missions, whereby a church endorses a missionary who is supported directly by the church and also possibly by other congregations. At times they have established benevolent institutions, such as a retirement home or orphanage, but have had limited success in this area.

Old Missionary Baptist associations included in the *Religious Congregations and Membership* study in 2000 number around 40,000 in a few over 300 churches. One cluster that includes the Enon, Wiseman, Siloam, Edmonson, and Barren River Associations is in northern Middle Tennessee and the Pennyroyal south-central area of Kentucky, including the Upper Cumberland of both states. Because of controversy over exchanging letters with Southern Baptist churches, most churches in the Wiseman Association left, which greatly increased unaffiliated churches in the region to fifty-six with an estimated membership of 8,000 in Tennessee and Kentucky.

Other Old Missionary Baptist associations also include: the Southwestern District

Association in West Tennessee; the Pine Mountain Association in eastern Kentucky; the Bear Creek Association in northern Alabama; and Bethel Association in Indiana. In addition, Georgia has five including: Chetatee, Coosawattee, Ellijay, Original Smyrna, and Pleasant Grove. Missouri has eight in the Ozark region including: Baptist Old Path, Cane Creek, Cedar County, County Line, Dallas County, Old Time Camden County, Polk County, and St. Clair County.

Wayne Trail Missionary Baptist Association, listed separately in the 2000 study, is also in this category. This association, located primarily in northern Ohio, was founded by migrants from the South in the 1940s. It has 2,192 members in thirteen churches. Its churches have a mourner's bench or altar, and a number observe footwashing. Three other associations in northern Georgia, also listed under their own names in the 2000 study, are: Jasper, Pleasant Valley, and New Hope, with 7,790 members in fifty-one churches. They simply carry "Baptist" in their associational names. All three are independent of conventions. They practice footwashing. Pleasant Valley and Jasper have mourner's benches but New Hope does not. They generally use musical instruments, but only Jasper has Sunday schools of any number.

Outside the 2000 study are three rural Regular Baptist associations in northwest Arkansas and northeastern Oklahoma. They include: East Washington Regular (1,527 in ten churches), Salem Regular (114 in two churches), and King's River Regular United (222 in two churches). They are similar to Old Missionary Baptists and not to be confused with the Old Regular Baptists of Appalachia that are more Calvinistic and primitive in church practice. Like Old Missionary Baptists, they reject conventions, are moderately Calvinistic, and use the mourner's bench or altar. Like most Old Missionary Baptists they are also amillennial. They call their pastors "elder," most of whom are untrained and are bivocational. They use musical instruments in worship and support Sunday schools. Another association outside the 2000 study is the Mt. Carmel Missionary Baptist Association in northern Alabama. The Association consists of eight churches and a total attendance of 370.

Including Old Missionary Baptist associations in the 2000 study, whether under the Old Missionary label or their own name, as well as the Regular Baptists in Arkansas and Oklahoma and the Mt. Carmel Association in Alabama, the total is 444 churches with over 60,000 members. The average church is small and is generally located in rural areas except for a number of churches in the Wayne Trail Association and some churches in the suburban areas in Davidson and Sumner Counties in Tennessee.

Bibliography

H. C Vanderpool, a leader among Old Missionary Baptists, has written, *Twentieth Century Baptists*, vol. 2, printed in Scottsdale, Kentucky, by Gerald Printing Company, 1999, which provides histories of churches, biographical sketches, and an account of the cooperative work of this group.

Clifford A. Grammich, Jr., "'Old' Missionary Baptists," in *Local Baptists, Local Politics*, (Knoxville: University of Tennessee Press, 1999), 71-76, is an account that concentrates on Old Missionary Baptists in Kentucky and Tennessee. Also see Albert W. Wardin, Jr., "Old Missionary Baptists," *Tennessee Baptist History*, IV/1 (Fall, 2002), 26-31.

Enterprise Baptists (1894)

The Enterprise Association of Regular Baptist Churches of Jesus Christ was formed in 1894 in Enterprise, Johnson County, Kentucky. Their churches carry the name "Enterprise Baptist." This body broke from the Regular Baptists by rejecting predestination. They have become Arminian in doctrine. They are similar to Free Will Baptists, unlike most other Old-Time Baptists who are mildly Calvinistic. The association does not correspond with other associations except with the Bethel Association of United Baptists in Missouri.

Their churches include altars for prayer and practice footwashing. Most churches have Sunday schools. The association maintains an associational camp at White Oak, Ohio. They have no mission program. As most Old Mission Baptists, they are also amillennial. They number 4,300 members in sixty-five churches. They are located primarily in northeastern Kentucky and southern Ohio. One church is in Indiana.

Bibliography

See John Sparks, *The Roots of Appalachian Christianity,* (Lexington: University Press of Kentucky, 2001), 248, for a short reference to Enterprise Baptists.

United Baptists

United Baptists are a group of independent associations that carry the name "United Baptist." In the union of the Regular and Separate Baptists in the late eighteenth and early nineteenth centuries, Baptists in the South tended to assume the name "United Baptist." This designation was dropped in time by most Baptists.

United Baptists exhibit much diversity. Some associations, such as Stockton Valley, West Union, Green River, and South Fork in northeastern Tennessee and southern Kentucky are much like the Old Missionary Baptists and mildly Calvinistic. Second North Concord Association of United Missionary Baptist Churches in Kentucky (with both "United" and "Missionary" in its name) may also be placed in this category. The Cumberland River Association, which identifies with the American Baptist Association, a national Landmark body, is progressive in supporting Sunday schools, missions, and musical instruments in worship and is not listed in the website "United Baptists Today." Some United Baptists reject Sunday schools and musical instruments, and some of them are Arminian and practice open communion.

United Baptists are traditional in rejecting centralized denominational organizations and benevolent and educational institutions. Their pastors are not theologically trained and are bivocational. While some support missions, others are non-missionary. Numbers of them also observe footwashing.

Because of different lists, it is not entirely clear as to the number of United Baptist associations. United Baptist associations have also experienced numerous splits. By conflating the list of United Baptist associations in *Churches and Church Membership in the United States,* 1990,[207] which lists twenty-four of them, with the listing by Robert L. Vaughn of Mt. Enterprise, Texas, who notes twenty-nine, one is able to identify thirty-two such associations. By including splits, John Sparks adds another eight, and "United Baptists Today"[208] adds another six for a total of forty-six.

The 1990 study, which listed twenty-four associations, recorded 436 churches with 54,248 members, which is an undercount. If one added twenty-two additional associations, assuming these associations average about the size of the others, the total figure might possibly be from 90,000 to 100,000 members in around 800 churches. The 1990 study found that United Baptists were well represented in Kentucky, in Appalachia and the Pennyroyal section, with 35,000 United Baptists in 250 churches. It included the Cumberland River Association. Smaller numbers lapped over into West Virginia, Ohio, Indiana, Tennessee, Arkansas, and Alabama. Through migration United Baptists are also in Missouri in the Bethel and Central Missouri Associations. Some United Baptist associations cooperate in a National Association of United Baptists of America, which held its first session in 1964 in Huntington, West Virginia.

Bibliography

Arthur C. Piepkorn, *Profiles in Belief,* (New York: Harper & Row), 1978, II, 442-43. Clifford A. Grammich, Jr., *Local Baptists, Local Politics,* (Knoxville: University of Tennessee Press, 1999), 88-93. Grammich includes Jasper and Pleasant Valley Associations of Georgia that do not carry the United Baptist name. John Sparks, *The Roots of Appalachian Christianity,* (Lexington: University Press of Kentucky), 2001), 228-39. Sparks is a minister of the United Baptists.

X. Primitivists[209]

	MEMBERSHIP	CHURCHES
Primitive Baptists—Old Line (1827)	46,954	1,381
Primitive Baptists—Predestinarian (1827)	1,882	243
Primitive Baptists—Universalists (1924)	378	18
Old Regular Baptists (1854)	15,218	326
Regular Baptists	3,938	41
Two-Seed-in-the-Spirit Predestinarian Baptists (1826)	55	5
TOTAL	**68,425**	**2,014**

Primitive Baptists

Primitive Baptists are traditionalists, wedded to a Baptist faith and practice of the late eighteenth and early nineteenth centuries. Primitive Baptists often called themselves "Old School Baptists," while opponents would refer to them as "Hardshell Baptists." Their separation from other Baptists first occurred in 1827 and was well completed by 1840. Primitive Baptists were primarily rural and wedded to a pre-industrial society, feeling threatened by the new age of the factory and the locomotive. They feared concentrations of power and wealth—economic, political, and social.

Primitive Baptists opposed the numerous innovations that appeared in Baptist life in the first decades of the nineteenth century. They rejected institutions beyond the local church and the association. They believed that societies, boards, and conventions with their incessant appeals for money were unbiblical and a threat to local church autonomy. As a consequence they rejected home and foreign mission societies, Bible societies, and tract societies.

Their pastors, who were largely untrained farmer-preachers, generally supported themselves. They looked upon the appearance of educated home missionaries with set salaries as a threat, entering a field where they had already labored. Pastors received no formal theological training since it was believed that a pastor was called by God who would give him the inspiration and message without the need of such training. On the other hand, Primitive Baptists were not opposed to education as such, and some of the pastors were professional men or self-taught. Pastors were students of Scripture and when a novice would study with other pastors. Primitive Baptists, by and large, opposed paying their pastors a set salary but provided them with gifts in money or kind. Most pastors were bivocational. Primitive Baptists continued to call their pastors "elders," a title used by all Baptists in the past.

Primitive Baptists were also wedded to the traditional in worship and practice and have maintained rather successfully these patterns. Particularly in Appalachia, their preaching style, with other Baptist subgroups, is often a rhythmic sing-song. Singing is a cappella. Many practice footwashing but some do not, particularly in the North. It was never a test of fellowship. They felt that Sunday schools were unbiblical, unnecessary, and a human means to produce Christians.

In their reaction against innovations, they became defensive and hardened in their theological views. The Calvinist strand in Baptist theology, which acknowledged God's sovereignty and man's depravity, was heightened. In theory, they were not opposed to preaching the gospel, but it was to edify the saints and not convert sinners, which was God's work. No means were necessary. In opposition to mission organizations, they became anti-missionary, opposing them on theological grounds.

In their lack of evangelistic effort, including revivalism, opposition to Sunday schools and youth organizations, maintenance of traditional worship patterns, rural orientation, and aging membership, the Primitivists face decline and numerous churches and associations have disbanded. They, however, continue to have some strength in the rural South. Their indigenous strength in the Northeast, Upper Midwest, and West has practically disappeared, and their presence there is due primarily to Southern migration. Division and factionalism have also beset them over theological differences, the acceptance of excluded members, and the autocratic authority of associational moderators.

Some changes, however, have occurred in more recent years, and they have shown some limited growth in urban centers. Although their church buildings are plain without inner adornment or stained glass, many congregations today have improved facilities, adding parking lots, air conditioning, indoor rest rooms, carpets, and kitchens or fellowship halls. In the past, monthly preaching with a business session and service on the preceding Saturday was the norm, but today the number of preaching services has significantly increased in many of the churches. Although elders are still generally bivocational, some elders today receive half support if not full support. Younger elders not only study with older elders or follow the preaching of others but also may listen to sermons on cassette tapes.

Services, however, remain simple and traditional, primarily composed of preaching, congregational singing (no choirs or soloists), and prayer. Sermons generally last almost an hour. Pastors, by and large, speak extemporaneously with a few using notes. Singing lasts a half hour and is unaccompanied by musical instruments and led by a song leader who sets the pitch. Primitive Baptists retain the hymnody of the past by singing the old gospel hymns, often in a distinctive sound and style, with shape notes. After the initial hymn, members in the congregation call out hymns to be sung. At the end of the service, worshippers move about extending the right hand of fellowship.

Churches observe the Lord's Supper quarterly, twice a year, or annually. Wine is used for the cup; some using the common cup while others individual cups. The bread, which is unleavened, is baked at home. Only Baptists of like faith and order are invited to participate. Baptism may be in a baptistry or, as in the past, in an open stream. Baptism from Missionary Baptists is not accepted. Besides continuing to publish periodicals, they also now use radio.

With few exceptions, memberships are extremely small. Visiting brethren and individuals who are not members augment attendance. Since baptism often occurs later in life, nonmembers may provide an important segment of the worshippers. Larger gatherings occur at annual associational meetings and union meetings. Unlike the past, many churches today are not members of any association, and union meetings have declined. Some independent churches, however, may invite other churches to a fellowship meeting in the absence of an associational moderator.

Bibliography

Two very fine dissertations on Primitive Baptists are by Julietta Haynes, *A History of the Primitive Baptists,* (Ph.D. dissertation, University of Texas, 1959), which includes a listing of Primitive Baptist periodicals, and Byron Cecil Lambert, *The Rise of the Anti-Mission Baptists: Sources and Leaders, 1800–1840,* (Ph.D. dissertation, University of Chicago, 1957; New York: Arno Press, 1980). The article by Arthur C. Piepkorn, "The Primitive Baptists of North America," *Concordia Theological Monthly,* XLII/5, (May, 1971), 297-324, was reprinted in *Baptist History and Heritage,* VII/1, (January, 1972), 33-51, and provides valuable information. An excellent account of Primitive Baptists past and present is by John G. Crowley, "The Primitive or Old School Baptists," in Jonas, *The Baptist River,* (Macon: Mercer University Press, 2006), 158-181. An old-fashioned Primitive Baptist history with statistical data is Sylvester Hassell,

History of the Church of God, (Middletown, NY: Gilbert Beebe's Sons, 1886, reprinted by Turner Lassetter, Atlanta, 1948, 1955). An excellent study of Primitive Baptist singing with a description of Primitive life and practice is the work by Beverly Bush Paterson, *The Sound of the Dove: Singing in Appalachian Primitive Baptist Churches,* (Urbana and Chicago: University of Illinois Press, 1995). Primitive Baptist libraries are located at Elon College, North Carolina, and Carthage, Illinois. With its acquisition of the Primitive Baptist library at Atwood, Tennessee, the Southern Baptist Historical Library and Archives, Nashville, Tennessee, has one of the most extensive collections of Primitive Baptist materials, including associational minutes, periodicals, and books.

Primitive Baptists—Old Line (1827)

The largest and most distributed Primitive Baptist body is the Old Line Primitive Baptists. They are more moderate than the Absolute Predestinarians. They believe in divine election but teach "conditional time salvation," *i.e.* the rewards of a Christian in this life are conditioned upon one's obedience to God's laws.

The *Primitive Baptist Church Directory,* 1996 edition, lists 1,381 Old-Line churches both in associations and independent congregations. With an estimated average membership of thirty-four, based on associational records, their total membership is around 47,000. Their strongest state is Georgia, followed in descending order by Alabama, Texas, and Tennessee. They are extremely weak outside the South but have some congregations in the Great Lakes region and California. Their associations number probably over 120, if all divisions were located. Forty-eight percent of their churches are independent of any association.

One of the foremost converts to the Primitive Baptist cause is Elder Lasserre Bradley, Jr., a Baptist minister who was rebaptized in 1958. He and fifty-four others constituted the Cincinnati Primitive Baptist Church. Bradley maintains a radio ministry, the "Baptist Bible Hour," a weekly broadcast that began in 1953 and that is also on the internet.

Primitive Baptists—Predestinarian (1827)

Predestinarian Primitive Baptists, called at times Absoluters, broke with Old Line Primitive Baptists over the extent of God's predestination, insisting that it extended over all of life. They deny making God the author of sin since man sins voluntarily, but by His will God allows sin for a greater good.

According to Julietta Haynes, the controversy over the extent of predestination began around 1880 with churches and associations dividing between 1884 and 1935 across the nation except in the Northeast, an area under control of the Absoluters. As a result the Primitive Baptist movement was irrevocably rent with cutting all fellowship between the two groups.[210]

In 2000, Predestinarian Baptists had 243 congregations and thirty-nine associations. Even with these numbers, it is an extremely small body. An investigation of associational records reveals an average church membership of a little less than eight, resulting in a total of less than 2,000. Attendance at services is often augmented by visitors from other congregations. Its greatest strength is in North Carolina with eighty-three churches and Virginia with fifty-two. Almost twenty-four percent of its churches are not members of any association.

This body includes the oldest Primitive Baptist church in the nation, the Welsh Tract Baptist Church in New Castle County, Delaware, formed in 1701, which has fifteen members. It also includes the Kehukee Association of North Carolina, the first association in 1827 to separate from the Missionary Baptists, which in 2001 had only eleven members in four churches. The oldest continuing Primitive Baptist periodical, a Predestinarian publication, is the *Signs of the Times,* which was founded in 1832. Predestinarian Baptists have a library at Elon College, North Carolina.

Primitive Baptists—Universalists (1924)

A small group of Primitive Baptists in Appalachia is the Primitive Baptist Universalists, known also as the "No Hellers." The elect of God enjoy His grace on earth in the present, while the non-elect suffer a hell on earth by their separation from God. Christ's atonement is universal, and at the resurrection everyone, elect and non-elect, will gain heaven without distinction. There is no literal hell.

Universalism first appeared to trouble the Washington District Association of Upper East Tennessee and Southwest Virginia in 1907. The association, however, did not split until 1924 when it refused to seat messengers from churches accepting universalism. The disfranchised Universalists then formed their own Washington District Association. By this time, universalism had also penetrated the Three Forks of Powell's River Association and Stoney Creek Association, which is now extinct.

Washington District and Three Forks of Powell's River still exist along with Elkhorn Association. A second Elkhorn Association also exists but is not in fellowship with the other three. At present, the three associations in fellowship total fourteen churches and 258 members, a significant drop from 1994 when they had thirty-six churches and 571 members. The second Elkhorn Association has four churches and 120 members, thus making a grand total of eighteen churches and 378 members. Half of the churches are in Buchanan County in Virginia and McDowell County in West Virginia. A single congregation is located in each of the following states: Kentucky, Tennessee, Ohio, and Pennsylvania.

Bibliography

An excellent study of the history, theology, and practices of the Universalists is by Howard Dorgan, *In the Hands of a Happy God: The No-Hellers of Central Appalachia,* (Knoxville: University of Tennessee Press, 1997).

Old Regular Baptists (1854)

Old Regular Baptists, a Baptist subdenomination in Appalachia, exhibit many of the same characteristics as Primitive Baptists. Their church buildings are plain. Their pastors, also called elders, are bivocational, unpaid, and untrained. They oppose Sunday schools. Footwashing is practiced. As other Baptists in the early nineteenth century, Old Regular Baptists continue to observe monthly preaching with a business meeting and service on the previous Saturday. Services, which are more emotional than those among Primitive Baptists, are three hours long with sermons by three or more elders. Preaching is improvised often in a rhythmic sing-song pattern. Congregational singing, led by a song leader, is a cappella, sung slowly and often in mournful tones.

Their theology has Calvinistic roots. They teach an "election by grace" stating that "God gives opportunity for individuals to respond to His offer of grace, but the recipient must personally experience it to obtain it." Old Regular Baptists reject the predestination of all things of the Predestinarian Primitive Baptists and God's predetermined election of salvation of the Old Line Primitive Baptists.

Old Regular Baptists oppose women sporting bobbed hair and wearing modern fashions and men with long hair. Women are permitted no pastoral roles; in business session they remain silent, not engaging in debate or deliberation.

Old Regular Baptists descend primarily from the New Salem Association in eastern Kentucky and its associational offshoots. This association was formed in 1825 and was United Baptist but in time became increasingly separated from other United Baptists who accepted organized missions and innovations in church practice. In 1854, the association took the name, "Regular United." In 1891, the name was changed to "Old Regular."

The study, *Churches and Church Membership in the United States*, 1990, recorded seventeen Old Regular associations, primarily in Kentucky, West Virginia, and Virginia, particularly in the area where these states converge. Their membership was a bit over 15,000 in over three hundred churches. These figures included the Bethel Association, which was out of fellowship with other Old Regular Baptists, but not the Kyova Association, another association out of fellowship. Because of migration, Old Regular Baptists may be found in the Great Lakes region and in Washington State.

Average membership is less than fifty per church, but attendance at monthly services is augmented by numbers of unbaptized and visitors from neighboring congregations. As among Primitive Baptists, baptism often occurs late in life. Old Regular Baptists hold associational meetings, union meetings, and memorial meetings to commemorate those who have died, often drawing large crowds.

Bibliography

An excellent study of Old Regular Baptists is the work by Howard Dorgan, *The Old Regular Baptists of Central Appalachia* (Knoxville: University of Tennessee Press, 1989), which relates their history, theology, and church practices. An informative description is by Ron Short, reared an Old Regular Baptist, "'We believed in the family and The Old Regular Baptist Church,'" in *Southern Exposure*, IV/3, (Fall, 1976), 60-65, printed as well in Samuel S. Hill, Jr., ed., *On Jordan's Stormy Banks*, (Macon: Mercer University Press, 1983), 101-107. Also see, "The Old Regular Baptists," in John Sparks, *The Roots of Appalachian Christianity,* (Lexington: University Press of Kentucky, 2001), 251-64. An old-fashioned work by a Regular Baptist on some of the Regular Baptist associations is Rufus Perrigan, *History of Regular Baptists and Their Ancestors and Accessors,* (Haysi, Virginia: Author, 1961).

Regular Baptists

Regular Baptists are in theological agreement with Old Regular Baptists but are more open to modern developments in church practice and also to other Baptist subdenominations. Although generally singing a cappella in their regular worship services, their hymns and style tend to be more contemporary and may even use instruments in informal settings. They hold revivals and may also sponsor Sunday schools. On the other hand, as Old Regular Baptists their pastors are untrained and bivocational. They also observe footwashing. In the study, *Churches and Church Membership in the United States*, 1990, they were found to have almost 3,000 members in forty-one churches. The great majority is in North Carolina.

Bibliography

See Howard Dorgan, *Giving Glory to God In Appalachia: Worship Practices of Six Baptist Subdenominations,* (Knoxville: University of Tennessee Press, 1987), 28-29, for differences between Regular and Old Regular Baptists.

Two-Seed-in-the-Spirit Predestinarian Baptists (1826)

Daniel Parker (1781–1844), a Primitive Baptist, is the progenitor of this subgroup with his doctrine of the two seeds, a type of Manichaeism. He propounded his theological views in three pamphlets in 1826. He believed that one is born with either the good seed, implanted by God in Adam and Eve, or the evil seed, which Satan implanted at the fall. The seeds are "in the spirit" and not of the flesh. The followers of Parker went beyond him to reject a corporeal resurrection. They taught that Christ appeared in a spiritual body and did not suffer physical death or a physical resurrection. God resurrects His children spiritually as they die to the flesh, and their spirits go to God after death. After death, the spirits of those with the evil seed remain eternally in a spiritual hell.

With his publication, *A Public Address to the Baptist Society*, in 1820, which attacked the

Triennial Convention, Parker became a leading foe of organized missions. His own theology, which regarded missions as useless, reinforced the anti-mission cause. In 1833, he led a congregation from Illinois into Texas, the first Baptist church in this territory.

The great majority of Primitive Baptists opposed two-seedism, and it was strongly fought in such places as Texas and Tennessee. Two-Seed Baptists, however, have at times been confused with regular Primitive Baptists since their practices are the same. Associations that accepted two-seedism generally did not include any explicit two-seed doctrine and almost without exception never included "Two-Seed" in their names. Two-Seed associations were dispersed over a wide area, including Florida, the Upper South, Indiana, and Texas. One of its most successful areas was a belt from southern Kentucky through Middle Tennessee into northern Alabama where it affected three associations.

This body has precipitously declined. The U.S. religious census in 1906 recorded fifty-five churches and 781 members. In 1961, it had only twelve congregations. Today there is only one remaining association—Trinity River, which includes two churches—Little Hope near Jacksboro, Texas, and Otter Creek in Putnam County, Indiana, with a membership of forty. A third church, Concord Church (twelve members) is located in the Highland District near McMinnville, Tennessee, and meets each Sunday. A fourth church, Mt. Moriah (three members) at Athens, Alabama, has services only twice a year with the Concord Church. A fifth church is a division of the Little Hope Church of Jacksboro, whose membership is unknown.

Bibliography

Joe Early, Jr., "Daniel Parker: A Common Man for the Common People," *American Baptist Quarterly*, XXIII/1, (March, 2004), 50-64. Albert W. Wardin, Jr., "Two-Seed-in-the-Spirit Predestinarian Baptists," *Baptist History and Heritage*, XXXVII/3, (Summer/Fall, 2002), 97-99. For an account of the Otter Creek Church, see Terry E. Miller, "Voices from the Past: The Singing and the Preaching at Otter Creek Church," *Journal of American Folklore*, LXXXVIII/349, (July–September, 1975), 266-82, and "Otter Creek Church, Indiana; Lonely Bastion of Daniel Parker's 'Two-Seedism,'" *Foundations*, XVIII/4, (October–December, 1975), 358-76. For a description of Two-Seedism in South Georgia and Florida, see John G. Crowley, *Primitive Baptists of the Wiregrass South*, (Gainesville: University Press of Florida, 1998), 118-33.

XI. Progressive Primitive

	Membership	Churches
1. Progressive Primitive Baptists (1897)	7,739	121
2. Central Baptist Association (1956)	3,678	33
3. Eastern District Association of Primitive Baptists (1848)	6,468	67
TOTAL	**17,885**	**221**

Some Primitive Baptists have shifted from their former styles of worship and polity and in some cases even theology. They have moved from the traditional to a transitional stage of development. An early such movement began in Georgia, but today similar developments have appeared among some Primitive Baptists in Appalachia.

Progressive Primitive Baptists (1897)

Around 1897, a progressive movement began in Georgia among Primitive Baptists when some churches started to use organs and a few years later began to hold extended meetings. Tensions developed with the Old Liners who refused to countenance any innovations and who passed resolutions of nonfellowship. By the 1920s, the Old Liners refused all efforts of reconciliation.

Today, Progressive Primitive Baptists accept Sunday schools, Bible conferences, nursing facilities, youth camps, a campground, a ministers' school, a builders organization (for building churches), and, of course, musical instruments in worship. They formed a Primitive Baptist Foundation and established a ministry in Ukraine. In 1954, they opened Birdwood College but relinquished control in 1976. Today, it continues as Thomas University, an independent non-sectarian school.

On the other hand, they are still Calvinists, teaching particular and unconditional election, and observe footwashing. In spite of their innovations, other Primitive Baptists, although not in fellowship with them, still recognize them as part of the Primitive Baptist fraternity.

Progressive Primitive Baptists have thirteen associations with over 7,700 members in 121 churches. Seventy-five percent of their membership is in Georgia. Smaller groups are in other Southern states with also a few churches in Indiana and Illinois. Its periodical, *The Banner-Herald*, began in 1894 as *The Pilgrim's Banner* and in 1918 merged with *The Pilgrim's Herald*, which had started in 1916. It also maintains a Progressive Primitive Baptist Archive.

Bibliography

See Julietta Haynes, *A History of the Primitive Baptists,* (Ph.D. dissertation, University of Texas, 1959), 240-44, 263-76.

Central Baptist Association (1956)

In 1956, Central Baptist Association was founded by churches that separated from the Eastern District Association of Primitive Baptists. It chose the name "Central" for theological rather than geographical reasons—to stray neither to the right or left. They teach that God's plan of salvation was predetermined, but an individual may resist God's grace for salvation. A majority of their churches observe footwashing. Some of their pastors are called "elders." Their churches have Sunday schools and use musical instruments in worship. Women are prohibited from pastoral ministry and except for special circumstances are silent in church.

The association has formed Mt. Moriah Ministries, located in the fellowship hall of the Riverside Baptist Church of Kingsport, Tennessee. Its program includes the operation of a summer camp at Jasper, Virginia, and a mission interest in Jamaica. It began an orphans' home, which, however, it no longer operates. The association is comparatively small with a little more than 3,500 members in thirty-three churches. The congregations are concentrated in northeast Upper Tennessee and southwestern Virginia. A few churches are in Kentucky, South Carolina, and Indiana.

Bibliography

See "Central Baptists," in Clifford A. Grammich, Jr., *Local Baptists, Local Politics*, (Knoxville: University of Tennessee Press, 1999), 60-65.

Eastern District Association of Primitive Baptists (1848)

Although it identifies itself as a Primitive Baptist association, it is not a typical association of this order. First, it does not hold to unconditional election. It also does not correspond with other Primitive Baptist associations, and its congregations are typically much larger.

The Central Association broke from it because of its conservatism, but today it is a transitional body, but not going as far as the former body. It has no foreign mission interests nor institutions. It also continues to observe foortwashing, and women are prohibited from expression on associational affairs. On the other hand, it has Sunday schools, conducts revivals, and does not ban musical instruments in worship.

As the Central Association, its greatest strength is in northeast Upper Tennessee and southwest Virginia where eighty percent of its churches and members are located. It has a few churches in Kentucky and Ohio. It is more rural than the Central Association.

Bibliography

"Eastern District Primitive Baptist Association," Clifford A. Grammich, Jr., *Local Baptists, Local Politics,* (Knoxville: University of Tennessee Press, 1999), 83-88.

XII. Neo-Calvinist

	Membership	Churches
1. Reformed Baptists (1967)	12,000	200
2. Sovereign Grace Baptists (1954)	8,000	200
3. Strict Baptists (1907)	21	3
TOTAL	**20,021**	**403**

Reformed/Sovereign Grace Baptists

Neo-Calvinists adhere to the ecclesiology and doctrines of the Particular Baptists of England of the seventeenth century. Although this tribal group, by and large, is a comparatively recent manifestation of Baptist life in the United States, its roots are in the life and thought of the first Calvinistic Baptists. In a sense, Neo-Calvinists have come full circle, bringing to life in the twentieth and twenty-first centuries Baptist confessions three hundred or more years from the past.

Neo-Calvinists are adherents of God's particular redemption. They oppose, however, Primitive Baptists for their hyper-Calvinism and anti-missionism. They follow an evangelical Calvinism that supports the preaching of the gospel to all. They approve mission organizations, Bible and pastors' conferences, Sunday schools, and Christian Schools, and even revivals, if properly conducted. On the other hand, they oppose the techniques of modern evangelism as too superficial.

They are strong advocates of the independence of the local church and oppose complex denominational structures. Some churches have a plurality of elders while others have only one pastor. The movement tries to some extent to recover the practice of church discipline, lost today among major Baptist bodies. With roots in Reformed theology, they tend to oppose premillennialism. They also reject Landmarkism.

Reformed/Sovereign Grace Baptists appeared in the middle of the 1950s. One source was from the efforts of Rolfe Barnard, an independent Baptist evangelist. A second source was the publications of Arthur W. Pink. In 1954, Henry Mahan, pastor of Thirteenth Street Baptist Church of Ashland, Kentucky, an alumnus of Tennessee Temple College, convened at his church the first meeting of the Sovereign Grace Bible Conference. Other conferences have followed in various parts of the nation. Participants may include non-Baptists but of the Reformed tradition. In addition to conferences, books and periodicals have advanced the movement.

Neo-Calvinists are in two basic strands—Reformed Baptists who adhere to the Second London Confession of 1689 of English Particular Baptists and Sovereign Grace Baptists who adhere to the First London Confession of 1646. The 1689 confession follows more closely the Westminster Confession of Faith and covenant theology and is thus more Puritan in its expression, while the 1646 confession puts a greater stress on grace and the New Covenant. A local church in either camp may carry the name Baptist, Reformed

Baptist, Sovereign Grace Baptist, or even no denominational name. The local name is no sure indicator of a church's alignment.

It has been difficult to compile a full listing of Reformed and Sovereign Grace churches since neither group has a central authority or has compiled an official directory. Some help is gained through periodicals and the internet. One can only estimate the total number of churches and membership. Congregations are generally small and with some exception probably average forty members each.

The Neo-Calvinist movement among Baptists is broader than just incorporating Reformed, Sovereign Grace, and Strict Baptists. A renewed interest in Calvinist tenets has appeared among other Baptist bodies, such as Southern Baptists, with pastors holding such tenets remaining with their respective church bodies.[211] In addition, a surprising number of Landmark Sovereign Grace congregations have appeared, unaffiliated with any national organization but because of their Landmarkism are listed with other Landmark bodies.

Bibliography

David Scott, "A Survey of Particular Baptists: Their Origins, Doctrine, Dissension and Revival," *Baptist Reformation Review,* III/1, (Spring, 1974), 9-26. John Thornbury, "Calvinistic Baptists in America," *Banner of Truth,* November, 1968, 32-36. "Sovereign Grace Baptists," *Yearbook of American & Canadian Churches,* 1991, 115.

Reformed Baptists (1967)

A center of Reformed Baptist strength is in Pennsylvania and surrounding areas. This was also a center of strength for Baptists in the colonial period where also the Philadelphia Confession of Faith (or Second London Confession) was adopted. In 1967, the Grace Baptist Church of Carlisle, Pennsylvania, began an annual pastors' conference under the leadership of its pastor, Walter Chantry, a graduate of Westminster Theological Seminary. A few years later Reformed Baptists established an annual Reformed Baptist Family Conference. Ten churches, including congregations in Pennsylvania, Delaware, and New Jersey, adopted the Philadelphia Confession and formed a Reformed Baptist association.

In 1985, delegates from Reformed Baptist congregations established in Anderson, Indiana, Reformed Baptist Mission Services (RBMS), a mission agency. The RBMS adopted the London Confession of 1689 to which contributing churches and missionaries must subscribe. In the *Mission Handbook,* 2004–2006, the RBMS reported income for overseas of $300,000 with sixteen U.S. personnel and nine non-U.S. personnel serving in nine foreign countries.

In Mesa, Arizona, in 1997, Reformed Baptists formed the Association of Reformed Baptist Churches of America, incorporating the RBMS into it. The association fosters fellowship and missions and has plans for a seminary and a publishing house. It began with a charter membership of twenty-four churches but today has forty-four congregations, primarily in the North and West from Massachusetts to California. A Reformed Baptist Church Directory on the internet lists about 200 churches widely dispersed in forty-seven states with no one state having more than eighteen churches. Pennsylvania, New Jersey, New York, and California have the largest concentrations with some strength in the South, especially in Texas, Florida, and Georgia.

Sovereign Grace Baptists (1954)

In 1954, the first Sovereign Grace Bible Conference was held in Ashland, Kentucky. Because of doctrinal differences beginning in 1980, Sovereign Grace and Reformed Baptists developed into two distinct movements. Sovereign Grace Baptists adhere more closely to the First London Confession of 1646 than the Second London Confession of 1689. Like Reformed Baptists, the local church is sovereign. A number of their churches do not carry the name Baptist. The strength of the Sovereign Grace movement is in the region of the Great Lakes and South.

The Sovereign Grace movement is not cohesive, consisting of a number of independent circles with separate Bible conferences. One of the early participants in the movement is Jon Zens, who does not use the name Baptist. He is editor of *Searching Together*, which was founded as *Baptist Reformation Review* in 1972 in Nashville, Tennessee, by Norbert Ward, a former Primitive Baptist. In 1976, Zens became co-editor and two years later editor, moving the paper to Oregon and then to Wisconsin and now publishing it in Minnesota and changing it to its present name. Searching Together Bible Conferences are also held.

Don Fortner, pastor of the Grace Baptist Church of Danville, Kentucky, and an author, heads another Sovereign Grace circle. His church hosts an annual Sovereign Grace Bible Conference. In addition, two Particular Baptist conferences exist in the Carolinas and Georgia.

Sovereign Grace Baptists have been slow in organizing fellowships or associations, but some have appeared. In March, 2001, in Nashville, Tennessee, eleven pastors/elders adopted a constitution and by-laws for a Sovereign Grace Baptist Fellowship. Participants were from five Southern states and Missouri. One of the leaders was Gary Long of Springfield, Missouri, the head of Particular Baptist Press. Either a church or a pastor may be a member. The Fellowship meets annually in conjunction with a missionary or Bible conference. The organ of the fellowship is *The Sovereign Grace Messenger*.

In 1984, pastors in Michigan, who beginning in 1972, had cooperated in retreats and a camp program, formed the Great Lakes Baptist Association. In an effort to become more national, members of the association transformed it in 1989 into the Sovereign Grace Baptist Association. Today the association has seventeen churches in seven states that at least partially border the Great Lakes from Minnesota to New York. Continental Baptist Churches, a small group formed in 1983, with headquarters in Roanoke, Virginia, on the basis of the First London Confession, ceased as an association in 2003.

Strict Baptists (1907)

With Strict Baptists one comes full circle both theologically and geographically with early Particular or Regular Baptists in colonial America who had migrated from the British Isles. Strict Baptists are an import from England who separated from the Baptist Union in Great Britain for its departure from Calvinistic tenets and toleration of broad theological views and practices.

English immigrants began the first Strict Baptist church in the United States in 1907 in Cleveland, Ohio. It was aligned with the Gospel Standard Strict Baptists. Although this church has ceased to exist, its second pastor, Sidney Sumsion, formed in 1947 the Hope Strict Baptist Church of Grand Rapids, Michigan, which exists today as the Zion Strict Baptist Church.

Two other Strict Baptist churches have been formed. Hope Baptist Church of Sheboygan, Wisconsin, has its roots in Dutch immigrants who came under Strict Baptist influence. Old Paths Strict Baptist Church of Choteau, Montana, first began as a Reformed congregation but, after its exclusion by that denomination, began practicing believer's baptism by immersion. After cooperating for a time with Reformed Baptists, it joined the Strict Baptists. The membership of the three congregations is small, totaling only twenty-one but average attendance is 115.

Bibliography

"Strict Baptists," *Encyclopedia of American Religions,* 1999, 6th ed., 490. "Strict Baptists" in Albert W. Wardin, *Baptists Around the World* (Nashville: Broadman & Holman, 1995), 432.

Distribution of Baptists by Region and State

This section is a comparative study of Baptists by region and state. The ten regions, by and large, follow the census regions of the United States with some modification. Delaware is located in the Middle Atlantic region instead of the South Atlantic region and Missouri is placed in the Trans-Mississippi South region instead of the Great Plains (or West North Central) region. The South Atlantic and East South Central regions are divided into Upper South and Lower South regions. California and Hawaii are in their own region, separated from the other Pacific states.

Material in each region is divided into three sections. The first section is a listing of the membership and churches of the Baptist tribes in that region, including in some cases average attendance. The second section is a general description of the characteristics and strength of Baptists in the region. The Third section lists each state in turn with the membership and churches and in some cases also average attendance of each Baptist body.

New England

	MEMBERSHIP	ATTENDANCE	CHURCHES
Ecumenical Mainline*	138,200	60,110	746
National*	37,800		122
Conservative Evangelical (N)	26,751	27,108	190
Fundamental (N)**	5,177	6,791	70
Conservative Evangelical (S)	20,569	13,017	157
Fundamental (S)***	12,915	12,915	141
Landmark	216		11
General/Free Will	210		3
Neo-Calvinist	600		15
TOTAL	**242,438**		**1,455**
Dual: Ecumenical-National*	-17,700		-63
Fundamental (N)-(S)**/***	-629	-629	-7
Fundamental (S)***	-590	-590	-6
TOTALS	**223,519**		**1,379**

New England is historic ground for Baptists. In the seventeenth century, Baptists formed here their first churches. They entered every New England state by the mid-eighteenth century. Regular Baptists, General Six Principle Baptists, Seventh Day Baptists, a Separate Baptist movement, and a Freewill body first appeared in this area. Baptists formed Rhode Island College (now Brown University), the first Baptist college in the nation. New England Baptists were leaders in home and foreign missions and provided support for anti-slavery.

Baptists are located in every county in the region except two in Vermont (Grand Isle and Lamoille), a state, by the way, which has less Baptists and Baptist churches than any other state in the United States. Baptists are the largest Protestant denomination in Maine and

Rhode Island. On the other hand, the United Church of Christ is the largest Protestant body in the region. In addition, the Roman Catholic Church dominates the religious scene, claiming over forty percent of the population, which leaves Baptists with less than a quarter of a million, a distinct minority.

American Baptist Churches/USA is the largest Baptist body in the region, leading in all states and most counties except for National Baptists in the Connecticut Valley and the metropolitan area near New York City. It has been losing membership, numbering 225,000 at the end of World War II, but now listing only 138,000 and an average attendance of 60,000. Its center for theological studies is Andover Newton Theological Seminary in Newton Centre, Massachusetts. Seventh Day Baptists have only five churches, and the General Six Principle Baptists no longer exist as a body; its remaining three churches now identify with conservative evangelicals.

Even though the area is not particularly open to conservative evangelicalism, northern conservative bodies, such as Conservative Baptists and Baptist General Conference, have a noticeable presence. Conservative Baptists maintain New England Bible College in Maine. Conservative evangelicalism also receives support from Gordon-Conwell Theological Seminary, a multidenominational school with Baptist roots. In recent decades southern-oriented bodies, notably the Southern Baptist Convention and the Baptist Bible Fellowship, have had some success in planting new congregations. The latter body has established Boston Baptist College.

Even with the entry of southern-oriented bodies, Baptists of all kinds today are less than the number which the American Baptist Churches alone had over a half century ago. Baptist churches are generally small. Growth is more often found among ethnic populations rather than the native Anglo population.

Bibliography

Andrew Walsh and Mark Silk, eds., *Religion and Public Life in New England,* (Walnut Creek, CA: AltaMira Press, 2004).

Maine (1682/1768)

	Membership	Attendance	Churches
Ecumenical Mainline			
ABC	21,620	10,837	164
Conservative Evangelical (N)			
BG	208	127	2
CBA	5,562	5,562	36
Fundamental (N)			
FBF*	792	924	11
GARBC	434	504	6
Conservative Evangelical (S)			
SBC	1,945	1,030	13
Fundamental (S)			
BBF*	1,730	1,730	23
Landmark			
ABA	60		2
BMA	16		1
General/ Free Will			
Free Will	70		1
Neo-Calvinist			
REF	80		2
TOTALS	**32,517**		**261**
Dual: *FBF with one BBF			
	-75	-75	-1
TOTALS	**32,442**		**260**

New Hampshire (1755)

	Membership	Attendance	Churches
Ecumenical Mainline			
ABC*	13,236	5,986	90
National			
NBC*	400		2
Conservative Evangelical (N)			
CBA	3,614	3,614	26
Fundamental (N)			
FBF	441	585	9
GARBC	98	130	2
IBFNA	49	65	1
Conservative Evangelical (S)			
SBC	2,718	1,654	14
Fundamental(S)			
BBF	1,300	1,300	15

Landmark			
ABA	20		1
BMA	20		1
General/Free Will			
	140		2
Neo-Calvinist			
REF	80		2
TOTALS	**22,116**		**165**
Dual:*ABC with 2 NBC			
	-400		-2
TOTALS	**21,716**		**163**

Vermont (1768)

	MEMBERSHIP	ATTENDANCE	CHURCHES
Ecumenical Mainline			
ABC	6,835	2,656	59
Conservative Evangelical (N)			
BGA	150	340	1
CBA	260	260	4
Fundamental (N)			
FBF	147	147	3
IFCA	49	49	1
Conservative Evangelical (S)			
SBC	824	727	17
Fundamental (S)			
BBF *	655	655	10
IBFI*	65	65	1
WBF	65	65	1
Landmark			
ABA	40		2
Neo-Calvinist			
REF	40		1
TOTALS	**9,130**		**100**
Dual:*IBFI with one BBF			
	-65	-65	-1
TOTALS	**9,065**		**99**

Massachusetts (1663)

	MEMBERSHIP	ATTENDANCE	CHURCHES
Ecumenical Mainline			
ABC*	43,015	22,279	244
National			
NBC/PNB*	15,600		48
Conservative Evangelical (N)			
BGC	4,123	4,323	33
CBA	6,852	6,852	43
Fundamental (N)			
FBF**	483	504	7
GARBC	413	431	6
IBFNA	138	144	2
Conservative Evangelical (S)			
SBC	8,941	6,814	73
Fundamental (S)			
BBF**	5,000	5,000	49
Landmark			
IL	n/a		1
Neo-Calvinist			
REF	160		4
SG	120		3
TOTALS	**84,845**		**513**
Dual: *ABC with 14 NBC/PNB			
	-2,500		-14
**FBF with 2 BBF			
	-204	-204	-2
TOTALS	**82,141**		**497**

Rhode Island (1638)

	MEMBERSHIP	ATTENDANCE	CHURCHES
Ecumenical Mainline			
ABC*	17,104	6,337	73
National			
NBC/PNB*	2,000		6
Conservative Evangelical (N)			
BGC	140	120	2
CBA	1,350	1,350	8
SD	299	135	3
Independent	229	284	2
Fundamental (N)			
FBF**	92	140	2
GARBC	46	70	1
Conservative Evangelical (S)			
SBC	1,559	609	8
Fundamental (S)			
BBF**/***	2,000	2,000	16
WBF***	375	375	3
Landmark			
ABA	20		1
Neo-Calvinist			
REF	40		1

TOTALS	**25,254**		**126**
Dual: *ABC with 6 NBC/PNB			
	-2,000		-6
**FBF with 1 BBF			
	-125	-125	-1
***WBF with 3 BBF			
	-375	-375	-3
TOTALS	**22,754**		**116**

Connecticut (1704)

	Membership	Attendance	Churches
Ecumenical Mainline			
ABC*	36,390	12,015	116
National			
NBC/PNB*	19,800		66
Conservative Evangelical (N)			
BGC	2,410	2,596	13
CBA	1,487	1,487	14
NAB	10	8	1
SD	57	50	2
Fundamental(N)			
FBF**	1,365	2,119	13
GARBC	525	816	5
IFBNA	105	163	1
Conservative Evangelical (S)			
SBC	4,582	2,183	32
Fundamental (S)			
BBF**/***	1,350	1,350	18
IBFI***	75	75	1
SWBF***	150	150	2
WBF**	150	150	2
Landmark			
ABA	20		1
IL	20		1
Neo-Calvinist			
REF	80		2
TOTALS	**68,576**		**290**
Dual: *ABC with 41 NBC/PNB			
	-12,800		-41
**FBF with 2 BBF and 1 WBF			
	-225	-225	-3
***IFBI with 1 BBF; SWBF with 1 BBF			
	-150	-150	-2
TOTALS	**55,401**		**244**

Middle Atlantic

	Membership	Attendance	Churches
Ecumenical Mainline*	347,892	159,787	1,252
National	576,219		1,126
Conservative Evangelical (N)	42,784	42,634	300
Fundamental (N)**/***	42,050	48,579	376
Conservative Evangelical (S)	75,175	48,157	540
Fundamental (S)***	42,723	42,723	278
Landmark	2,533		56
General/Free Will	514		9
Primitive	232		12
Neo-Calvinist	5,835		53
TOTALS	**1,135,957**		**4,002**
Dual: Ecumenical-National*	-70,900		-253
Fundamental (N)-(S)**/***	-2,523	-2,592	-18
Fundamental (S)***	-5,059	-5,059	-34
TOTALS	**1,057,475**		**3,697**

The Middle Atlantic states include: New York, New Jersey, Pennsylvania, and Delaware but excludes Maryland because its white Baptist population is primarily related to Baptists in the South.

Appalachian Mountains divide the region between an eastern section, which borders on the Atlantic seaboard, and a western section, which includes Upper New York and central and western Pennsylvania. With forty-five million inhabitants, the region is well populated with much of the eastern section a megalopolis extending south from New England and including such great metropolitan centers as New York City, a great cultural and financial center, and Philadelphia. This area also includes large numbers of foreign born and Hispanics, particularly in New York and New Jersey. The western section is noted for its heavy industry, mining, and agriculture.

The region has had a heritage of religious toleration and accommodation that continues to the present. With about a third of the population, the Roman Catholic Church is the largest religious body. Jews number over five percent of the population and have established here many of their religious and social institutions. Mainline Protestant denominations are also well represented. The Federal Council of Churches is located in New York City.

Baptists considered Philadelphia and the surrounding area congenial territory. Baptists established their first churches in the area and also formed the Philadelphia Association in 1707. It became a standard for Baptists. The first Baptist church in the region appeared in Pennsylvania in 1684, followed by New Jersey in 1688, Delaware in 1703, and finally New York in 1714. The First and Second Great Awakenings enhanced Baptist growth, and in time Baptists spread over the whole territory. Today, Baptists are in every county but two in Pennsylvania—Forest and Pike counties. Baptists, however, have never gained dominance in the area and are not only greatly outnumbered by Roman Catholics and Jews, but in the white population they are third, if not fourth in comparison to other Protestant bodies. Methodists, the largest Protestant body, far outpaced them; among whites, Lutherans have greater numbers, and Presbyterians are of equal strength.

Baptists claim around a million members with over half of them National or African-American Baptists. In the twentieth century, African-Americans migrated in large numbers into the region and as a result have helped to maintain a viable Protestant presence in the metropolitan areas. In second place is the American Baptist Churches/USA with roots in the colonial period. With 350,000 members and over 1,200 churches, it is well distributed throughout the region. It is a multi-cultural body with probably at least twenty percent of its churches and members dually aligned with National Baptist bodies. It has suffered some decline since the end of the Second World War but not as precipitously as in New England. In the last decades, it has maintained about the same membership. Its headquarters is at Valley Forge, Pennsylvania. One of its seminaries is Colgate-Rochester/Bexley Hall/Crozier at Rochester, New York, and a second is Eastern Baptist Theological Seminary (today Palmer Theological Seminary) at Wynnewood, Pennsylvania. The diverse theological complexion of American Baptists is well represented by these two schools with the one in New York representing their more liberal legacy, while the one in Pennsylvania representing their conservative evangelical heritage. American Baptists also have Keuka College, in New York, and Eastern College, in Pennsylvania. Both the American Baptist Churches/USA and National Baptists are participants in the ecumenical movement.

Conservative and Fundamentalist Baptists, both groups outside the ecumenical movement, are a small minority in the general population as well as a minority among Baptists in the region. Southern Baptists are the largest conservative evangelical Baptist group in the region, but they, along with southern Fundamentalist bodies, have found the area not as productive as other regions because of the lack of significant southern migration. In any case, these southern bodies have nevertheless been able to establish 800 congregations here.

Both the northern Evangelical Conservatives and northern Fundamentalists, totaling almost

700 congregations, have siphoned strength from the American Baptist Churches/USA but have also planted new churches. The Conservative Baptist Association has its greater strength in the eastern section of the region, while the fundamentalist General Association of Regular Baptist Churches has its greater strength in the west. The CBA supports Seminary of the East with centers at Philadelphia, New York City, Auburn, Massachusetts, and Baltimore, Maryland, while the GARBC maintains Baptist Bible College and Seminary at Clarks Summit, Pennsylvania.

A number of Baptist groups have a very small presence, including Seventh Day Baptists, Landmark Baptists, Free Will Baptists, and Primitive Baptists, who are almost extinct. Pennsylvania has the last surviving General Six Principle Baptist Church, located in Susquehanna County.

Bibliography

Neil R. Peirce and Michael Barone, *The Mid-Atlantic States of America,* (New York: W. W. Norton, 1972), 11-21. Randall Balmer and Mark Silk, *Religion and Public Life in the Middle Atlantic Region,* (Walnut Creek, CA: AltaMira Press, 2006).

New York (1714)

	Membership	Attendance	Churches
Ecumenical Mainline			
ABC*	164,420	68,105	541
National			
NBC/PNB*	250,000		430
Conservative Evangelical (N)			
BGC	2,563	2,468	17
CBA	13,971	13,971	109
NAB	1,309	1,545	10
SD	692	468	10
Fundamental (N)			
FBF**	1,800	1,980	20
GARBC**	13,081	14,356	145
IFCA**	810	890	9
NTA	250	250	1

Conservative Evangelical(S)			
SBC	19,644	13,579	219
Fundamental (S)			
BBF**/***	12,200	12,200	72
IBFI***	510	510	3
SWBF***	680	680	4
WBF***	1,360	1,360	8
Landmark			
ABA	80		4
BMA	136		3
IL	270		9
IL-SG	40		1
Primitive			
PR	7		4
Neo-Calvinist			
REF	2,100		17
SG	120		3
TOTALS	**486,043**		**1,639**
Dual: *ABC with NBC/PNB	-38,000		-127
**FBF with 1 BBF; IFCA with 1 GARBC	-260	-269	-2
***IBFI with 2 WBF; SWBF with 1 BBF; WBF with 2 BBF	-850	-850	-5
TOTALS	**446,933**		**1,505**

New Jersey 1688)

	Membership	Attendance	Churches
Ecumenical Mainline			
ABC*	70,955	26,952	262
National			
NBC/PNB*	69,000		254
NPR	1,132		9
Conservative Evangelical (N)			
BGC	262	242	2
CBA	8,626	8,626	53
NAB	155	200	3
SD	465	194	4
Fundamental (N)			
FBF**	1,639	2,233	11
GARBC	4,325	5,892	29
IBFNA	447	609	3
IFCA	1,341	1,827	9
NTA	23	23	1
Conservative Evangelical (S)			
SBC	14,446	9,969	76

Fundamental (S)			
BBF**/***	5,200	5,200	32
SWBF***	1,296	1,296	8
WBF***	162	162	1
Landmark			
ABA	40		2
BMA	172		2
IL	50		2
General/Free Will			
FW	n/a		3
Neo-Calvinist			
REF	1,250		10
SG	40		1
TOTALS	**181,026**		**777**
Dual: *ABC with 65 NBC/PNB			
	-18,000		-65
**FBF with 3 BBF			
	-486	-486	-3
***SWBF with 6 BBF; WBF with 1 BBF			
	-1,134	-1,134	-7
TOTALS	**161,406**		**702**

Pennsylvania (1684)

	Membership	Attendance	Churches
Ecumenical Mainline			
ABC*	108,132	62,416	435
National			
NBC/PNB*	250,000		400
NBCA*	1,930		13
NPR	229		1
Conservative Evangelical (N)			
BGC	2,265	2,930	16
CBA	9,256	9,256	57
NAB	2,198	1,882	13
SD	158	93	3
Fundamental (N)			
FBF**/***	6,696	7,506	54
GARBC**	7,932	8,908	64
IBFNA**	1,736	1,946	14
IFCA	1,116	1,251	9
Conservative Evangelical (S)			
SBC	36,007	22,133	226
Fundamental (S)			
BBF**/***	8,820	8,820	64
IBFI***	1,932	1,932	14
SBF**/***	1,932	1,932	14
WBF**/***	5,796	5,796	42
Landmark			
ABA	900		16
IL	715		13
IL-SG	40		1
General/Free Will			
Freewill	297		3
SIX PR	20		1
Primitive			
OL	136		4
UN	6		1
Neo-Calvinist			
REF	2,000		16
SG	200		5
TOTALS	**450,449**		**1,499**
Dual: *ABC with 57 NBC/PNB, 1 NBCA			
	-14,000		-58
**FBF with 6 BBF, 1 SBF, 2 WBF			
	-1,104	-1,104	-8
**IBFNA with 2 FBF, 2 GARBC			
	-496	-556	-4
***IBFI with 3 BBF, 7 WBF			
	-1,380	-1,380	-10
***SBF with 4 BBF			
	-552	-552	-4
***WBF with 7 BBF			
	-966	-966	-7
TOTALS	**431,951**		**1,408**

Delaware (1703)

	Membership	Attendance	Churches
Ecumenical Mainline			
ABC*	4,385	2,314	14
National			
NBC/PNB*	3,928		19
Conservative Evangelical (N)			
BGC	764	659	2
CBA	100	100	1
Fundamental (N)			
FBF**	244	260	2
GARBC	610	648	5
Conservative Evangelical (S)			
SBC	5,078	2,476	19
Fundamental (S)			
BBF**/***	1,950	1,950	11

SBF	708	708	4
WBF***	177	177	1
Landmark			
ABA	60		2
IL	30		1
General/Free Will			
FW	197		2
Primitive			
OL	68		2
PR	15		1
Neo-Calvinist			
REF	125		1
TOTALS	**18,439**		**87**
Dual: *ABC with 3 NBC/PNB			
	-900		-3
**FBF with 1 BBF			
	-177	-177	-1
***WBF with 1 BBF			
	-177	-177	-1
TOTALS	**17,185**		**82**

Great Lakes

	Membership	Attendance	Churches
Ecumenical Mainline*	318,441	137,958	1,211
National*	919,061		1,975
Conservative Evangelical(N)	61,025	66,378	370
Fundamental (N)** /***	210,651	197,752	1,193
Conservative Evangelical (S)	554,039	204,499	2,168
Fundamental (S)**/***	199,240	199,240	951
Landmark	17,090		279
General/ Free Will	41,546		562
Old-Time	12,106		134
Progressive Primitive	712		11
Primitive	5,532		168
Neo-Calvinist	1,940		50
TOTAL	**2,341,383**		**9,072**
Dual: Ecumenical-National*	- 26,176		-97
Fundamental (N)-(S)**/***	-31,055	-30,286	-181
Fundamental (S)**/***	-48,137	-48,137	-207
TOTAL	**2,236,015**		**8,587**

The Great Lakes region includes the states of Ohio, Indiana, Illinois, Michigan, and Wisconsin. Its territory is set apart from the nation by great waterways—the Great Lakes in the North, the Mississippi River in the West, and the Ohio River in the South. With its location in the heart of the nation, it represents, in many respects, a middle standard or composite of the country in its diversity, population, economic development, and religious distribution. The region includes large metropolitan areas and heavy industry but also productive agricultural areas, incorporating a southern hill country, a farm belt, and northern woodlands. With a diverse cultural heritage and migrations, it has become a political battleground as well as an area of diverse Baptist movements.

Its religious configuration is in part an extension of the Middle Atlantic region with a strong Roman Catholic presence, the leading religious body in each of the states, and strong mainline Protestant bodies, including Lutherans, Methodists, Presbyterians, and the United Church of Christ. With migration of Southerners, both African-American and white, Baptists of all kinds have become the largest

Protestant body in the region and in each state except Wisconsin. Among whites alone, however, Baptists are the largest Protestant group only in Indiana with Methodists in the lead in Ohio and Lutherans in Illinois, Michigan, and Wisconsin. White Baptists are particularly weak in Wisconsin, following not only Roman Catholics and Lutherans but also Methodists and the United Church of Christ.

Baptists were early settlers in the region, establishing their first church in Ohio in 1790. Churches followed in Illinois (1796), Indiana (1798), Michigan (1822), and finally in Wisconsin (1837). Baptists are well distributed, with no churches in only six counties including: Putnam, in Illinois, Keneenaw, in Michigan, and Calumet, Kewaunee, Marquette, and Menominee in Wisconsin. Because of southern migration and northern division, the region is a mélange of Baptist bodies and has more Baptist diversity than any in the nation.

American Baptist Churches/USA represents the earliest Baptists in the region and continues to have a significant although diminished presence. At the end of the Second World War, it had a bit over 400,000 members; today it has 318,000 members. The latter total includes 26,000 members that are also dually aligned with National Baptists. American Baptists have a strong band of churches through central Ohio, central and southern Indiana, and northern Illinois, frequently being the leading Baptist group in these areas but otherwise comparatively weak in the rest of the region. They have been squeezed between Baptist forces from the north and south. They have lost significant strength to northern fundamentalist groups in Indiana, Michigan, and Wisconsin and to the former ethnic Baptist General Conference in Upper Michigan and Wisconsin. In addition, southern–oriented Baptists have taken the lead in much of the southern areas. American Baptists sustain colleges in Indiana, Illinois, and Michigan and Northern Baptist Theological Seminary in Lombard, Illinois.

Southern influence has played a significant role in Baptist life in the region. With over 900,000 members, National Baptists, their figures swelled by migration in the twentieth century, are well represented in industrial centers. In the late eighteenth and early nineteenth centuries, white southern migrants settled much of the southern hill country, which left a southern imprint in the region. Because of theological and cultural differences, much of southern Illinois left the American (then Northern) Baptists in 1907 and then affiliated with the Southern Baptist Convention. During the Second World War, large numbers of southerners settled in the industrial areas of the region, which provided a base for the establishment of numerous Southern Baptist and southern Fundamentalist Baptist congregations. Besides southern Illinois, Southern Baptists are particularly strong in southwest Ohio and southwest Indiana and except for Upper Michigan and Wisconsin are well distributed throughout the region. Because of original southern settlement or later migration, numerous small southern-oriented Baptist groups are also present, such as Landmark, General, Free Will, Old-Time, and Primitive Baptists.

Except for the Baptist General Conference in Wisconsin and Illinois, northern Conservative Evangelicals are very weak. Conservative Baptists lost their state organizations in four of the five states to fundamentalists and today number only 18,000 and 82 churches in the whole region. Besides, they have moved their national headquarters from Illinois to Colorado. On the other hand, this region includes more northern Fundamentalists than any other in the nation. The General Association of Regular Baptist Churches has 105,000 members in over 600 churches and is particularly strong in Michigan, where it leads all other Baptists in attendance, and in Indiana. The New Testament Association of Independent Baptist Churches together with independent Fundamentalist state organizations number 74,000 in 386 churches. In addition, there are 88 churches of the Fundamental Baptist Fellowship unassociated with either the GARBC or NTAIBC and related bodies and another 36 congregations unassociated with any of the above three groups.

Bibliography

Neal R. Peirce and John Keefe, *The Great*

Lakes States of America, (New York and London: W.W. Norton, 1972). Philip Barlow and Mark Silk, *Religion and Public Life in the Midwest*, (Walnut Creek, CA: AltaMira Press, 2004).

Ohio
(1790)

	Membership	Attendance	Churches
Ecumenical Mainline			
ABC*	94,696	42,359	323
National			
NPC/PNB*	232,000		672
NBCA	2,640		22
NPR	772		5
Conservative Evangelical (N)			
BGC	2,801	3,172	15
CBA	2,357	2,357	12
NAB	2,087	2,150	7
SD	47	49	1
Fundamental (N)			
FBF**	6,086	5,712	34
GARBC	32,172	30,258	180
IBFNA	179	168	1
IFCA**	716	672	4
Conservative Evangelical (S)			
SBC	150,034	60,977	514
Fundamental (S)			
BBF**/***	63,200	63,200	213
IBFI***	17,820	17,820	60
SWBF***	7,722	7,722	26
WBF**/***	42,768	42,768	144
Landmark			
ABA	650		13
BMA	150		1
IL	1,500		26
IL-SG	1,440		36
General/Free Will			
FW	10,210		167
FW-IND	20		1
SEP	79		1
Old-Time			
ENT	1,612		28
OM	149		3
UNI	3,772		49
WT	1,898		11
Progressive Primitive			
PrE	393		4
Primitive			
OL	1,200		35
UN	29		2
OR	785		22
Neo-Calvinist			
REF	200		5
SG	200		5
TOTALS	**682,384**		**2,642**
Dual: *ABC with NBC/PNB			
	-13,257		-45
**FBF with 8 BBF, 1 WBF; IFCA with 1 BBF			
	–2,970	-2,970	-10
***IBFI with 28 BBF, 1 SWBF, 13 WBF; SWBF with 7 BBF, 7 WBF; WBF with 68 BBF			
	-37,125	-37,125	-125
TOTALS	**629,032**		**2,462**

Indiana
(1798)

	Membership	Attendance	Churches
Ecumenical Mainline			
ABC*	92,325	36,024	362
National			
NBC/PNB*	130,000		193
NBCA*	4,100		55
NMBC	18,706		105
NPR	61		1
Conservative Evangelical (N)			
BGC	268	232	4
CBA	750	750	6
NAB	60	30	1
Fundamental (N)			
FBF**	6,612	7,076	29
GARBC**	27,585	29,563	121
IFCA**	1,824	1,952	8
NTA/IN	25,200	18,900	126
Conservative Evangelical (S)			
SBC	100,140	34,265	345
Fundamental (S)			
BBF***	13,000	13,000	133
IBFI***	1,078	1,078	11
SWBF***	1,764	1,764	18
WBF***	1,568	1,568	16
Landmark			
ABA	1,520		23
BMA	373		4
IL	1,400		20

IL-SG	400		10
General/Free Will			
FW	1,400		26
FW-IND	912		11
GEN	12,117		122
SEP	2,219		30
Old-Time			
ENT	39		1
OM	1,541		14
UNI	2,435		20
Progressive Primitive			
CEN	188		3
PRO	131		4
Primitive			
OL	1,258		37
OR	384		17
T-S	16		1
Neo-Calvinist			
REF	280		7
SG	120		3
TOTALS	**451,774**		**1,887**
Dual: *ABC with 7 NBC/PNB, 1 NBCA	-1,847		-8
**FBF with 6 BBF, 1 WBF, 16 NTA/IN; IFCA with 2 BBF, 1 NTA/IN; NTA/IN with 38 BBF, 1 SWBF, 2 WBF, 8 GARBC	–10,124	-9,402	-75
***BBF with 1 GARBC; IBFI with 6 BBF; SWBF with 7 BBF; WBF with 8 BBF	-2,286	-2,302	-22
TOTALS	**437,517**		**1,782**

Illinois
(1796)

	Membership	Attendance	Churches
Ecumenical Mainline			
ABC*	70,916	28,244	296
National			
NBC/PNB*	77,000		174
NBCA*	190,000		150
NPR	532		5
Conservative Evangelical (N)			
BGC	13,652	14,060	78
CBA	7,575	7,575	33
NAB	1,594	1,213	11
SD	65	30	1
Fundamental (N)			
FBF**	4,620	4,242	42
GARBC**	7,631	6,975	69
IBFNA**	220	202	2
IFCA**	880	808	8
NTA/ILL**	20,000	20,000	89
Conservative Evangelical (S)			
SBC	247,810	86,615	981
Fundamental (S)			
BBF**/***	15,000	15,000	81
IBFI**/***	740	740	4
SWBF**/***	1,295	1,295	7
WBF**/***	925	925	5
Landmark			
ABA	920		19
BMA	952		14
IL	1,767		31
IL-SG	560		14
General/Free Will			
FW	3,521		41
GEN	5,734		89
SEP	480		8
Old-Time			
OM	n/a		1
UNI	29		1
Primitive			
OL	1,122		33
OR	54		2
Neo-Calvinist			
REF	120		3
SG	160		4
TOTALS	**675,874**		**2,296**
Dual: *ABC with 22 NBC/PNB, 1 NBCA	-5,673		-23
**FBF with 18 NTA/ILL, 7 BBF, 1 WBF; IBFNA with 1 GARBC; IFCA with 1 GARBC, 2 BBF; NTA/ILL with 14 BBF, 1 IBFI, 3 SWBF	-9,450	-9,432	-48
***IBFI with 1 BBF; SWBF with 3 BBF; WBF with 3 BBF	-1,295	-1,295	-7
TOTALS	**659,456**		**2,218**

Michigan
(1822)

	Membership	Attendance	Churches
Ecumenical Mainline			
ABC*	47,486		159
National			
NBC/PNB*	185,000		400

NBCA	6,500		21
NMBC	31,500		90
NPR	250		4
Conservative Evangelical (N)			
BGC	6,676	7,232	59
CBA	5,710	5,710	20
NAB	4,686	4,680	22
SD	176	117	2
Fundamental (N)			
FBF**	6,327	5,254	37
GARBC**	34,077	28,174	199
IBFNA	171	142	1
IFCA**	2,394	1,988	14
NTA/MICH**	16,000	16,000	59
Conservative Evangelical (S)			
SBC	44,656	18,430	264
Fundamental (S)			
BBF**/***	15,000	15,000	106
IBFI**/***	3,834	3,834	27
SWBF	568	568	4
WBF**/***	8,520	8,520	60
Landmark			
ABA	850		17
BMA	2,323		16
IL	1,344		14
IL-SG	520		13
General/Free Will			
FW	3,141		44
GEN	1,678		21
Old-Time			
OM	302		2
UNI	26		1
WT	294		2
Primitive			
OL	272		8
OR	412		11
Neo-Calvinist			
REF	200		5
SG	520		13
ST	14		1
TOTALS	**431,427**		**1,716**

Dual: *ABC with 17 NBC/PNB
-4,749 -17

** FBF with l BFF, 16 NTA/MICH; IFCA with 1 GARBC, 1 NTA/MICH; NTA/MICH with 3 BBF, 1 IBFI, 2 WBF -5,772 -5,743 -25

***IBFI with 10 BBF, 5 WBF; WBF with 28 BBF, 5 IBFI -6,816 -6,816 -48

TOTALS	**414,090**		**1,626**

Wisconsin (1837)

	Membership	Attendance	Churches
Ecumenical Mainline			
ABC*	13,018	6,961	71
National			
NBC*	40,000		78
Conservative Evangelical (N)			
BGC	7,282	12,016	68
CBA	1,817	1,817	11
NAB	2,922	2,891	14
SD	500	297	5
Fundamental (N)			
FBF**	1,380	1,830	15
GARBC	3,492	4,643	38
IBFNA	276	366	3
NTA/WIS**	12,759	12,759	112
Independent	50	68	2
Conservative Evangelical (S)			
SBC	11,399	4,212	64
Fundamental (S)			
BBF**/***	3,700	3,700	30
IBFI***	123	123	1
SWBF**	123	123	1
WBF***	492	492	4
Landmark			
ABA	170		3
IL	171		3
IL-SG	80		2
General/Free Will			
FW	35		1
Old-Time			
UNI	9		1
Neo-Calvinist			
REF	80		2
SG	40		1
ST	6		1
TOTALS	**99,924**		**531**

Dual: *ABC with 4 NBC
-650 -4

**FBF with 3 BBF, 10 NTA/WIS; NTA-WIS with 9 BBF, 1 SWBF–2,739 -2,739 -23

***IBFI with 1 BBF; WBF with 4 BBF
-615 -615 -5

TOTALS	**95,920**		**499**

Great Plains

	Membership	Attendance	Churches
Ecumenical Mainline*	98,504	42,382	484
National*.	73,699		249
Conservative Evangelical (N)	57,500	70,677	384
Fundamental (N)**/***	29,424	29,921	306
Conservative Evangelical (S)	116,854	49,602	497
Fundamental (S)**/***	38,287	38,287	288
Landmark	4,644		86
General/Free Will	346		16
Old-Time	n/a		2
Primitive	336		10
Neo-Calvinist	360		9
TOTAL	**419,954**		**2,331**
Dual: Ecumenical-National*	-3,634		-16
Fundamental (N)-(S)**/***	-1,724	-1,710	-15
Fundamental (S)**/***	-7,765	-7,765	-57
TOTAL	**406,831**		**2,243**

The Great Plains region includes the six states of Minnesota, Iowa, North Dakota, South Dakota, Nebraska, and Kansas. Geographically Missouri belongs with these states, but religiously, and particularly for Baptists, it relates far more with the Trans-Mississippi West and is therefore considered there. This region is a land of rolling terrain and wide open spaces and noted for climatic extremes of heat and cold with drought and tornadoes and flooding, forcing hardy pioneers to adapt to a daunting environment. Agriculture continues as a leading industry but light industry is also important as well as mining in Minnesota. For some time, the region has experienced slow population growth and even loss in some areas with many people leaving the land and small towns.

Although Puritan stock settled from the East, a significant portion of the settlers were of Scandinavian and German stock with the latter including large numbers of Germans from the Russian Empire. Roman Catholics and Lutherans dominate the religious scene. Roman Catholics number about one-third of the religious adherents, while Lutherans range from twenty-four percent in Iowa to forty-five percent in North Dakota with the remaining states, except for Kansas, between these two parameters. As in the Great Lakes region, Methodism also has a significant presence.

Baptists were early in the region. Baptists formed an Indian church in Kansas as early as 1832, but continuous Baptist work did not begin here until 1855. Baptist churches first began in Iowa in 1834, Minnesota in 1849, Nebraska in 1855, South Dakota in 1864, and finally North Dakota in 1879. Except for Kansas, which borders two strong Southern Baptist states, Baptists are comparatively weak and seriously divided. About half of the Baptist constituency in the region resides in Kansas. The Great Plains has more counties without a Baptist church than any other in the nation. Nebraska leads the nation with thirty-three such counties, followed by North Dakota and South Dakota each with thirteen, and Minnesota with seven. On the other hand, Iowa with Adair County and Kansas with Rush County each have only one such county.

American Baptist Churches/USA with almost 100,000 members and almost 500 churches continues to have a significant presence in Iowa, Nebraska, and Kansas. It has four regional bodies in the region. On the other hand, it has lost significant strength, dropping from 166,000 members at the end of the Second World War. At one time, it had practically a monopoly in both membership and attendance in each of the states; today it leads in membership only in Iowa and South Dakota and does not lead in attendance in any of them. It maintains some institutional strength with colleges in South Dakota and Kansas and Central Baptist Theological Seminary in Kansas City, Kansas. National Baptists have same strength in metropolitan areas with a notable presence in all the states except the two Dakotas.

The Baptist General Conference with its Swedish roots and the North American Baptist Conference with its German roots are particularly important segments of the Baptist population in the northern reaches of the area. The Baptist General Conference is the leading Baptist body in Minnesota and supports a university and seminary in St. Paul. As small as it is, the North American Baptist Conference is the leading body in North Dakota and leads in attendance in South Dakota. In South Dakota these two conferences double the attendance of the American Baptist Churches. The North American Conference maintains a seminary at Sioux Falls, South Dakota.

The fundamentalist controversy in the American Baptist Churches seriously divided the Minnesota Baptist State Convention with the result that it is the most divided and weakened state convention in the nation. In its separation from American Baptists, the convention became Conservative Baptist, and then it suffered a further division when fundamentalists gained control and later changed its name to the Minnesota Baptist Association. The Minnesota Baptist Association maintains Pillsbury Baptist Bible College in Owatonna, and its constituency also supports Central Baptist Theological Seminary in Minneapolis.

Except for Iowa, where the General Association of Regular Baptists leads in attendance, northern Fundamentalists are weak in the region, particularly in comparison to their strength in the Great Lakes region. Churches in the Minnesota Association and Minnesota churches with sole membership in the national New Testament Association total less than 8,000 members, and their very small association in South Dakota no longer holds annual sessions. The Conservative Baptists are also very weak, maintaining limited strength in Minnesota and Iowa with never having had much strength in the remaining states.

With their comity with Northern Baptists, Southern Baptists did not formally enter the region until after the Second World War. In 1946, they formed a Kansas Convention, which became the Kansas-Nebraska Convention in 1973. They experienced some success in Kansas but more limited progress in Nebraska, both states where Southern Baptists lead in both membership and attendance. In time, Southern Baptists entered the remaining states but with only limited success. They formed a Minnesota-Wisconsin Convention, an Iowa Convention, and finally transformed its Dakota Fellowship into a convention in January, 2004. Southern Baptists maintain Midwestern Baptist Theological Seminary in Kansas City, Missouri. Southern Fundamentalists are very weak in the region except in Kansas and Iowa.

Bibliography

Neil R. Peirce, *The Great Plains States of America,* (New York: W.W. Norton, 1972), 15-28. Philip Barlow and Mark Silk, *Religion and Public Life in the Midwest,* (Walnut Creek, CA: AltaMira Press, 2004).

Minnesota (1849)

	Membership	Attendance	Churches
Ecumenical Mainline			
ABC*	9,427	3,837	35
National			
NBC/PNB*	20,000		28
Conservative Evangelical (N)			
BGC	26,629	41,060	150
CBA	5,090	5,090	38
NAB	1,098	933	11
SD	96	55	1
Fundamental (N)			
FBF**	910	910	7
GARBC	2,453	2,476	26
IFCA	390	390	3
NTA-MIN**	7,524	7,524	58
Independent	70	75	2
Conservative Evangelical (S)			
SBC	4,380	2,780	45
Fundamental (S)			
BBF**/***	625	625	6
IBFI	104	104	1
SWBF**	104	104	1
WBF**/***	208	208	2
Landmark			
IL	320		8
IL-SG	80		2
Neo-Calvinist			
REF	40		1
TOTAL	**79,548**		**425**
Dual: *ABC with 7 NBC/PNB			
	-1,885		-7
**FBF with 5 NTA/MIN			
	-650	-650	-5
***BBF with 1 NTA/MIN; SWBF with 1 FBF; WBF with 1 BBF, 1 FBF			
	-494	-494	-4
TOTAL	**76,519**		**409**

Iowa (1834)

	Membership	Attendance	Churches
Ecumenical Mainline			
ABC*	20,787	8,345	113
National			
NBC*	8,000		37
Conservative Evangelical (N)			
BGC	5,014	4,909	31
CBA	2,615	2,615	12
NAB	1,874	1,561	14
Fundamental (N)			
FBF**	148	148	4
GARBC	11,048	11,860	101
IFCA	37	37	1
NTA**	110	110	3
Conservative Evanelical (S)			
SBC	10,836	6,070	75
Fundamental (S)			
BBF***	4,000	4,000	30
IBFI***	400	400	3
WBF***	931	931	7
Landmark			
ABA	30		1
IL	150		5
IL-SG	40		1
General/Free Will			
FW	n/a		2
Primitive			
OL	200		6
Neo-Calvinist			
REF	40		1
SG	80		2
TOTAL	**66,340**		**449**
Dual: *ABC with 2 NBC			
	-416		-2
**FBF with 1 NTA			
	-37	-37	-1
***IBFI with 1 BBF; WBF with 3 BBF	-531	-531	-4
TOTAL	**65,356**		**442**

North Dakota (1879)

	Membership	Attendance	Churches
Ecumenical Mainline			
ABC*	1,698	614	16
Conservative Evangelical (N)			
BGC	299	351	5
CBA	409	409	3
NAB	4,443	3,803	32
Fundamental (N)			
Independent	1,163	1,171	17
Conservative Evangelical (S)			
SBC	2,520	1,455	27
Fundamental (S)			
BBF	255	255	5
IBFI	50	50	1
WBF	50	50	1
Landmark			
IL	400		10
IL-SG	40		1
TOTAL	**11,327**		**118**

South Dakota (1864)

	Membership	Attendance	Churches
Ecumenical Mainline			
ABC	5,035	3,073	35
Conservative Evangelical (N)			
BGC	2,840	2,843	15
NAB	3,474	3,302	23
Fundamental (N)			
FBF	110	110	2
GARBC	96	132	4
NTA/SD	275	275	5
Independent	20	40	1
Conservative Evangelical (S)			
SBC	5,251	2,201	47
Fundamental (S)			
BBF*	700	700	7
SWBF	100	100	1
WBF*	200	200	2
Landmark			
ABA	60		3
IL	40		2
General/Free Will			
FW			1
Neo-Calvinist			
REF	40		1
TOTAL	**18,241**		**149**
Dual: *WBF with 1 BBF			
	-100	-100	-1
TOTAL	**18,141**		**148**

Nebraska (1855)

	Membership	Attendance	Churches
Ecumenical Mainline			
ABC*	10,185	4,985	61
National			
NBC*	8,000		37
NPR	150		1
Conservative Evangelical (N)			
BGC	2,122	2,359	32
CBA	96	96	2
NAB	143	90	3
SD	120	87	1
Fundamental (N)			
FBF**	624	616	8
GARBC**	1,058	1,074	14
IBFNA**	78	77	1
IFCA	78	77	1
Independent	25	26	2
Conservative Evangelical (S)			
SBC	13,547	8,343	49
Fundamental (S)			
BBF**/***	1,400	1,400	20
IBFI***	280	280	4
WBF***	630	630	9
Landmark			
ABA	58		2
IL	29		1
General/Free Will			
GEN	35		1
Primitive			
OL	68		2
Neo-Calvinist			
SG	40		1
TOTAL	**38,766**		**254**
Dual: *ABC with 2 NBC			
	-306		-2
**FBF with 2 BBF; IFNA with 1 GARBC			
	-218	-217	-3
***IBFI with 2 BBF, 1 WBF; WBF with 4 BBF			
	-490	-490	-7
TOTAL	**37,752**		**242**

Kansas (1832/1855)

	Membership	Attendance	Churches
Ecumenical Mainline			
ABC*	51,372	21,228	224
National			
NBC*	28,748		117
NBCA	8,776		28
NPR	25		1
Conservative Evangelical (N)			
NAB	1,091	875	10
SD	47	39	1
Fundamental (N)			
FBF**	828	720	12
GARBC**	1,865	1,613	27
IBFNA	207	180	3
IFCA	207	180	3
NTA**	100	100	1
Conservative Evangelical (S)			
SBC	80,320	28,753	254
Fundamental (S)			
BBF**/***	20,000	20,000	133
IBFI***	2,250	2,250	15
SWBF***	300	300	2
WBF**/***	5,700	5,700	38
Landmark			
ABA	848		18
BMA	1,129		10
IL	1,260		18
IL-SG	160		4
General/Free Will			
FW	311		10
Old-Time			
OM	n/a		2
Primitive			
OL	68		2
Neo-Calvinist			
REF	80		2
SG	40		1
TOTAL	**205,732**		**936**
Dual: *ABC with 5 NBC			
	-1,027		-5
**FBF with 3 BBF, 1 WBF, 1 GARBC; NTA with 1 BBF	-819	-810	-6
***IBFI with 12 BBF, 2 WBF; SWBF with 1 BBF; WBF with 26 BBF			
	-6,150	-6,150	-41
TOTAL	**197,736**		**884**

Upper South

	Membership	Attendance	Churches
Ecumenical Mainline*	252,762	101,573	762
National*	1,324,347		5,106
Conservative Evangelical (N)	7,012	5,946	30
Fundamental(N)**/***	24,727	25,937	239
Conservative Evangelical (S)*	3,979,780	1,414,735	11,392
Fundamental (S)**/***	136,736	136,736	873
Landmark****	25,480		293
General/Free Will	265,234		2,055
Old-Time****	84,285		621
Progressive Primitive	9,549		98
Primitive	32,890		892
Neo-Calvinist.	2,160		54
TOTAL	**6,144,962**		**22,415**
Ecumenical-National*	-55,225		-94
Ecumenical-National-Conservative Evangelical (S)*	-28,000		-40
Ecumenical-Conservative Evangelical (S)*	-19,835		-37
Fundamental (N)-(S)**/***	-8,841	-8,841	-58
Fundamental (S)***	-16,237	-16,237	-105
Landmark-Old-Time****	-4,000		-16
TOTAL	**6,012,824**		**22,065**

The Upper South includes the six states of Maryland, Virginia, West Virginia, North Carolina, Kentucky, and Tennessee and the District of Columbia. It is one of three southern regions of the nation where Baptists with 6,000,000 members are the leading denomination. They are present in every county. Baptists came into the region comparatively late, not establishing their first church until 1714. They were among the first with the Westward movement into Kentucky and Tennessee.

Although Baptists lead by far in the region as a whole, they hold no monopoly and have contended with Roman Catholics, Methodists, and the Stone-Campbell movement. Roman Catholics lead Baptists in Maryland, and among the white population Methodists lead them in Maryland and about equal them in West Virginia. The Stone-Campbell movement is strongly represented in Kentucky and Tennessee.

The area is diverse in geography, culture, economic development, and racial distribution. From east to west it includes the tidewater, the piedmont, the Appalachian range bisected by a great valley, and then followed by rolling plains and bluegrass country until it ends at the Mississippi Valley. Agriculture has been a predominating industry, ranging from large plantations to the small acreages of independent farmers and sharecroppers with cotton and tobacco as leading crops. The textile industry became well established in the piedmont, while coal mining has been a leading industry in Appalachia.

Because of their comparative isolation in the area, Appalachia and the Upper Cumberland are distinct sub-regions with their own folkways and religious configuration. As a result, besides national Baptist bodies, they contain a number of many small Baptist groups, some with significant strength, ranging from predestinarian to free-will doctrines and often representing older patterns of Baptist life.

The Southern Baptist Convention leads in a majority of the counties of all the states except West Virginia. It established its headquarters and its publishing house, LifeWay Christian Resources, in Nashville and its International Mission Board in Richmond. Besides a number of colleges, it also has two seminaries in the region. Southern Baptists divide somewhat ideologically between the coastal area and areas west of Appalachia. Virginia and North Carolina tend to be more moderate and include a number of adherents of the Alliance of Baptists and the Cooperative Baptist Fellowship who have broken with the Southern Baptist Convention. Southern Baptists tend to become more Landmark in sentiment farther to the west, particularly in West Kentucky and West Tennessee.

The American Baptist Churches/USA leads in West Virginia, due to West Virginia's adherence to the Union cause in the Civil War. The District of Columbia Baptist Convention, whose churches are primarily in both the District and Maryland, is aligned with three Baptist bodies: American, Southern, and Progressive National Baptists.

National Baptists are the leading Baptist body in some counties of the Tidewater in Maryland, Virginia, and North Carolina. They also have significant strength in metropolitan areas such as Louisville, Nashville, and Memphis. The National Baptist Convention, USA, Inc. built its magnificent headquarters in Nashville, which adjoins American Baptist College, a training school for pastors and other Christian workers. A number of National Baptist churches are dually affiliated with American Baptists.

Southern Fundamentalists are well represented with northern Fundamentalists showing some limited strength. Northern Conservative Evangelicals, however, are extremely weak. Free Will Baptists show surprising numbers throughout the region and lead in three counties in Kentucky and two in West Virginia. Original Free Will Baptists and African-American Free Will Baptists are strong in eastern North Carolina. Free Will Baptists in the National Association and Independent Free Will Baptists show particular strength in Appalachia and the Upper Cumberland. Kentucky includes a number of General Baptists and Separate Baptists; Tennessee also has a number of the former group.

Old-Time Baptists are stronger in this region

than any other and lead in seven counties in Kentucky, two in Tennessee, and one in West Virginia. Primitive Baptists maintain strength in all the states except Maryland and West Virginia. Progressive Primitive Baptists are particularly strong in Virginia, Kentucky, and Tennessee. Old Regular Baptists show strength in Virginia, West Virginia, and Kentucky and Regular Baptists in North Carolina.

Bibliography

Wilma Dykeman and James Stokely, *The Border States,* (New York: Time-Life Books, 1968), 9-16. Charles Reagan Wilson and Mark Silk, *Religion and Public Life in the South* (Walnut Creek, CA: AltaMira Press, 2005).

Maryland (1742)

	Membership	Attendance	Churches
Ecumenical Mainline			
ABC*/**	35,904	16,075	85
National			
NBC/PNB*	169,000		159
NBCA	4,000		18
Conservative Evangelical (N)			
BGC	4,805	3,860	5
CBA	480	480	3
SD	29	23	1
Fundamental (N)			
FBF***	1,404	1,404	12
GARBC	1,522	1,517	13
IBFNA	117	117	1
IFCA***	117	117	1
Conservative Evangelical (S)			
SBC**	113,662	45,612	405
Fundamental (S)			
BBF***/****	6,800	6,800	47
IBFI****	290	290	2
SWBF***	2,320	2,320	16
WBF****	580	580	4
Landmark			
IL	n/a		2
General/Free Will			
FW	395		4
Primitive			
OL	238		7
PR	32		4
Neo-Calvinist			
REF	40		1
TOTAL	**341,735**		**790**
Dual: *ABC with NBC/PNB			
	-1,795		-4
**ABC with SBC			
	-9,335		-22
***FBF with 2 BBF, 1 SWBF; IFCA with 1 BBF			
	-580	-580	-4
**** IBFI with 1 BBF, 1 WBF; WBF with 1 BBF			
	-435	-435	-3
TOTAL	**329,590**		**757**

District of Columbia (1802)

	Membership	Attendance	Churches
Ecumenical Mainline			
ABC*/**/***/****			
	43,457	16,243	62
National			
NBC/PNB*/***/****			
	43,000		95
Conservative Evangelical (N)			
CBA	65	65	1
SD	43	43	1
Conservative Evangelical (S)			
SBC**/***/****			
	32,572	9,758	49
TOTAL	**119,137**		**208**
Dual: *ABC with 5 NBC/PNB			
	-3,500		-5
**ABC with 15 SBC			
	-10,500		-15
***ABC with 20 NBC/PNB and SBC			
	-14,000		-20
**** SBC with 20 NBC/PNB and ABC			
	-14,000		-20
TOTAL	**77,137**		**148**

Virginia
(1714)

	Membership	Attendance	Churches
Ecumenical Mainline			
ABC*	46,414	18,057	98
National			
NBC/PNB*	253,000		1,148
NBCA*	75,000		350
NPR	352		4
Conservative Evangelical (N)			
BGC	290	325	3
CBA	130	130	1
Fundamental (N)			
FBF**	5,635	5,635	49
GARBC	922	925	8
IFCA**	345	345	3
Conservative Evangelical (S)			
SBC	629,586	219,421	1,660
Fundamental (S)			
BBF**/***	25,000	25,000	159
IBFI***	471	471	3
SWBF**/***	6,280	6,280	40
WBF***	2,826	2,826	18
Landmark			
ABA	550		7
BMA	177		1
IL	360		4
IL-SG	360		9
General/Free Will			
FW	4,255		51
FW-IND	2,689		46
SEP	89		3
Old-Time			
OM	29		1
Progressive Primitive			
CEN	727		15
PrE	1,556		24
PRO	45		1
Primitive			
OL	3,400		100
OR	1,886		45
PR	557		52
REG	271		3
UN	166		9
Neo-Calvinist			
REF	320		8
SG	240		6
TOTAL	**1,063,928**		**3,929**

Dual: *ABC with 40 NBC/PNB, 1 NBC/PNB and NBCA, 3 NBCA

	–20,886		-44

**FBF with 17 BBF, 3 SWBF; IFCA with 1 BBF

	-3,297	-3,297	-21

***IBFI with 1 BBF, 1 WBF; SWBF with 16 BBF; WBF with 2 BBF

	-3,140	-3,140	-20
TOTAL	**1,036,605**		**3,844**

West Virginia
(1775)

	Membership	Attendance	Churches
Ecumenical Mainline			
ABC	89,863	35,284	463
National			
NBC	12,000		250
Conservative Evangelical (N)			
CON	285	285	2
SD	325	119	3
Fundamental (N)			
FBF*	3,286	2,635	31
GARBC	1,803	1,442	17
IFCA	106	85	1
Conservative Evangelical (S)			
SBC	36,231	13,314	165
Fundamental (S)			
BBF**	3,315	3,315	51
IBFI**	195	195	3
SWBF	910	910	14
WBF	3,185	3,185	49
Landmark			
ABA	1,020		7
IL	1,000		7
IL-SG	1,280		32
General/Free Will			
FW	9,047		179
SEP	60		1
Old-Time			
OM	69		3
UNI	2,426		19
Primitive			
OL	1.224		36
OR	1,750		34
PR	68		6
UN	144		5
Neo-Calvinist			

REF	40		1
SG	240		6
TOTAL	**169,872**		**1,385**
Dual: *FBF with 5 BBF, 1 SWBF			
	-390	-390	-6
**IBFI with 1 BBF, 1 WBF; SWBF with 6 BBF; WBF with 9 BBF			
	-1,105	-1,105	-17
TOTAL	**168,377**		**1,362**

North Carolina (1727)

	Membership	Attendance	Churches
Ecumenical Mainline			
ABC*	31,146	13,657	40
National			
NB*	425,000		1,700
NPR	4,873		20
Conservative Evangelical (N)			
BGC	39	110	1
NAB	70	102	1
SD	211	148	3
Fundamental (N)			
FBF**	6,174	7,560	63
GARBC	98	120	1
IFCA	98	120	1
Conservative Evangelical (S)			
SBC	1,225,077	486,244	3,717
Fundamental (S)			
BBF**/***	22,270	22,270	131
IBFI**/***	510	510	3
SWBF**/***	12,580	12,580	74
WBF**/***	2,720	2,720	16
Landmark			
ABA	100		1
BMA	100		1
IL	1,000		10
IL-SG	240		6
General/Free Will			
FW	21,085		202
FW-IND	2,490		40
FW-OR	37,039		234
UNAFWB	100,000		500
Primitive			
OL	3,196		94
OR	20		2
PR	563		83
REG	3,321		34
UN	23		1
Neo-Calvinist			
REF	280		7
SG	200		5
TOTAL	**1,900,523**		**6,991**
Dual:*ABC with 31 NB			
	-24,000		-31
**FBF with 13 BBF, 1 IBFI, 4 SWBF, 1 WBF			
	-3,230	-3,230	-19
***IBFI with 1 BBF, 1 WBF; SWBF with 17 BBF, 2 WBF; WBF with 5 BBF			
	-4,420	-4,420	-26
TOTAL	**1,868,873**		**6,915**

Kentucky (1781)

	Membership	Attendance	Churches
Ecumenical Mainline			
ABC*	2,428	912	5
National			
NB*	160,000		649
NPR	672		13
Conservative Evangelical(N)			
CBA	200		1
Fundamental (N)			
FBF	n/a		4
GARBC	n/a		2
IFCA	n/a		1
Conservative Evangelical (S)			
SBC	794,040	245,922	2,424
Fundamental (S)			
BBF**	14,235	14,235	61
IBFI**	1,165	1,165	5
SWBF**	2,796	2,796	12
WBF**	1,864	1,864	8
Landmark			
ABA***	5,250		21
BMA	97		1
IL	5,000		52
IL-SG	3,080		77
General/Free Will			
FW	16,711		133
FW-IND	3,277		39
GEN	23,811		190
SEP	5,540		54

Old-Time			
DK	32		1
ENT	2,659		36
OM	13,989		74
UNI***	35,945		250
Progressive Primitive			
CEN	486		3
PrE	871		9
Primitive			
OL	2,210		65
OR	9,562		181
PR	30		3
UN	23		1
Neo-Calvinist			
REF	120		3
SG	320		8
TOTAL	**1,106,413**		**4,386**
Dual: *ABC with 2 NB			
	-1,771		-2
**IBFI with 1 BBF, 1 WBF; SWBF with 3 BBF, 1 WBF; WBF with 3 BBF			
	-2,097	-2,097	-9
.***ABA with 16 UNI			
	-4,000		-16
TOTAL	**1,098,545**		**4,359**

Tennessee (1779)

	Membership	Attendance	Churches
Ecumenical Mainline			
ABC*	3,550	1,345	9
National			
NBC/PNB*	139,393		470
NBCA	25,369		134
NMBC	6,373		9
NPR	6,315		87
Conservative Evangelical(N)			
SD	40	36	4
Fundamental (N)			
FBF**	2,600	3,250	26
GARBC	200	250	2
IFCA	300	375	3
Conservative Evangelical (S)			
SBC	1,148,612	394,464	2,972
Fundamental (S)			
BBF***	15,000	15,000	89
IBFI**	840	840	5
SWBF**	7,224	7,224	43
WBF**	3,360	3,360	20
Landmark			
ABA	2,372		21
BMA	1,454		10
IL	1,600		13
IL-SG	440		11
General/Free Will			
FW	22,091		227
FW-IND	9,780		110
GEN	6,845		40
SEP	30		2
Old-Time			
DR	6,932		71
OM	16,357		124
UNI	5,847		42
Progressive Primitive			
CEN	1,845		9
PrE	3,648		30
PRO	371		7
Primitive			
OL	4,100		115
PR	54		9
REG	19		1
T-S	10		1
UN	23		1
Neo-Calvinist			
REF	200		5
SG	160		4
TOTAL	**1,443,354**		**4,726**
Dual: *ABC with 8 NBC/PNB.			
	-3,273		-8
**FBF with 6 BBF, 2 SWBF			
	-1,344	-1,344	-8
***IBFI with 2 BBF; SWBF with 16 BBF, I IBFI, 2 WBF; WBF with 9 BBF			
	-5,040	-5,040	-30
TOTAL	**1,433,697**		**4,680**

Lower South

	MEMBERSHIP	ATTENDANCE	CHURCHES
Ecumenical Mainline*	22,399	8,015	54
National*	2,573,688		7,707
Conservative Evangelical (N)	4,577	4,805	52
Fundamental (N)**/***	24,754	24,754	159
Conservative Evangelical (S)	5,005,004	1,809,784	12,350
Fundamental (S)**/***	132,885	132,895	875
Landmark	82,881		683
General/Free Will	55,521		617
Old-Time	29,312		201
Progressive Primitive	7,113		104
Primitive	18,590		581
Neo-Calvinist	2,520		63
TOTAL	**7,959,244**		**23,446**
Ecumenical-National*	-12,985		-27
Fundamental (N)-(S)**/***	-4,083	-4083	-23
Fundamental (S)***	-26,264	-26,264	-171
TOTAL	**7,915,912**		**23,225**

The Lower South includes the five states of South Carolina, Georgia, Florida, Alabama, and Mississippi. Approaching 8,000,000 members, it includes more Baptists than any other region with churches in every county. Baptists established their first church as early as the late seventeenth century in South Carolina, but largely because of later settlement they did not enter the other states until seventy-five years or more later.

Since the Second World War, the region has experienced a significant change from a predominantly underdeveloped rural area of low income and few cities to an area of economic development with increase of manufacturing and metropolitan growth. A modern textile industry and chemicals have come to the fore, and "King Cotton" no longer rules the economy. With the Civil Rights movement and legislation, race relations between white and black have noticeably improved. Northerners, both white and black, have been moving into the area, and a large Cuban population now resides in Florida. Florida has become a magnet for vacationers as well as a home for many retirees.

Baptists dominate throughout the region except in the peninsular coasts of Florida with its large Roman Catholic Hispanic population. Methodists are rather well spread throughout the region but in smaller number. Except for predominantly black counties, primarily extending westward from South Carolina and on to Mississippi and in the Mississippi Valley, Southern Baptists with five million members are the leading Baptist group. Two exceptions, however, are two counties in Mississippi where the Baptist Missionary Association leads (Itawamba and Stone) and in two counties in southern Florida where National Baptists predominate (Broward and Dade). Southern Baptists have established their home mission agency, the North American Baptist Mission Board, in the Atlanta area and their Woman's Baptist Missionary Union at Birmingham.

National Baptists claim two and a half million members. In each state, The National Baptist Convention, USA, Inc. relates to a large state convention. The conventions range in size from 300,000 in Mississippi to 600,000 in Alabama besides additional smaller ones in the former state. The National Baptist Convention of America, Inc. has some strength in the area, while the National Baptist Primitive Baptist Convention maintains its largest constituency in Florida.

Southern Fundamentals are present with

some strength in each of the states, particularly in Florida. On the other hand, all northern-oriented groups are extremely weak as a whole even with the influx of northerners into the region. Slight exceptions are the GARBC with an attendance of 7,000 in forty-seven churches in Florida and the FBF that relates to thirty-eight churches in South Carolina due at least in part to connections with Bob Jones University. Primitive Baptists with almost 600 churches are particularly strong in Georgia and Alabama with their main strength in the former state. Old-Time Baptists with their primary strength in Georgia and Alabama are generally located in the Appalachian and piedmont areas rather than the coastal plains.

Bibliography

John Osborne, *The Old South,* (New York: Time-Life Books, 1968), 6-14. Charles Reagan Wilson and Mark Silk, *Religion and Public Life in the South,* (Walnut Creek, CA: AltaMira Press, 2005). Morton D. Winsberg, *Atlas of Race, Ancestry and Religion in 21st-Century Florida,* (Gainesville: University Press of Florida, 2006).

South Carolina (1696)

	Membership	Attendance	Churches
Ecumenical Mainline			
ABC*	2,360	1,675	4
National			
NB*	400,000		1,700
Conservative Evangelical (N)			
CBA	100	100	1
SD	211	148	3
Fundamental (N)			
FBF**	8,094	8,094	38
NTA	45	45	1
Conservative Evangelical (S)			
SBC	747,092	272,515	1,878
Fundamental (S)			
BBF**/***	10,000	10,000	47
IBFI***	639	639	3
SWBF**/***	5,954	5,954	28
WBF***	1,278	1,278	6
Landmark			
ABA	672		9
IL	300		4
IL-SG	160		4
General/Free Will			
FW	6,103		123
FW-IND	18		1
FW-OR	159		3
UAFWB-CONF	900		6
Progressive Primitive			
CEN	432		3
Primitive			
OL	340		10
PR	23		3
Neo-Calvinist			
REF	80		2
SG	80		2
TOTAL	**1,185,040**		**3,879**
Dual: *ABC with 3 NB	-1,770		-3
**FBF with 5 BBF, 5 SWBF	-2,130	-2,130	-10
***IBFI with 1 WBF; SWBF with 7 BBF, 1 WBF; WBF with 4 BBF	-2,769	-2,769	-13
TOTAL	**1,178,371**		**3,853**

Georgia (1772)

	Membership	Attendance	Churches
Ecumenical Mainline			
ABC*	9,060	2,220	18
National			
NB*	500,000		800
NPR	1,391		22
Conservative Evangelical (N)			
BGC	18	12	1
SD	39	30	1
Fundamental (N)			
FBF**	4,455	4,455	27
GARBC	600	250	2
IFCA	330	330	2
Conservative Evangelical (S)			
SBC	1,362,799	493,967	3,233
Fundamental (S)			
BBF**/***	15,000	15,000	91

IBFI***	1,485	1,485	9
SWBF**/***	11,880	11,880	72
WBF**/***	4,785	4,785	29
Landmark			
ABA	2,128		31
IL	1,000		14
IL-SG	280		7
General/Free Will			
FW	9,619		120
Old-Time			
DR	73		1
JAS & PV	5,659		31
NH	2,131		10
OM	13,498		78
Progressive Primitive			
PRO	5,806		85
Primitive			
OL	7,500		216
PR	26		3
Neo-Calvinist			
REF	360		9
SG	520		13
TOTAL	**1,960,442**		**4,925**
Dual: *ABC with 10 NB			
	-5,000		-10
**FBF with 3 BBF, 2 SWBF, 1 WBF			
	-990	-990	-6
***IBFI with 2 BBF, 1 SWBF, 1 WBF; SWBF with 15 BBF; WBF with 6 BBF			
	-4,125	-4,125	-25
TOTAL	**1,950,327**		**4,884**

Florida
(1821)

	Membership	Attendance	Churches
Ecumenical Mainline			
ABC*	4,007	1,286	26
National			
NBC/PNB	500,000		728
NBCA	70,000		203
NPR	17,895		174
Conservative Evangelical (N)			
BGC	2,364	2,789	25
CBA	835	835	9
NAB	675	575	3
SD	239	215	5
Fundamental (N)			
FBF**	3,720	3,720	24
GARBC	5,626	7,066	47
IBFNA	240	300	2
IFCA	310	310	2
Conservative Evangelical (S)			
SBC	1,057,240	414,835	2,054
Fundamental (S)			
BBF**/***	34,100	34,100	220
IBFI**/***	7,905	7,905	51
SWBF**	8,060	8,060	52
WBF**	16,275	16,275	105
Landmark			
ABA	15,626		123
BMA	973		12
IL	1,845		15
IL-SG	1,200		30
INTER	117		1
General/Free Will			
FW	6,096		74
GEN	338		3
SEP	20		1
UAFWB-CONF	9,150		61
Old-Time			
OM	n/a		3
Progressive Primitive			
PRO	449		10
Primitive			
OL	2,500		74
PR	22		4
Neo-Calvinist			
REF	440		11
SG	320		8
TOTAL	**1,768,587**		**4,160**
Dual: *ABC with 7 NBC/PNB, 4 NBCA			
	-1,683		-11
**FBF with 4 BBF, 1 IBF			
	-775	-775	-5
***IBFI with 20 BBF, 1 SWBF, 13 WBF; SWBF with 32 BBF; WBF with 46 BBF			
	-17,360	-17,360	-112
TOTAL	**1,748,769**		**4,032**

Alabama (1808)

	Membership	Attendance	Churches
Ecumenical Mainline			
ABC*	6,622	2,774	3
National			
NBC/PNB	645,000		2,555
NBCA	21,852		133
NPR	13,552		113
Conservative Evangelical (N)			
CBA	15	15	1
SD	36	33	1
Fundamental (N)			
FBF**	846	846	9
IFCA	188	188	2
Conservative Evangelical (S)			
SBC	1,112,560	382,473	3,148
Fundamental (S)			
BBF**/***	6,000	6,000	64
IBFI**	940	940	10
SWBF**/***	1,974	1,974	21
WBF**	1,410	1,410	15
Landmark			
ABA	5,038		36
BMA	1,676		17
IL	900		7
IL-SG	880		22
INTER	926		7
General/Free Will			
FW	19,252		165
FW-IND	127		3
Old-Time			
DR	3,151		26
OM	4,800		46
Progressive Primitive			
PRO	426		6
Primitive			
OL	5,000		147
PR	176		36
T-S	3		1
Neo-Calvinist			
REF	120		3
SG	360		9
TOTAL	**1,853,830**		**6,606**
Dual: *ABC with 2 NBC/PNB			
	-4,415		-2
**FBF with 1 BBF, 1 SWBF			
	-188	-188	-2
***IBFI with 2 BBF, 1 WBF; SWBF with 5 BBF; WBF with 7 BBF			
	-1,410	-1,410	-15
TOTAL	**1,847,817**		**6,587**

Mississippi (1791)

	Membership	Attendance	Churches
Ecumenical Mainline			
ABC*	350	60	3
National			
NBC/PNB*	367,000		917
NBCA	36,059		346
NPR	939		16
Conservative Evangelical (N)			
SD	45	53	2
Fundamental (N)			
FBF	300	300	3
Conservative Evangelical (S)			
SBC	725,313	245,994	2,037
Fundamental (S)			
BBF**	4,000	4,000	40
IBFI**	200	200	2
SBF**	500	500	5
WBF**	500	500	5
Landmark			
ABA	4,360		41
BMA	32,246		186
IL	1,450		9
IL-ASSN	2,286		14
IL-SG	640		16
INTER	8,178		78
General/Free Will			
FW	3,658		56
GEN	81		1
Old-Time			
OM	n/a		6
Primitive			
OL	3,000		87
Neo-Calvinist			
REF	120		3
SG	120		3
TOTAL	**1,191,345**		**3,876**
Dual: *ABC with 1 NBC/PNB			
	-117		-1
**IBFI with 1 BBF; SWBF with 1 BBF; WBF with 4 BBF			
	-600	-600	-6
TOTAL	**1,190,628**		**3,869**

Trans-Mississippi South

	MEMBERSHIP	ATTENDANCE	CHURCHES
Ecumenical Mainline*	22,519	7,948	67
National*	1,224,560		5,395
Conservative Evangelical (N)	2,811	2,774	38
Fundamental (N)**/ ***	4,350	4,410	50
Conservative Evangelical (S)*	5,332,620	1,637,053	11,242
Fundamental (S)**/***	239,515	239,515	1,413
Landmark	395,747		2,471
General/Free Will**	85,960		1,012
Old-Time	11,056		158
Progressive Primitive	455		6
Primitive	8,921		289
Neo-Calvinist	1,760		44
TOTAL	**7,330,274**		**22,185**
Ecumenical Mainline-National*	-5,138		-15
Ecumenical Mainline-Conservative Evangelical (S)*	-1,822		-5
Fundamental (N)-(S)**/***	-1,019	-1,004	-8
Fundamental (S)***	-68,705	-68,705	-402
TOTAL	**7,253,590**		**21,755**

The Trans-Mississippi South includes the states of Missouri, Arkansas, Louisiana, Oklahoma, and Texas. Missouri is included because of its cultural and religious affinity to this region, although geographically it is considered a state of the Mid-West or Great Plains. This region stretches over an extended territory from the well-watered Mississippi Valley to the dry high plains of the West. It includes the rather isolated highlands of the Ozarks, a subregion in Missouri and Arkansas lapping into Oklahoma, which has carried much of the same characteristics of Appalachia in the East. The region has produced wealth in cotton, wheat, and cattle and in gushing oil wells.

The region includes a complexity of populations. Europeans first appeared with settlement by the French and Spanish. The onrush of Americans brought into the northern and central areas of the region peoples from the Upper South. Along with a large rural population, it has also developed a number of notable metropolitan centers. With its large Anglo population, it includes numerous sub-groups including Indian tribes, blacks, Creoles and Cajuns of French origin, Americans of German descent in the hill country of Texas, and a large and growing Hispanic population. From its early history as a frontier region, its population, often contentious, is very individualistic.

Baptists were among the first Anglo pioneers in the territory that had first been controlled and settled by France and Spain and later controlled by Mexico. Baptist churches appeared in each of the states during the first decades of the nineteenth century. Although facing Roman Catholic populations among French and Spanish populations and competition from other Protestants, such as Methodists and the Stone-Campbell Movement, Baptists developed a Baptist empire in the area, which has included Indian and Hispanic converts. Baptists of all kinds, including black Baptists, number over 7,000,000 and are the largest denomination in the region. Their churches are in every county except two in Texas—Kenedy and Loving. With traditionally strong populations in Missouri, Louisiana, and Texas, Roman Catholics closely follow Baptists and continue to grow with a large immigrant Hispanic population. Today, Pentecostal and Charismatic groups have a growing presence in the region.

For Baptists, the region is noted for its conservative orthodoxy with a strong infusion of Landmarkism, a high-church movement that considers only Baptists as truly apostolic. It is not surprising that the region with its proclivity for controversy and individualism has given birth to several independent Landmark bodies and independent Fundamentalist fellowships, both stressing the independence of the local church. Texas provided much of the leadership that shifted the Southern Baptist Convention to a stricter conservative position.

The Southern Baptist Convention, with over five million members, leads in all counties in Texas, Oklahoma, and most of Missouri, but National Baptists lead in a number of counties in Louisiana and independent Landmark Baptists in many counties in Arkansas. The conservative Southern Baptist party, by and large, controls in each state, except Texas, where the old state convention is under the control of moderates but faces a rival Southern Baptist state convention that is in full alignment with the national leadership. Missouri Baptists have been in contention between moderates and conservatives over control of state agencies. Besides numerous colleges, Southern Baptists support three of their seminaries in the region besides establishing their relief and annuity board, GuideStone Financial Resources, in Fort Worth.

Independent Landmark bodies with almost 400,000 members and approximately 2,500 churches have a strong rural base and are particularly strong in Arkansas, leading in thirteen counties, as well as in the Piney-Woods area of eastern Texas. These bodies are fundamentalist in theology and exclusive in polity, not only not recognizing other denominations as true churches but also consider other Baptists as deviant for not following strict Landmark principles. Independent Southern Fundamentalist bodies, which include three fellowships that trace their origins to the iconoclastic activity of J. Frank Norris, have, excluding dual affiliations, an estimated membership of 170,000 in 1,000 churches. These Independents, fundamentalist in theology and separationist in polity, are, however, more open in ecclesiology and far more geared to metropolitan centers than the independent Landmarkers.

National Baptists are a strong presence in a belt of counties in southern and eastern Arkansas, northern Louisiana, and eastern Texas. They are also well represented in the larger metropolitan areas of the region. As in Appalachia, Old-Time Baptists appear in the Ozarks with such groups as Old-Time Missionary Baptists and United Baptists as well as some Independent Free Will Baptists. Primitives are present in each of the states with Texas housing half of their congregations. General Baptists, extending into southern Missouri, where they have their headquarters, and Arkansas, number more than 20,000, while Free Will Baptists with more than 60,000 maintain their major strength in Missouri, Arkansas, and Oklahoma. The American Baptist Churches/USA, northern Conservative Evangelicals, primarily represented by members of the North American Baptist Conference, and northern Fundamentalists, are extremely weak.

Bibliography

Lawrence Goodwyn, *The South Central States,* (Time-Life Books, 1967), 6-33. William Lindsey and Mark Silk, eds., *Religion and Public Life in the Southern Crossroads,* (Walnut Creek, CA: (AltaMira Press, 2005). Terry G. Jordan-Bychkov, *The Upland South,* (Santa Fe, NM, and Harrisonburg, VA: Center for American Places, 2003).

Missouri
(1804)

	MEMBERSHIP	ATTENDANCE	CHURCHES
Ecumenical Mainline			
ABC*	10,715	4,968	29
National			
NPC/PNB*	127,000		772
NBCA	11,500		65
NPR	95		2
Conservative Evangelical(N)			
BGC	595	785	6
NAB	114	120	1
SD	109	67	2
Fundamental (N)			
FBF**	388	388	4
GARBC	1,259	1,262	13
IFCA	194	194	2

Conservative Evangelical (S)*			
SBC	642,093	195,093	1,884
Fundamental (S)			
BBF***	23,000	23,000	149
IBFI***	2,325	2,325	15
SWBF***	620	620	4
WBF***	1,085	1,085	7
Landmark			
ABA	1,744		26
BMA	8,421		90
IL	2,112		24
IL-SG	160		4
General/Free Will			
FW**	15,723		185
FW-IND	499		11
GEN	15,525		230
Old-Time			
OM	6,906		85
UNI	2,514		30
Progressive Primitive			
PRO	232		2
Primitive			
OL	1,462		43
Neo-Calvinist			
REF	40		1
SG	200		5
TOTAL	**876,630**		**3,691**
Dual; *ABC with 2 NBC/PNB			
	-750		-2
*ABC with 5 SBC			
	-1,822		-5
**FBF with 1 FW			
	-85	-85	-1
***IBFI with 4 BBF; SWBF with 6 BBF; WBF with 6 BBF	-2,480	-2,480	-16
TOTAL	**871,493**		**3,667**

Arkansas
(1818)

	Membership	Attendance	Churches
Ecumenical Mainline			
ABC	128		1
National			
NBC	90,027		944
NBCA	3,200		40
Conservative Evangelical (N)			
SD	31		1
Fundamental (N)			
FBF*	100	100	1
GARBC	440	305	9
IFCA	49	34	1
NTA	40	40	1
Conservative Evangelical (S)			
SBC	534,534	163,772	1,372
Fundamental (S)			
BBF***	4,800	4,800	48
IBFI**	600	600	6
SWBF**	300	300	3
WBF**	400	400	4
Landmark			
ABA	93,560		570
BMA	70, 123		359
IL	4,678		28
IL-SG	440		11
INTER	36		2
General/Free Will			
FW	21,178		209
GEN	5,712		57
UAFWB-CONF	450		3
Old-Time			
OM	426		8
UNI	1,210		20
Primitive			
OL	1,564		46
PR	30		3
Neo-Calvinist			
REF	40		1
SG	240		6
TOTAL	**834,336**		**3,754**
Dual: *FBF with 1 BBF			
	-100	-100	-1
**IBFI with 3 BBF; SWBF with 1 BBF; WBF with 4 BBF	-800	-800	-8
TOTAL	**833,436**		**3,745**

Louisiana (1812)

	Membership	Attendance	Churches
Ecumenical Mainline			
ABC*	2,134	675	7
National			
NBC/PNB*	200,000		500
NBCA	84,900		290
Conservative Evangelical (N)			
NAB	99	80	1
Fundamental (N)			
FBF**	84	84	1
GARBC	20	15	1
Conservative Evangelical (S)			
SBC	609,259	182,455	1,435
Fundamental (S)			
BBF**/***	3,100	3,100	37
IBFI***	1,260	1,260	15
SWBF***	252	252	3
WBF***	1,848	1,848	22
Landmark			
ABA	10,405		76
BMA	7,131		35
IL	1,738		11
IL-SG	440		11
General/Free Will			
FW	68		4
UAFWB-CONF	750		5
Old-Time			
OM	n/a		7
Progressive Primitive			
PRO	64		1
Primitive			
OL	714		21
PR	45		5
Neo-Calvinist			
REF	40		1
SG	240		6
TOTAL	**924,591**		**2,495**
Dual: *ABC with 1 NBC/PNB			
	-299		-1
**FBF with 1 BBF			
	-84	-84	-1
***IBFI with 9 BBF, 3 WBF; SWBF with 3 BBF; WBF with 10 BBF			
	-2,100	-2,100	-25
TOTAL	**922,108**		**2,468**

Oklahoma (1832)

	Membership	Attendance	Churches
Ecumenical Mainline			
ABC*	4,024	1,398	14
National			
NBC/PNB*	60,000		300
NBCA	4,500		45
NMBC	10,000		100
Conservative Evangelical (N)			
NAB	303	219	5
SD	45	20	1
Fundamental (N)			
FBF**	100	70	2
GARBC	50	35	1
Conservative Evangelical (S)			
SBC	776,847	207,276	1,578
Fundamental (S)			
BBF**/***	22,000	22,000	98
IBFI***	7,650	7,650	34
SWBF***	225	225	1
WBF***	4,050	4,050	18
Landmark			
ABA	11,521		114
BMA	7,528		48
IL	3,000		26
IL-SG	320		8
General/Free Will			
FW	23,173		245
FW-IND	134		2
GEN	507		8
Old-Time			
OM	n/a		5
Primitive			
OL	850		25
PR	18		2
Neo-Calvinist			
REF	200		5
SG	120		3
TOTAL	**937,165**		**2,688**
Dual: *ABC with 1 NBC/PNB			
	-282		-1
**FBF with 1 BBF-50		-35	-1
***IBFI with 15 BBF, 5 WBF; SWBF with 1 BBF; WBF with 10 BBF			
	-6,975	-6,975	-31
TOTAL	**929,858**		**2,655**

Texas (1834)

	Membership	Attendance	Churches
Ecumenical Mainline			
ABC*	5,518	837	16
National			
NBC/PNB*	225,000		750
NBCA	404,798		1,525
NPR	3,540		62
Conservative Evangelical (N)			
BGC	241	228	5
NAB	1,224	1,192	13
SD	50	38	3
Fundamental (N)			
FBF**	1,050	1,050	6
GARBC	504	729	7
IFCA	72	104	1
Conservative Evangelical (S)			
SBC	2,769,887	888,457	4,973
Fundamental (S)			
BBF***	75,000	75,000	429
IBFI***	47,600	47,600	272
SWBF***	2,275	2,275	13
WBF***	41,125	41,125	235
Landmark			
ABA	48,768		380
BMA	98,015		473
IL	24,535		149
IL-SG	1,000		25
INTER	72		1
General/Free Will			
FW	2,241		53
Old-Time			
OM	n/a		3
Progressive Primitive			
PRO	159		3
Primitive			
OL	4,000		118
PR	211		24
T-S	27		2
Neo-Calvinist			
REF	400		10
SG	240		6
TOTAL	**3,757,552**		**9,557**
Dual: *ABC with 4 NBC/PNB, 7 NBCA	–3,807		-11
**FBF with 3 BBF, 1 WBF	-700	-700	-4
***IBFI with 144 BBF, 28 WBF; SWBF with 9 BBF, 1 WBF; WBF with 140 BBF	-56,350	-56,350	-322
TOTAL	**3,696,695**		**9,220**

Mountain

	Membership	Attendance	Churches
Ecumenical Mainline*	51,502	26,442	243
National*	46,105		206
Conservative Evangelical (N)	45,336	48,067	277
Fundamental (N)**	24,062	27,147	259
Conservative Evangelical (S)	361,694	140,372	1,316
Fundamental (S)**/***	35,559	35,559	310
Landmark	6,598		132
General/Free Will	865		33
Old-Time	n/a		3
Primitive	442		13
Neo-Calvinist	566		15
TOTAL	**572,729**		**2,807**
Ecumenical Mainline-National*	-4,549		-17
Fundamental (N)-(S)**/***	-7,814	-7,814	-70
Fundamental (S)***	- 5,434	-5,434	-49
TOTAL	**554,932**		**2,671**

The Mountain states include Montana, Wyoming, Idaho, Colorado, Utah, Nevada, New Mexico, and Arizona. It is a rugged territory of mountains, basins, and plains with a serious water deficit but yet sustains a growing population of miners, ranchers, farmers, and city dwellers.

With its dry climate, it has attracted many retirees, and its rugged beauty brings many tourists. It is a land that still carries characteristics of its pioneer past. In the nineteenth century the area experienced an influx of miners and ranchers followed by homesteaders, who in turn were confronted by native Indians and earlier Hispanic settlers in the southern section. Its inhabitants continue to include a cross-section of Anglos, Hispanics, and Indians.

Baptists established their first churches in the region in the midst of the nineteenth century, from 1853 to 1881, during the years of American migration into the region. It was no easy task with shifting populations and long distances. Roman Catholics were already well represented among the Indian and Hispanic populations, and Mormons were firmly established in Utah, two denominational bodies that today lead in the area. In 1936, white Baptists and white Presbyterians were about equal in strength, while white Methodists were forty or more percent larger than either body. Because of Southern migration and church planting, particularly by Southern Baptists, Baptists today have a modest yet respectable membership of over a half million. They are now the third largest religious denomination in the region.

Baptists are in every county but sixteen. The exclusions include seven in Montana, three in Idaho, three in Utah, two in Colorado, and one in Nevada. Baptists are particularly weak in the northern tier of states and in Utah in the middle tier but aside from Mormons are the largest Protestant body in each state except Montana and Wyoming.

Up to the early twentieth century, Northern (today American) Baptists had a Baptist monopoly and established a state convention in each state. In 1912, they withdrew from New Mexico in favor of Southern Baptists. In 1936 they numbered 45,000 in 260 churches and in 1946 65,000 in 303 churches. Because of defections to Conservative Baptists, which included loss of control of the Arizona state convention, and to other Fundamentalist Baptist bodies, the American Baptists have been reduced to about 52,000 with attendance of 26,000, which includes seven churches of more than 4,000 members dually affiliated with National Baptists. Except for a block of counties in Idaho, they lead in only a few other scattered counties. Except for the Rocky Mountains Region of Colorado and Wyoming, American Baptists have no other regional convention within the area. Pacific Coast regions cover the remaining territory.

Southern Baptists are by far the leading Baptist body in each of the states and a majority of the counties. Their greatest strength is in New Mexico, Arizona, and Colorado. They have conventions in each state except that Utah and Idaho are in one state body. They have a college in Montana and a conference center in New Mexico. Southern Fundamentalists, led by the Baptist Bible Fellowship, have their greatest strength in the same three states as Southern Baptists. Because of the lack of a strong African-American population, National Baptists are weak but show some strength in the metropolitan areas of Colorado, Arizona, and Nevada.

Northern Conservative Evangelicals about equal American Baptists in membership but with 48,000 far outrank them in attendance. Except in Montana, Conservative Baptists are the leading body among northern Conservative Evangelicals and northern Fundamentalists. Their main strength is in Colorado and in Arizona. Their national agencies are now located in the Denver area, where they moved from Illinois. A leading theological seminary in the region is Denver Seminary, founded by Conservative Baptists, but today has only nominal denominational ties. Northern Fundamentalists are much weaker than Conservative Evangelicals although they lead them in Montana.

Bibliography

Neal R. Peirce, *The Mountain States of America,* (New York: W. W. Norton, 1972), 15-28. Jan Shipps and Mark Silk, eds., *Religion and Public Life in the Mountain West,* (Walnut Creek, CA: AltaMira Press 2004).

Montana (1870)

	Membership	Attendance	Churches
Ecumenical Mainline			
ABC	2,472	1,665	26
Conservative Evangelical (N)			
BGC	216	316	4
CBA	758	758	6
NAB	266	258	3
Fundamental (N)			
FBF*	504	504	6
GARBC	992	1,279	13
IFCA	84	84	1
NTA*	1,845	1,845	22
Conservative Evangelical (S)			
SBC	12,377	6,159	105
Fundamental (S)			
BBF**	1,300	1,300	14
IBFI*/**	186	186	2
WBF*/**	279	279	3
Landmark			
ABA	156		9
IL	34		2
General/Free Will			
FW	16		2
Neo-Calvinist			
REF	40		1
ST	6		1
TOTAL	**21,531**		**220**
Dual: *FBF with 5 NTA			
	-420	-420	-5
**IBFI with 1 BBF, 1 NTA; WBF with 1 BBF, 1 NTA			
	-354	-354	-4
TOTAL	**20,757**		**211**

Wyoming (1870)

	Membership	Attendance	Churches
Ecumenical Mainline			
ABC	2,904	1,492	26
National			
NBC	1,300		9
Conservative Evangelical (N)			
BGC	652	1,020	6
CBA	1,909	1,909	13
Fundamental (N)			
FBF*	1,548	1,548	18
GARBC	86	86	1
NTA*	430	430	5
Conservative Evangelical (S)			
SBC	13,694	4,169	105
Fundamental (S)			
BBF**	950	950	10
IBFI*/**	285	285	3
SBF*/**	190	190	2
WBF**	380	380	4
Landmark			
ABA	70		3
IL	46		2
General/Free Will			
FW	n/a		1
Neo-Calvinist			
REF	40		1
TOTAL	**24,484**		**209**
Dual: *FBF with 1 NTA			
	-86	-86	-1
*IBFI with 1 BBF, 1 FBF, 1 WBF; SBF with 1 BBF; 1 FBF; WBF with 3 BBF			
	-742	-742	-8
TOTAL	**23,656**		**200**

Idaho (1864)

	Membership	Attendance	Churches
Ecumenical Mainline			
ABC*	5,738	3,328	37
National			
NBC*	250		2
Conservative Evangelical (N)			
BGC	165	180	1
CBA	1,596	1, 596	12
NAB	251	305	2
Fundamental (N)			
FBF	210	282	6
GARBC	1,227	1,383	13
Conservative Evangelical (S)			
SBC	12,135	4,960	66
Fundamental (S)			
BBF**	2,125	2,125	17
IBFI**	500	500	4
WBF**	500	500	4

Landmark			
ABA	279		3
IL	279		3
IL-SG	40		1
General/Free Will			
FW	251		6
Old-Time			
OM	n/a		2
Neo-Calvinist			
REF	40		1
TOTAL	**25,586**		**180**
Dual: *ABC with 1 NBC			
	-172		-1
**IBFI with 1 BBF, 1 WBF; WBF with 3 BBF			
	-625	-625	-5
TOTAL	**24,789**		**174**

Colorado

(1863)

	Membership	Attendance	Churches
Ecumenical Mainline			
ABC*	21,887	10,662	77
National			
NBC*	15,650		40
Conservative Evangelical (N)			
BGC	5,640	6,703	31
CBA	10,488	10,488	51
NAB	332	320	5
SD	213	148	3
Fundamental(N)			
FBF**	5,390	5,390	49
GARBC**	1,378	1,384	14
IFCA	110	110	1
NTA/MS**	5,700	5,700	52
Conservative Evangelical (S)			
SBC	68,064	31,240	243
Fundamental (S)			
BBF**/***	9,000	9,000	71
IBFI**/***	635	635	5
SWBF***	127	127	1
WBF**/***	1,524	1,524	12
Landmark			
ABA	404		11
BMA	168		3
IL	880		22
IL-SG	80		2
General/Free Will			
FW	210		7
Old-Time			
OM	n/a		1
Neo-Calvinist			
REG	40		1
SG	40		1
TOTAL	**147,960**		**703**
Dual: *ABC with 7 NBC			
	-1,970		-7
**FBF with 8 BBF, 1 IBFI, 27 NTA/MS; GARBC with 4 NTA/MS; NTA/MS with11 BBF, 1 WBF			
	6,077	-6,077	-52
***IBFI with 1 BBF; SWBF with 1 BBF; WBF with 6 BBF			
	-1,016	-1,016	-8
TOTAL	**138,897**		**636**

Utah

(1881)

	Membership	Attendance	Churches
Ecumenical Mainline			
ABC*	1,582	1,203	9
National			
NBC*	1,200		7
Conservative Evangelical(N)			
CBA	1,660	1,660	11
Fundamental (N)			
FBF**	330	330	6
GARBC	181	200	5
Conservative Evangelical (S)			
SBC	9,989	5,120	62
Fundamental (S)			
BBF**/***	700	700	12
IBFI**	174	174	3
SWBF***	174	174	3
WBF	174	174	3
Landmark			
ABA	70		3
IL	115		5
General/Freewill			
FW	n/a		2
TOTAL	**16,349**		**131**
Dual: *ABC with 1 NBC			
	-174		-1
**FBF with 2 BBF, 1 IBFI			
	-174	-174	-3
***SWBF with 1 BBF			
	–58	-58	-1
TOTAL	**15,943**		**126**

Nevada (1873)

	Membership	Attendance	Churches
Ecumenical Mainline			
ABC*	6,216	2,486	21
National			
NPB/PNB*	10,150		14
Conservative Evangelical (N)			
CBA	1,140	1,140	8
Fundamental (N)			
FBF	62	107	1
GARBC	185	320	3
Conservative Evangelical (S)			
SBC	31,952	13,888	111
Fundamental (S)			
BBF	1,500	1,500	8
Landmark			
ABA	636		4
BMA	68		1
IL	420		3
Neo-Calvinist			
REF	40		1
TOTAL	**52,369**		**175**
Dual:*ABC with 4 NBC/PNB			
	-1,181		-4
TOTAL	**51,188**		**171**

New Mexico (1853/1880)

	Membership	Attendance	Churches
Ecumenical Mainline			
ABC*	1,168	520	3
National			
NBC*	1,650		22
NBCA	730		11
Conservative Evangelical(N)			
CBA	670	670	5
SD	6	6	1
Fundamental (N)			
FBF**	560	560	5
GARBC	261	400	5
IFCA	52	80	1
Conservative Evangelical (S)			
SBC	103,847	34,972	301
Fundamental (S)			
BBF***	5,600	5,600	50
IBFI***	672	672	6
WBF**/***	1,680	1,680	15
Landmark			
ABA	627		6
BMA	204		5
IL	600		8
IL-SG	120		3
General/Free Will			
FW	44		4
Primitive			
OL	272		8
Neo-Calvinist			
REF	40		1
TOTAL	**118,803**		**460**
Dual: *ABC with 1 NBC			
	-385		-1
**FBF with 2 WBF			
	-224	-224	-2
***IBFI with 3 BBF, 1 BBF; WBF with 10 BBF			
	-1,568	-1,568	-14
TOTAL	**116,626**		**443**

Arizona (1880)

	Membership	Attendance	Churches
Ecumenical Mainline			
ABC*	9,535	5,086	44
National			
NBC*	5,400		36
NBCA*	3,775		21
NMBC	6,000		44
Conservative Evangelical (N)			
BGC	2,012	3,228	11
CBA	17,362	17,362	104
Fundamental (N)			
FBF**	1,666	1,666	14
GARBC	981	1,135	14
IBFNA	70	81	1
IFCA**	140	162	2
NTA	70	81	1
Conservative Evangelical (S)			
SBC	109,636	40,864	323
Fundamental (S)			
BBF**/***	5,000	5,000	42
IBFI**/***	833	833	7
WBF***	1,071	1,071	9
Landmark			
ABA	980		24

BMA	122	4
IL	200	5
General/Free Will		
FW	306	9
GEN	38	2
Primitive		
OL	170	5
Neo-Calvinist		
REF	200	5

SG	80		2
TOTAL	**165,647**		**729**
Dual: *ABC with 2 NBC, 1 NBCA			
	-667		-3
**FBF with 5 BBF, 1 IBFI; IFCA with 1 BBF			
	-833	-833	-7
***IBFI with 2 BBF; WBF with 7 BBF			
	-1,071	-1,071	-9
TOTAL	**163,076**		**710**

Pacific Northwest

	Membership	Attendance	Churches
Ecumenical Mainline*	37,853	18,752	183
National*	20,610		132
Conservative Evangelical (N)	70,091	75,014	362
Fundamental (N)**	13,165	17,564	123
Conservative Evangelical (S)	93,678	38,728	415
Fundamental (S)**/***	23,023	23,023	141
Landmark	4,831		109
General/Free Will	345		6
Old-Time	n/a		2
Primitive	72		6
Neo-Calvinist	600		15
TOTAL	**264,268**		**1,494**
Dual: Ecumenical Mainline-National*	-10,245		-48
Fundamental (N)-(S)**/***	-978	-1,074	-8
Fundamental (S)***	-4,230	-4,230	-30
TOTAL	**248,815**		**1,408**

Baptists entered the three Pacific Northwest states of Oregon, Washington, and Alaska in the nineteenth century.

They were among the earliest settlers of Oregon and Washington, forming their first church in the former state in 1844 and in the latter state in 1859. They entered Alaska much later when the Woman's American Baptist Home Mission Society established a mission on Kodiak Island in 1896. A second beginning in Alaska began when Southern Baptists formed their first church in 1943 in Anchorage

The Pacific Northwest lacks a dominant religious tradition. Much of the population sought freedom from the constraints of other regions, and their individualism and mobility together with the appeal of an inviting environment have made the region more indifferent to institutional religion than other areas.

According to the *Religious Congregations and Membership* study in 2000, Oregon with religious adherents at 31 percent and Washington with 33 percent were the lowest states with religious affiliation in the United States. According to the American Religious Identification Survey of 2001, although a significant percentage of non-adherents identify with some religious heritage, a large number, around thirty percent, reject any identification.

The Roman Catholic Church is the largest denomination in the region but claims only eleven percent of the population. With about a quarter million members in 1,400 churches, Baptists are the largest Protestant body. They are also rather well distributed, lacking only one county in Washington and five county equivalents in Alaska. On the other hand, most other denominational families are also well represented, including Holiness and Pentecostal bodies with growing constituencies. In addition, Mormons claim as large a constituency as Baptists although far less within the population in self-identification.

Baptists have not had the advantage of as strong a Southern migration as other regions. In addition, Baptists are very fragmented and in recent years have not shown significant growth Before the Second World War, American Baptists, except for a limited number of Landmark Baptists, had a practical monopoly. By losing the majority of their churches in Oregon and with a lack of church planting, impeded in part by comity agreements, American Baptists, who claimed almost 57,000 in 1946, today have about 38,000 with over 10,000 of these dually related to National Baptists. Linfield College in McMinnville, Oregon, the pioneer Baptist college in the area, maintains a traditional tie to American Baptists.

National Baptist have strength in large metropolitan areas with The National Baptist Convention, USA, Inc. the leading National body in Washington and Alaska, while the National Baptist Convention of America, Inc. leads in Oregon. Southern Baptists claim the largest membership in the region, leading in Washington and far in the lead in Alaska, but whose average attendance is far behind northern Conservative Evangelicals.

Southern Fundamentalists and Landmark Baptists are represented with some strength. Northern Conservative Evangelicals are the leaders in attendance in Oregon and Washington. Conservative Baptists are the largest Baptist body in Oregon, leading in almost every county, and have a significant number of members in Washington.

Conservative Baptists have a leading seminary in the area, Western Seminary, but their small college, Judson Baptist College in The Dalles, Oregon, was forced to close. The Baptist General Conference has an important constituency in Washington. With the exception of the GARBC in Washington, which supports Northwest Baptist Seminary in Tacoma, northern Fundamentalists are very weak in the region. Western Baptist College (now Corbin College) in Salem, Oregon, which was related to the GARBC, is now independent.

Bibliography

Patricia O'Connell Killen and Mark Silk, eds., *Religion and Public Life in the Pacific Northwest* (Walnut Creek, CA: AltaMira Press, 2004).

Oregon
(1844)

	MEMBERSHIP	ATTENDANCE	CHURCHES
Ecumenical Mainline			
ABC*	10,966	5,695	50
National			
NBC*	975		2
NBCA/NMBC*	3,819		17
NB-Independent	350		2
Conservative Evangelical (N)			
BGC	1,634	1,533	14
CBA	36,017	36,017	183
NAB	1,674	1,438	13
SD	25	28	1
Fundamental (N)			
FBF**	444	512	4
GARBC	1,438	1,658	13
IFCA	111	28	1
Conservative Evangelical (S)			
SBC	26,258	10,222	126
Fundamental (S)			
BBF**/***	5,000	5,000	32
IBFI***	624	624	4
WBF**/***	780	780	5
Landmark			
ABA	856		19
BMA	196		4
IL	1,080		24
IL-SG	120		3
General/Free Will			
FW	207		3
Primitive			
OL	49		4
Neo-Calvinist			
REF	240		6
SG	40		1
TOTAL	**92,903**		**531**
Dual: *ABC with 1 NBC, 7 NBCA/NMBC	-2,120		-8

	Membership	Attendance	Churches
**FBF with 1 BBF, 1 WBF			
	-312	-312	-2
***IBFI with 3 BBF; WBF with 4 BBF			
	-1,092	-1,092	-7
TOTAL	**89,379**		**514**

	Membership	Attendance	Churches
Dual: *ABC with 25 NBC, 11 NBCA/NMBC			
	-7,525		-36
**FBF with 2 BBF, 1 WBF			
	-450	-450	-3
***IBFI with 8 BBF, 1 WBF; WBF with 10 BBF			
	-2,850	-2,850	-19
TOTAL	**131,254**		**740**

Washington (1859)

	Membership	Attendance	Churches
Ecumenical Mainline			
ABC*	25,085	12,199	121
National			
NBC*	8,100		36
NBCA/NMBC*	4,400		22
NMBC	966		33
Conservative Evangelical (N)			
BGC	10,411	15,362	46
CBA	16,594	16,594	70
NAB	2,431	2,757	23
SD	125	73	3
Fundamental (N)			
FBF**	1,287	1,749	11
GARBC	7,747	10,478	66
IBFNA	351	477	3
IFCA	117	159	1
Conservative Evangelical (S)			
SBC	49,715	21,283	220
Fundamental (S)			
BBF**/***	7,800	7800	52
IBFI***	1,500	1,500	10
SWBF	300	300	2
WBF**/***	2,400	2,400	16
Independent	90	90	1
Landmark			
ABA	924		22
BMA	355		6
IL	500		11
IL-SG	440		11
General/Free Will			
FW	138		2
Old-Time			
OM	n/a		1
Primitive			
OL	23		2
Neo-Calvinist			
REF	280		7
TOTAL	**142,079**		**798**

Alaska (1896)

	Membership	Attendance	Churches
Ecumenical Mainline			
ABC*	1,802	858	12
National			
NBC*	2,000		20
Conservative Evangelical (N)			
BGC	260	292	4
CBA	920	920	5
Fundamental (N)			
FBF**	1,080	1,560	15
GARB	506	727	7
IBFNA	72	104	1
Independent	12	12	1
Conservative Evangelical (S)			
SBC	17,705	7,223	69
Fundamental (S)			
BBF**/***	4,000	4,000	11
WBF**/***	504	504	7
Independent	25	25	1
Landmark			
IL	240		6
IL-SG	120		3
General/Free Will			
FW	n/a		1
Old-Time			
OM	n/a		1
Neo-Calvinist			
REF	40		1
TOTAL	**29,286**		**165**
Dual: *ABC with 4 NBC			
	-600		-4
**FBF with 2 BBF, 1 WBF			
	-216	-216	-3
***WBF with 4 BBF			
	-288	-288	-4
TOTAL	**28,182**		**154**

Pacific Southwest

	MEMBERSHIP	ATTENDANCE	CHURCHES
Ecumenical Mainline*	127,471	98,258	559
National*	284,605		904
Conservative Evangelical (N)	100,404	134,949	430
Fundamental (N)**/***	34,773	37,468	254
Conservative Evangelical (S)	382,626	178,944	1,463
Fundamental (S)***	25,905	25,905	169
Landmark	14,079		216
General/Free Will	4,897		84
Old-Time	n/a		2
PRIMITVE	853		26
Neo-Calvinist	1,040		26
TOTAL	**976,653**		**4,133**
Dual: Ecumenical Mainline-National*	-11,428		-49
Fundamental (N)-(S)**/***	-11,423	-11,449	-74
Fundamental (S)***	-1,727	-1,727	-11
TOTAL	**952,075**		**3,999**

California and Hawaii, the two states of the Pacific Southwest, have been magnets for Caucasian migration with California as an Eldorado, a land of opportunity, and Hawaii, a Pacific paradise. Both harbor a multitude of religious expressions from Roman Catholicism and traditional Protestantism to Eastern religions and non-traditional spirituality.

Many people, however, claim no religious identity or are just loosely attached to a religious tradition. The Roman Catholic Church in California is by far the largest religious body, claiming thirty percent of the population. It is also the leading body in Hawaii, claiming about twenty percent of the population.

Baptists formed their first church in California in 1849, soon after the opening of the territory to American settlement. On the other hand, not until 1930 Baptists had established their first church in Hawaii, over a century after the arrival of the first missionaries. Baptists with over 900,000 are the second largest denomination in California, but in Hawaii with only 19,000 they are outnumbered by the United Church of Christ and Mormons and bested by the Assemblies of God and Foursquare Gospel in attendance. Baptists are well distributed in both states, lacking churches in only two extremely small counties—Alpine in California and Kalawao in Hawaii.

In California Baptists have grown from both migration and aggressive programs of evangelism and church planting. With the diverse population of the state, Baptists in California include a multi-ethnic constituency of Hispanic, Asiatic, and African-American members. California also has attracted a large spectrum of Baptist bodies with some of them developing constituencies of considerable strength. In 1936, the American Baptists, known earlier as Northern Baptists, had 63,000 members, including ethnic Baptists, and except for some Landmark and African-American Baptists controlled the Baptist scene. Although claiming 127,00 members in over 500 churches in 2000, Southern Baptists and National Baptists have overtaken them. Today, they lead in only two counties in the state. They are particularly strong in the southern part but lack churches in some of the less populated counties in the northern section. Their northern region, ABC of the West, has shown significant signs of rejuvenation, but American Baptists are now facing serious division in the state over homosexuality. The Pacific Southwest region and possibly other churches are withdrawing. In Berkeley they maintain the American Baptist Seminary of the West and in Redlands the University of Redlands.

Because of strong migration, National Baptists, approaching 300,000 in four bodies with around 900 churches, are well represented in Baptist ranks. Their greatest strength is in the metropolitan areas of the central and southern sections of the state. Southern Baptists have grown to become the largest Baptist body in California through migration and a program of church planting. They are located in every county but three. They support Golden Gate Baptist Theological Seminary in Mill Valley, just north of San Francisco, and California Baptist University at Riverside in the south.

Northern Conservative Evangelicals with 100,000 in membership and 135,000 in attendance have found California a fruitful field. The Conservative Baptist Association with two regional associations claims 55,000 members. Western Seminary in Portland, Oregon, maintains branches in Sacramento and San Jose. The Baptist General Conference has 31,000 members but claims an attendance of twice this number. The North American Baptist Conference, helped by migration, has found northern California one of its prime areas outside of its home area of the Dakotas.

In contrast to the Great Lakes region, northern Fundamental bodies are comparatively weak in the state. The GARBC, with around 11,500 members is about equally divided between the northern and southern sections. Its seminary and college in the state moved to the Pacific Northwest. The Fellowship of Fundamental Baptists of California is located primarily in the northern section. Its constituency supports Ironwood Christian Camp at Newberry Springs and Lucerne Christian Conference Center at Clear Lake, but its San Francisco Baptist Seminary ceased around 1992.

Southern Fundamentalists are also comparatively weak. Landmark Missionary Baptists as well are comparatively small. A majority of their churches associate with the American Baptist Association, but fifty of them are unaffiliated with a national body either in independent associations or as completely independent congregations.

In Hawaii, eighty-eight percent of the churches and sixty-nine percent of the members are Southern Baptist. Other Baptist groups have barely more than token representation.

Bibliography

Wade Clark Roof and Mark Silk, eds., *Religion and Public Life in the Pacific Region,* (Walnut Creek, CA: AltaMira Press, 2005).

California (1849)

	Membership	Attendance	Churches
Ecumenical Mainline			
ABC*	126,983	97,821	556
National			
NBC/PNB*	115,000		525
NBCA*	43,750		125
NMBC	125,000		250
NPR	855		4
Conservative Evangelical (N)			
BGC	31,025	61,626	155
CBA	55,435	55,435	215
NAB	13,049	17,233	45
SD	555	262	10
Fundamental (N)			
FBF**	6,665	6,665	43
GARBC**	11,598	14,293	102
IBFNA**	465	465	3
IFCA	775	775	5
NTA/CAL**	14,855	14,855	96
Conservative Evangelical			
SBC	365,675	171,448	1,392
Fundamental (S)			
BBF**/***	21,000	21,000	134
IBFI**/***	2,041	2,041	13
SWBF**/***	785	785	5
WBF***	1,413	1,413	9
Landmark			
ABA	8,985		131
BMA	1,280		15
IL	3,123		50
IL-SG	440		11
General/Free Will			
FW	2,985		62
GEN	1,863		21

Old-Time			
OM	n/a		2
Primitive			
OL	850		25
PR	3		1
Neo-Calvinist			
REF	720		18
SG	240		6
TOTAL	**957,413**		**4,029**
Dual: *ABC with 34 NBC/PNB, 15 NBCA			
	-11,428		-49
**FBF with 39 NTA/CAL; IBFNA with 1 GARBC; NTA/CAL with 29 BBF, 2 IBFI, 2 SWBF			
	-11,340	-11,366	-73
***IBFI with 4 BBF; SWBF with 2 BBF; WBF with 5 BBF			
	-1,727	-1,727	-11
TOTAL	**932,918**		**3,896**

Hawaii (1930)

	Membership	Attendance	Churches
Ecumenical Mainline			
ABC	488	437	3
Conservative Evangelical (N)			
BGC	190	243	4
CBA	150	150	1
Fundamental (N)			
FBF*	249	249	3
GARBC	166	166	2
Conservative Evangelical (S)			
SBC	16,951	7,496	71
Fundamental (S)			
BBF	500	500	6
WBF*	166	166	2
Landmark			
ABA	139		5
IL	112		4
General/Free Will			
FW	49		1
Neo-Calvinist			
REF	80		2
TOTAL	**19,240**		**104**
Dual: *FBF with 1 WBF			
	-83		-1
TOTAL	**19,157**		**103**

Endnotes

Introduction

1. For county statistics of United Methodist, Roman Catholic, and Baptist predominance, see *Religious Congregations and Membership in the United States, 2000,* (Nashville: Glenmary Research Center, 2002), ix, xvii.

2. Robert G. Gardner, *Baptists of Early America: A Statistical History, 1639–1790,* (Atlanta: *Georgia Baptist Historical Society*, 1983), 211.

3. Ernest A. Payne, "The Baptist Scene Today in the United States," *The Quarterly Review,* XX/4, (October, 1963), 165, 170–75.

4. William G. McLoughlin, *Soul Liberty: The Baptists' Struggle in New England, 1620–1833,* (Hanover and London: Brown University Press, 1991), 13.

5. Fred Kniss, "Conflict and the Telling of North American Mennonite History," *Journal of Mennonite Studies,* XXIII, (2005), 101–10.

6. Donald B. Kraybill and C. Nelson Hostetter, *Anabaptist World USA,* (Scottdale, PA, and Waterloo, ON: Herald Press), 2001.

7. See Lydia Huffman Hoyle, "Baptist Americanus," in W. Glenn Jonas, Jr., *The Baptist River,* (Macon: Mercer University Press, 2006), 269–84.

8. Robert G. Gardner, "Baptist General Bodies in USA," *Baptist History and Heritage,* XII/2, (April, 1977), 92-94, 104.

9. Bill J. Leonard, *Baptist Ways: A History,* (Valley Forge: Judson Press, 2003), 1–15.

Chapter 1

1. Anthony Compolo, Jr., *A Denomination Looks at Itself,* (Valley Forge: Judson Press, 1971).

2. See the review of *Mission Handbook 2004–2006,* by Robert T. Coote in *International Bulletin,* January, 2005, 42, on the decline of foreign mission support by mainline denominations.

3. Compolo, 53, 57. Eileen R. Campbell-Reed and Pamela R. Durso, *The State of Women in Baptist Life–2005,* (Atlanta; Baptist Women in Ministry, 2006), 2, 4. *Christian Century,* April 18, 2006, 15.

4. See Compolo, 42-43.

5. Norman M. Green, Jr., "How American Baptists Have Changed in Thirty Years," *ABQ,* IX/2, (June, 1990), 61-70.

6. For a careful study of Northern Baptist attitudes toward immigrants and their outreach to them, see Lawrence B. Davis, *Immigrants, Baptists, and the Protestant Mind in America,* (Urbana, etc.: University of Illinois Press, 1973).

7. Northern Baptist Convention, *Annual,* 1920, 290-91; *1960 American Baptist Census,* 14; and Green, 64-65.

8. Green, 64-65.

9. See Compolo, 47-51.

10. William B. Lipphard, "Where Do We Go from Here?" *The Chronicle,* XV/4, (October, 1952), 149-58.

11. Howard Moody, "American Baptists: To Break the Bonds of Captivity," *The Christian Century,* April 10, 1963, 456-58. Also see Paul M. Harrison, *Authority and Power in the Free Church Tradition,* (Princeton: Princeton University Press, 1959), for a case study of the exercise of authority in the American Baptist Convention.

12. See Lucas Alan McBee, *The American Baptist Fellowship: A Case Study of Conservative Renewal,* (M.A. thesis, Baylor University, 1995), for material on both renewal organizations.

13. For statistics see Lipphard, 154-55, and Northern Baptist Convention, *Annual,* 1920, 290.

14. See Northern Baptist Convention, *Annual,* 1920, 290-91, and Green, 64-65. Green claims a loss of almost 350,000 white/Anglo members, starting from a different base and later date.

15. A helpful article on American Baptist identity is Eldon G. Ernst, "American Baptists: An Auto-biographical Quest for Identity," in Everett C. Goodwin, ed., *Baptists in the Balance,* (Valley Forge: Judson Press, 1997), 197-215.

16. Paul D. Borden, *Hit the Bullseye,* (Nashville: Abingdon Press, 2003).

Chapter 2

17. *Baptist Home Missions in America,* (New York: American Baptist Home Mission Society, 1883), 421.

18. For contemporary challenges, see William Banks, "Challenges Facing Blacks in America," *American Baptist Quarterly,* XXIII/2, (June, 2004), 123-36, and Aldon D. Morris and Shayne Lee, *The*

National Baptist Convention: Traditions and Contemporary Challenges, in David A. Roozen and James R. Nieman, eds., *Church, Identity, and Change,* (Grand Rapids and Cambridge, U.K.: William B. Eerdmans, 2006), 336-79.

19. For a contemporary survey of black life in the USA, see *The Economist,* August 6-12, 2005, 20-22.

20. *Mission Frontiers,* April, 2000, 14.

21. For internal struggles within the convention, see George W. Lucas, "Negro Baptists Sail a Stormy Sea," *Foundations,* IV/3, (July, 1961), 207-15.

22. For the Lyons affair, see Edward G. Gilbreath, "Redeeming Fire," *Christianity Today,* December 6, 1999, 38-47. Also see Morris and Lee, 364-68.

23. National Baptist Convention, USA, *Annual Report,* 1999–2001, 133.

24. For the work of the Foreign Mission Board, see William J. Harvey III, *Bridges of Faith Across the Seas,* (Philadelphia: Foreign Mission Board, National Baptist Convention, USA, 1989).

25. *Mission Handbook, 2004–2006,* 235.

26. The work of Bobby L. Lovett, *A Black Man's Dream: The First 100 years—Richard Henry Boyd and the National Baptist Publishing Board,* ([Nashville]: Mega Corporation, 1993), provides a study of the publishing company and its relation to various National Baptist bodies.

27. National Missionary Baptist Convention, *Journal,* 2000, 220.

Chapter 3

28. The standard history of the Baptist General Conference is Adolf Olson, *A Centenary History,* (Chicago: Baptist Conference Press, 1952). Subsequent volumes include David Guston and Martin Erickson, *Fifteen Eventful Years,* (Chicago: Harvest Publications, 1961), followed by volumes covering in turn the decades of the 1960s, 1970s, and 1980s. In September, 1987, the *American Baptist Quarterly,* VI/3, published an issue, *Swedish Baptists – American Baptists,* which included a colloquy and four incisive articles examining relations between Swedish and American Baptists. A helpful article is by Virgil A. Olson, "Neither Jew Nor Greek: A Study of an Ethnic Baptist Group, the Swedish Baptists, 1850–1950," *Baptist History and Heritage,* XXV/1, (January, 1990), 32-42.

29. See Norman A. Magnuson, "Along Kingdom Highways—American Baptists and Swedish Baptists in a Common Mission: An Introductory Essay," *American Baptist Quarterly,* VI/3, (September, 1987), 130-35.

30. For a helpful review of American Baptist attitudes toward Swedish Baptist work, see William H. Brackney, "To Be Lost in America: The Saga of Swedish Baptists from an American Baptist Perspective," *American Baptist Quarterly,* VI/3, (September, 1987), 149-55.

31. See Magnuson, 139-43, for a discussion of Swedish Baptist contributions to American Baptists.

32. For the formation of the foreign mission board and break with the ABFMS, see Joy A. Barnhardt and Luther (Lee) E. Barnhardt III, "The Baptist General Conference Foreign Mission Advance: An Investigation into the Causes of its Emergence," *American Baptist Quarterly, VI/3,* (September, 1987), 172-200.

33. A good discussion of the new spirit of Swedish Baptists in the 1940s is in the article by Virgil A. Olson, "An Interpretation of the Historical Relationships Between the American Baptist Convention and the Baptist General Conference," *American Baptist Quarterly,* VI/3, (September, 1987), 165-71.

34. The author was able to gain average attendance when working with the *Religious Congregations and Membership* study of 2000, but membership was not available except for churches in the Pacific Northwest. Therefore attendance figures are also used for membership.

35. The two works by Bruce L. Shelley, *Conservative Baptists: A Story of Twentieth-Century Dissent,* (Denver: Conservative Baptist Theological Seminary, 1960), and *A History of Conservative Baptists,* (Wheaton, Illinois: Conservative Baptist Press, 1971), provide helpful narratives with the first volume including in appendices a number of historical documents. The struggle of fundamentalist Baptists within the Northern Baptist Convention from a Conservative Baptist viewpoint is chronicled by Chester E. Tulga, *The Foreign Missions Controversy in the Northern Baptist Convention,* (Chicago: Conservative Baptist Fellowship, 1950).

36. The work by William Vance Trollinger, Jr., *God's Empire: William Bell Riley and Midwestern Fundamentalism,* (Madison: University of Wisconsin Press, 1990), is a valuable study. Also see the excellent biographies of William Bell Riley, John Roach Straton, and J. C. Massee in the work by C. Allyn Russell, *Voices of American Fundamentalism: Seven Biographical Studies,* (Philadelphia: Westminster Press, 1976). Riley's biography also appeared in *Minnesota History,* XLIII/1, (Spring, 1972), 14-38, and *Foundations,* XVIII/1, (January–March, 1975), 26-52.

37. For statistics, see Shelley (1960), 71, and G. Archer Weniger, *Questions and Answers about*

Conservative Baptists, (Minneapolis: C.B. Press, 1958).

38. See Shelley (1971), 68ff., and Sherman Roddy, "Separatist Baptists Today," *Foundations,* IV/3, (July, 1961), 225-30, for the controversy.

39. For statistics for 1982 and 1989, see the brochure, "The Conservative Baptist Association of America." For the ethnic composition of the churches in New York City, see Mark Marchak, "In Previews: Conservative Baptists and the New Song," *American Baptist Quarterly,* XIX/3, (September, 2000), 222-31.

40. *Mission Handbook, 2004–2006,* 103, 226-27. MTTA, *Harvest,* Spring, 2004, 4.

41. See the article by Bruce Shelley, "The Fruit of a Fundamentalist Fellowship," *Conservative Baptist,* Fall, 1982, 8-9, on the weakening of denominational identity of Conservative Baptists.

42. The most comprehensive history of the NABC is by Frank H. Woyke, *Heritage and Ministry of the North American Baptist Conference,* (Oakbrook Terrace, Illinois: North American Baptist Conference, 1979). An excellent work on the relationship of the German Baptist movement to American Baptists is Eric Henry Ohlmann's dissertation, *The American Baptist Mission to German-Americans: A Case Study of Attempted Assimilation,* (Th.D., Graduate Theological Union, 1973). Three other helpful sources are the centennial history, *These Glorious Years,* (Cleveland: Roger Williams Press, c. 1943); the article by Martin L. Leuschner, "North American Baptist General Conference," in *Baptist Advance,* (Nashville: Broadman Press, 1964), 227-50; and the article by Philip E. Thompson, "The North American Baptist Conference," in Jonas, *The Baptist River,* 182-205.

43. See Ohlmann for American Baptist contributions, 110ff., 199ff.

44. See Ohlmann, 252.

45. See Ohlmann, 165, 238, for the drain to English-speaking churches.

46. See Ohlmann, 239ff., 259ff., for factors for independence although he fails to recognize the theological factor.

47. Ohlmann, 134.

48. See Woyke, 362.

49. See David T. Priestly, "Doctrinal Statements of German Baptists in North America," *Foundations,* XXII/1, (January-March, 1979), 51-71, for a discussion of the confessional standards over the years of the German Baptists.

50. A standard work on Seventh Day Baptists is Don A. Sanford, *A Choosing People: The History of Seventh Day Baptists,* (Nashville: Broadman Press, 1992). A shorter work by Sanford is, *A Free People in Search of a Free Land,* (Janesville, WI: The Seventh Day Baptist Historical Society, 1987, third ed.). The latter work includes the Statement of Belief of Seventh Day Baptists, maps that show church locations and migration, and a genealogical table.

51. For the earlier statistics, see H. K. Carroll, *The Religious Forces of the United States,* (New York: The Christian Literature Co., 1893), 32, and *Religious Bodies: 1926,* II, 144. The author compiled the statistics for 2000, which were later sent to the office of the *Religious Congregations and Membership* study.

52. For women pastors in the SDB Conference, see Patricia A. Bancroft, "Chosen by God: Women Pastors on the Frontiers of the Seventh Day Baptist Denomination," *Baptist History and Heritage,* XL/3, (Summer/Fall, 2005), 17-26.

53. See Russel J.Thomsen, *Seventh Day Baptists—The Legacy to Adventists,* (Mountain View, CA, etc.: Pacific Press Publishing Association, 1971), for relations between Seventh Day Baptists and Adventists.

54. See H. Leon McBeth, *The Baptist Heritage,* (Nashville: Broadman Press, 1987), 724-49; Joshua Grijalva, *Ethnic Baptist History,* (San Antonio: Author, 1992; and "Ethnic Southern Baptists," *Baptist History and Heritage,* XXXVIII/3, (July, 1983) for accounts of ethnic bodies and ethnic mission work.

55. For Baptist mission work among Indians, see Torbet, 391-93, 489-90.

56. For Hispanic conventions and seminary related to American Baptists, see the letter of James I. Macias to Albert W. Wardin, July 30, 1979; Torbet, 1950, 503; Northern Baptist Convention, *Year Book,* 1947, 670-71; and Leland D. Hine, *Baptists in Southern California,* (Valley Forge: Judson Press, 1966), 161, 174. Hine lists 1923 for the organization of the convention in Southern California.

57. For Hispanic work by Southern Baptists in Texas and the Southwest, see McBeth, 736-41.

58. For Southern Baptists, see Peter Kung, "The Story of Asian Southern Baptists," *Baptist History and Heritage,* XVIII/3, (July, 1983), 49-58. See the issue entitled, "Exploring Asian American Christianity: Its Past, Present, and Future," *American Baptist Quarterly,* XXI/3, (September 2002), for American Baptist mission work among Asiatics.

59. See Lawrence B. Davis, *Immigrants, Baptists, and the Protestant Mind in America,* (Urbana, etc.: University of Illinois Press, 1973, 97ff.

60. For historical accounts of European ethnic bodies, see *The Chronicle,* (July, 1939), II/3, which includes articles on the Germans, Scandinavians, Italians, Czechoslovakians, Romanians, Hungarians, and Poles, and McBeth, 725-35. Also see Northern Baptist Convention, *Year Book,* 1946, 670-71, for a listing of ethnic Baptist organizations as related to Baptists in the North.

61. The author gained most of his information on Russian/Ukrainian Baptists through telephone interviews with leaders of their associational bodies.

62. Figures include, by and large, only membership in the USA.

Chapter 4

63. See Sherman Roddy, "Separatist Baptists Today," *Foundations,* IV/3, (July, 1961), 225-30, for differences among evangelical Baptists.

64. *Mission Handbook,* 2001-2003, 99, and 2004-2006, 69, 92-93, 153.

65. An early history of the GARBC is Joseph M. Stowell, *Background and History of the General Association of Regular Baptist Churches,* (Hayward, CA: Gospel Tracts Unlimited, 1949, c. 1954, 4th ed.). Paul N. Tassell wrote an official history, *Quest for Faithfulness,* (Schaumburg, IL: Regular Baptist Press, 1991). Curtis Wayne Wright produced in 1982 a Ph.D. dissertation at St. Louis University on the history of the GARBC to 1970 with a section on fundamentalist historiography and a theological analysis of this body.

66 For a history of the BBU, see Robert George Delnay, *A History of the Baptist Bible Union,* (Th.D. dissertation, Dallas Theological Seminary, 1963) that was printed in 1974 without documentation by Piedmont Bible College Press in 1974. GARBC histories also provide historical data on the BBU.

67. For differences between the two organizations, see "The Fundamentalists and the Bible Union," *The Watchman-Examiner,* April 19,1923, 487-88.

68. On the appearance of separatist associations, see Stowell, 28-29; Donald George Tinder, *Fundamentalist Baptists in the Northern and Western United States, 1920–1950,* (Ph.D. dissertation, Yale University, 1969), 400, 404-405; J. Murray Murdoch, *Portrait of Obedience: The Biography of Robert T. Ketcham,* (Schaumburg, IL: Regular Baptist Press, 1979), 118-23; and *Baptist Spokesman,* November, 1928, 16.

69. See George W. Dollar, *A History of Fundamentalism,* (Greenville, SC: Bob Jones University Press, 1973), for using the term "prima donna" for certain leaders.

70. See Tinder, 388-407, for a survey of the development of the GARBC to 1968, and Tassell, 422-23, for growth in the number of churches.

71. For a biography of Ketcham, see Murdoch.

72. For the foreign and home mission interests of the GARBC, see William J. Hopewell, Jr., *The Missionary Emphasis of the General Association of Regular Baptist Churches,* (Chicago: Regular Baptist Press, 1963), and Tinder, 342ff., 390-93.

73. See Tinder, 346, on relationships and mission giving of the GARBC constituency.

74. Tassell, 347-48. *Christianity Today,* September, 2006, 24-25.

75. See Tassell, 407-19, for results of the survey.

76. Tassell, 333-35.

77 Stowell, 59.

78. *Religious Bodies: 1936,* II, Part l, 254-55.

79. Ruth Ryburn of the GARBC office provided for the author complete statistics by state and county.

80. *Religious Congregations and Membership in the United States,* 2000, 4. Figures were extrapolated for non-reporting churches.

81. See the booklet, *What Happened to the GARBC at Niagra Falls?,* (Sellersville, PA: Bethel Baptist Press, c. 1990), for criticism of the GARBC.

82. For a survey of the FBF to the '60s, see Tinder, 439-42 and G. Archer Weniger, "A Brief History of the Conservative Baptist Fellowship," *The North Star Baptist,* April, 1965, 10-15, 18-9, and also printed as a brochure. See Shelley (1971), 86-99, for its controversy with Conservative Baptists from a Conservative Baptist viewpoint, and Richard V. Clearwaters, *The Great Conservative Baptist Compromise,* (Minneapolis: Central Seminary Press, n.d.) from the viewpoint of a FBF supporter. Also see "The Fundamental Baptist Fellowship and The Conservative Baptist Movement," in David O. Beale, *In Pursuit of Purity,* (Greenville, SC: Unusual Publications, 1986), 289-301, which includes a historical survey and current status of the FBF. For a helpful survey of the FBF, see the series of articles, "For the Faith," by Bob Whitmore and others in *Frontline Magazine,* May–June, 1998, 6-19.

83. See Tinder, 425-26, 431, 433, and Dollar, 227ff., 367, for references to Tulga's career. After joining a GARBC church, he joined the Landmark Baptists, was rebaptized, and taught two years in one of their schools, Eastern Baptist Institute, at Somerset, Kentucky. In 1963, he rejoined the Conservative Baptists, becoming a critic of the hard core party!

84. Shelley (1971), 96.

85. For an article on Weniger's life, see Bob Whitmore, "G. Archer Weniger, A Separatist Baptist Bulldog," *Frontline Magazine,* May–June, 1998, 18-9.

86. *New Testament Testimonies,* September–November, 1974, 1.

87. See Beale, 294-95.

88. For an account of NTA beginnings, see Richard V. Clearwaters, "The New Testament Association of Independent Baptist Churches of America," *Central Testimony,* VIII/1, (July–August, 1966). From a Conservative Baptist perspective, see Shelley (1971), 99-103, and from a hard core perspective, see

B. Myron Cedarholm, "Why a New Association of Churches Is Needed," *The North Star Baptist,* May, 1967, 3-21, and *Central Testimony,* IX/3, (November–December, 1967).

89. For Clearwaters's autobiography, see Richard V, Clearwaters, *On the Upward Road,* (Minneapolis: Author, n.d.). For the life of Cendarholm, see "B. Myron Cedarholm; Man of Character, Man of God," *Frontline Magazine,* May–June, 1999, 7-8.

90. See Bob Whitmore, "The Cedarholm/ Clearwaters Conflict," *Frontline Magazine,* May–June, 1999, 11-12. Some years later personal reconciliation was effected.

91. Shelley (1971), 102-103, and Richard V. Clearwaters, "The G.A.R.B. Guilt Complex of Dr. Merle R. Hull, Editor of *The Baptist Bulletin,*" *Central Testimony,* X/2, (September–October, 1968).

92. See Roy E. Shelpman, *Reflection of Conviction: The History of the IFBA of Michigan,* (Flint: Author, 1980), for documents on the division.

93. See "Conservative Baptist Cross Currents in Colorado," *Baptist Missionary-Evangelist,* May, 1962, and *Mountain States Baptist Messenger,* December, 1962, 2.

94. Tassell, 346-47. For addition material on Denver Baptist Bible College and Seminary, see Edward J. Fenlason and James M. Gemmill, *Ordered by the Lord: A Biography of John Widenaar,* (n.p.: Authors, 1993), 199-205.

95. For its history to 1992, see Edward J. Fenlason, *An Insider Looks Back: The Rise and Demise of the Inter-Mountain Fellowship, (1949–1992),* (n.p.: Author, n.d.). The author describes the differences between adherents of the IMBF and the Grace Fellowship.

Chapter 5

96. See Gardner, 21, for membership in 1790, subtracting, however, *German Seventh Day Baptists and Rogerenes*. For 1851, see *Baptist Home Missions in North America,* 555.

97. For a judicious account of the formation of the Southern Baptist Convention, see Lynn E. May, Jr., *Quarterly Review,* XXXI/1, (October–December, 1970), 51-64. For a survey of the views of various Baptist historians on the formation of the Southern Baptist Convention, see Walter B. Shurden and Lori Redwine Vanadoe, "The Origins of the Southern Baptist Convention: A Historiographical Study," *Baptist History and Heritage,* XXXXVII/1, (Winter, 2002), 71-96.

98. See James M. Morton, Jr., Leadership of W. B. Johnson in the "Formation of the Southern Baptist Convention," *Baptist History and Heritage,* V/1, (January, 1970), 3-12, 55, on Johnson's ecclesiology, but Morton goes too far in insisting "a new kind of convention" had then come into existence.

99. See Wardin, "Baptist Confessions: Use and Abuse," *American Baptist Quarterly,* XXI/4 (December, 2002), 467-83, for a discussion of confessional standards.

100. For Baptist support of the Confederacy, see David B. Chesebrough, "A Holy War: The Defense and Support of the Confederacy by Southern Baptists," *American Baptist Quarterly,* VI/1 (March, 1987), 17-30.

101. For effects of the war on Southern Baptists, see Jesse C. Fletcher, "Effect of the Civil War on Southern Baptist Churches," *Baptist History and Heritage,* XXXII/3-4, (July–October, 1997), 32-46.

102. See Hugh Wamble, "Landmarkism: Doctrinaire Ecclesiology Among Baptists," *Church History,* XXXIII/4, (December, 1964), 429-47, for a careful analysis of Landmarkism.

103. Rabun L. Brantley, "Southern Baptist Education," *Encyclopedia of Southern Baptists,* III, 1685.

104. A. B. Cash, "Mountain Mission Schools," *Encyclopedia of Southern Baptists,* II, 926-28,

105. See Robert A. Baker, *Relations Between Northern and Southern Baptists,* (Fort Worth: Seminary Hill Press, 1948), 183-216, on the principles of comity and territorial adjustments.

106. SBC *Annual,* 1921, 623.

107. For an example of the increase in gifts by Southern Baptists from the time of the Second World War, see *Southern Baptist Handbook, 1991,* 10.

108. For a discussion of migration from the South of both whites and blacks, see *Southerners Abroad, in Rural Worlds Lost: The American South, 1920–1960,* (Baton Rouge and London: Louisiana State University Press, 1987), 309-33.

109. SBC *Annual,* 1953, 446-51. Floyd Looney, *History of California Southern Baptists,* (Fresno: Board of Directors, Southern Baptist General Convention of California, 1954), 285.

110. See *Quarterly Review,* XV/3, (July–September, 1955), for articles on the early expansion of Southern Baptists as well as the article by John D. Raymond, "The Northward Expansion of the Southern Baptists," *Watchman-Examiner,* November 2, 1967, 684-86. For additional material on Southern Baptist expansion in the twentieth century, see the article by Tom J. Nettles, "Southern Baptists: Regional to National Transition," *Baptist History and Heritage,* XVII/3, (July, 1982), 32-54. For an account of Southern Baptist expansion into the Northeast, see

Donald L. Davidson, *A History of Southern Baptists in the Northeastern United States, 1950–1972,* (Th.D. dissertation, Southwestern Baptist Theological Seminary, 1974).

111. See Edwin Boling, "Social Factors in Church Extension: Southern Baptists in the North," *Foundations,* XVIII/2, (April–June, 1975), 146-52.

112. See Robert G. Torbet, "Historical Background of the Southern Baptist 'Invasion,'" *Foundations,* II/4, (October, 1959), 314-19. In the same issue, see Blake Smith, "The Southern Baptist 'Invasion': Right or Wrong?," 320-31, written by a Southern Baptist critic of the "invasion," claiming Southern Baptist misperceptions. Also see W. O. Carver, "Historical Background of Geographical Problems of American Baptists," *Quarterly Review,* XXVI/4, (Fourth Quarter, 1966), 5-17, a moderate view with some misgiving for denominational tensions. For a Southern Baptist view of Northern Baptist prejudice against the entry of Southern Baptists in California, see Looney, 17-18, 272.

113. For the conditions of rural churches, see J. Wayne Flynt, "Southern Baptists: Rural to Urban Transition," *Baptist History and Heritage,* XVI/1, (January, 1981), 24-34.

114. Samuel S. Hill, Jr., and Robert G. Torbet, *Baptists—North and South,* (Valley Forge, etc.: The Judson Press, 1963), 54.

115. See *Baptist and Reflector,* November 14, 2001, 24, and Richard Cimino, ed., *Lutherans Today,* (Grand Rapids, Michigan, and Cambridge, U.K.: William B. Eerdmans, 2003), 106-107.

116. For Southern Baptist work among ethnics, see Joshua Grijalva, *Ethnic Baptist History,* (Miami: Meta Publishers, n.d), and "Ethnic Southern Baptist Heritage," *Baptist History and Heritage,* XVIII/3, (July, 1983).

117. 1999 ACP Data in North American Mission Board, *Ethnic Profiles,* 2001–2002.

118. See Alan Scot Willis, *All According to God's Plan: Southern Baptist Missions and Race, 1945–1970,* (Lexington: University Press of Kentucky, 2005), for changing attitudes of Southern Baptists on race. For relations between Southern Baptists and African Americans, see the issue of *Baptist History and Heritage,* XVI/3, (July, 1981), entitled, "Black Southern Baptist Heritage," and *The Journal of African American Southern Baptist History,* I, (June, 2003). Among a number of valuable articles in the two periodicals, both include the very helpful article by Emmanuel L. McCall, "Home Mission Board Ministry in the Black Community."

119. Rufus B. Spain, *At Ease in Zion: A Social History of Southern Baptists, 1865–1899,* (Nashville: Vanderbilt University Press, 1967). John Lee Eighmy, *Churches in Cultural Captivity: A History of the Social Attitudes of Southern Baptists,* (Knoxville: University of Tennessee Press, 1972).

120. For a helpful discussion of the centralizing influences in the Southern Baptist Convention, see William Wright Barnes, *The Southern Baptist Convention: A Study in The Development of Ecclesiology,* (Fort Worth, Texas: Author, 1934).

121. LeRoy Moore, "Crazy Quilt: Southern Baptist Patterns of the Church," *Foundations,* XX/1, (January–March, 1977), 12-35.

122. James L. Sullivan, *Baptist Polity—As I See It,* (Nashville: Broadman Press, 1983), 196ff.

123. Wayne Flynt, "Not an Island Unto Itself: Southern Baptists and The New Theological Trends, (Liberalism, Ecumenism, and the Social Gospel), 1890–1940," *American Baptist Quarterly,* XXII/2, (June, 2003), 158-79.

124. See H. Cornell Goerner, W. O. Carver: "Man of Many Parts," *Baptist History and Heritage,* III/2, (July, 1968), 67-73, 114.

125. David Stricklin, *A Genealogy of Dissent: Southern Baptist Protest in the Twentieth Century,* (Lexington: University Press of Kentucky, 1999), 162-66.

126. See James Leo Garrett, Jr., E. Glenn Hinson, and James E. Tull, *Are Southern Baptists Evangelicals?* (Macon: Mercer University Press, 1983), for the debate. Also see, E. Glenn Hinson, "Baptists and Evangelicals: What Is the Difference?," *Baptist History and Heritage,* XVI/2, (April, 1981), 20-32; David S. Dockery, ed., *Southern Baptists and American Evangelicals,* (Nashville: Broadman and Holman, 1993); and Wayne Flynt's review of the Dockery book in *Church History,* LXV/1, (March, 1996), 151-52.

127. See Garrett, etc., 119-20, for a reply to Valentine.

128. Timothy P. Weber, "Evangelicalism North and South," *Review and Expositor,* XCII/3, (Summer, 1995), 299-317.

129. David S. Dockery and Mark A. Noll, eds., *Southern Baptists and American Evangelicals,* (Nashville: Broadman and Holman, 1993), 78-99.

130. One of the most balanced works on the conservative resurgence is the work by Barry Hankins, *Uneasy in Babylon: Southern Baptist Conservatives and American Culture,* (Tuscaloosa and London: The University of Alabama Press, 2002). For a helpful review of the resurgence with perspectives from both sides, see *Baptist History and Heritage,* XXVIII/4, (October, 1993), entitled, "The Southern Baptist Convention, 1979–1993: What Happened and Why?" A helpful article on the literature of the resurgence is by

Barry Hankins, "History Is Written by the Losers: A Case Study in Historiography and Religious Conflict," *Fides et Historia,* XXIX/3, (Fall, 1997), 50-65.

131. For "inerrancy," see Hankins, *Uneasy in Babylon,* 4-6. For "freedom," see Walter B. Shurden, *The Baptist Identity: Four Fragile Freedoms,* (Macon, Georgia: Smyth and Helwys, 1993).

132. James E. Wood, Jr., "The New Religious Right and Its Implications for Southern Baptists," *Foundations,* XXV/2, (April–June, 1982), 153-66.

133. On issues of church and state, see Barry Hankins, "The Evangelical Accommodationism of Southern Baptist Convention Conservatives," *Baptist History and Heritage,* XXXIII/1, (Winter, 1998), 54-65, and Ronnie Prevost, "SBC Resolutions Regarding Religious Liberty and the Separation of Church and State, (1940–1997): A Fundamental Shift," *Baptist History and Heritage,* XXIV/2, (Spring, 1999), 73-94. For the status of ordained women in Southern Baptist life, see Sarah Frances Anders, "Baptist Women Walking Together in America, 1950–2000," *Baptist History and Heritage,* XL/3, (Summer–Fall, 2005), 8-16, and Eileen R. Campbell-Reed and Pamela R. Durso, *The State of Women in Baptist Life-2005,* (Atlanta: Baptist Women in Ministry, 2006).

134. For the alliance between Southern Baptists and Southern Republicans, see Oran P. Smith, *The Rise of Baptist Republicanism,* (New York and London: New York University Press, 1997).

135. For an account of the rising interest in Calvinism, see Timothy George, "Southern Baptist Ghosts," *First Things,* May, 1999, 18-24. Also see Collin Hansen, "Young, Restless, Reformed," *Christianity Today,* September, 2006, 32-38.

136. Samuel S. Hill, Jr., "The Southern Baptists: Need for Reformulation, Redirection," *Christian Century,* January 9, 1963, 39.

137. See T. Edwin Boling, "Denominational Sectarians," *Foundations,* XXI/4, (October–December, 1978), 365-72, where he uses the term for Southern Baptists outside the South.

138. For Southern Baptist relations with other bodies, see the thematic issue, "Southern Baptists and Relationship with Other Denominations," *Baptist History and Heritage,* XXV/3, (July, 1990), and Jerry M. Stubblefield, "Principle and Expediency: Southern Baptist Ecumenical Attitudes, 1901–1977," *Quarterly Review,* XL/1, (October–December, 1979), 62-73, and Garrett, etc., 104-11.

139. In 1937, however, the Executive Committee authorized J. R. Sampey and three others to serve as representatives at a Faith and Order Conference in Edinburgh and a Conference on Church, State, and Community in Oxford.

140. See Keith Bassham, "IBN Meeting Report," *Baptist Bible Tribune,* November, 2004, 6-8, and Elmer Towns, "The Founding of the International Baptist Network," *National Liberty Journal,* April, 2005, 19, 21.

141. *Time,* February 7, 2005, 35-45.

142. Bill J. Leonard, "A Crumbling Empire: Is There a Baptist Future in the South," in Corrie E. Norman and Don S. Armentrout, eds., *Religion in the Contemporary South,* (Knoxville: University of Tennessee Press, 2005), 75-87.

143. *Mission Handbook,* 2004–2006, 15, 34. Nashville, *The Tennessean,* August 27, 2006, 9A.

144. For the principles and work of the Alliance, see *Baptists Today,* November 12, 1992, 11, and September, 2002, 9.

145. For historical data on the CBF, see Pamela R. Durso, *A Short History of the Cooperative Baptist Fellowship Movement,* (Brentwood, TN: Baptist History and Heritage Society, 2006), and Walter B. Shurden, "The Cooperative Baptist Fellowship," in W. Glenn Jonas, Jr., *The Baptist River* (Macon: Mercer University Press, 2006), 243-68.

146. "Application for Membership in the Baptist World Alliance" (typed ms.).

147. See "CBF and the 'D-Word,'" *Baptists Today,* June, 2002, 10-1.

148. See *Baptists Today,* May, 2002, 12.

149. For historical accounts of moderate Baptist agencies, see Walter B. Shurden, ed., *The Struggle for the Soul of the SBC,* (Macon: Mercer University Press, 1993).

150. For a description of Mainstream Baptists, see David R. Currie, "The Current Role of Mainstream Baptists," *The Baptist Studies Bulletin,* II/6 (June, 2003), 3-5, and John Pierce, "'Loose' Mainstream Group to Focus on Religious Liberty," *Baptists Today,* February, 2004, 16-17.

151. For questions on the future of moderates, see *Baptists Today,* May, 2002, 11, and August, 2002, 10-11. Also see Jim Jones, "Moderates Unite?," *Christian Century,* August 14-27, 2002, 30-34.

Chapter 6

152. Since Southern Fundamentalists, by and large, do not collect the memberships of their churches, it has been difficult to gain their statistics except by estimate. With the help of its state representatives, the author obtained for the *Religious Congregations and Membership* study, 2000, membership estimates of the BBFI. The survey produced an average local

church membership of between 159 and 160. The figure of 159 was then used as an estimate of the congregations of the other fellowships. Many fundamentalist churches are related to one or more fellowships and therefore multiple memberships were taken into account to get as correct an estimate as possible.

153. For an insightful article on Southern Fundamentalists, see Bill J. Leonard, "Independent Baptists: From Sectarian Minority to 'Moral Majority,'" *Church History,* LVI/4 (December, 1987), 504-17.

154. Billy Vick Bartlett, *A History of Baptist Separatism,* (Springfield, MO: Roark & Son Printing, 1972), 68.

155. *Mission Handbook,* 2004–2006, 90-92, 291, and IBFI *Directory*, 1998–2000, 60-62.

156. Two excellent critical studies of Norris are C. Allyn Russell, "J. Frank Norris: Violent Fundamentalist," *Southwestern Historical Quarterly,* LXXV/3 (January, 1972), 271-302, which was also published in the author's book, *Voices of American Fundamentalism,* (Philadelphia: Westminster Press, 1976), 20-46; and Barry Hankins, *God's Rascal: J. Frank Norris and the Beginnings of Southern Fundamentalism,* (Lexington: The University Press of Kentucky, 1996). Two articles by Leon McBeth dealing with Norris from a critical Southern Baptist viewpoint are "John Franklyn Norris: Texas Tornado," and "Two Ways To Be Baptist," *Baptist History and Heritage,* XXXII/2, (April, 1997), 23-38, 39-53. Among former Norris colleagues who have written on Norris, one might consult E. Ray Tatum, *Conquest or Failure? Biography of J. Frank Norris,* (Dallas: Baptist Historical Foundation, 1966).

157. See Ed Dobson and Jerry Falwell, *The Fundamentalist Phenomenon,* (Grand Rapids: Baker Book House, 1986, 2nd ed.), for neo-fundamentalist views. Also see Dobson's book, *In Search of Unity: An Appeal to Fundamentalists and Evangelicals,* (Nashville: Thomas Nelson, 1985). For a rejoinder to the second book, see Ernest Pickering, "Should Fundamentalists Seek Closer Ties With Evangelicals?," in *Sword of the Lord,* April 18, 1986, 14-20. Also see Curtis Hutson, editor of the *Sword of the Lord,* in his booklet, *Should Independent Baptists Reunite With the Southern Baptist Convention?*, and James O. Combs, editor of the *Bible Baptist Tribune*, "Should We Join the Southern Baptists?," in the *BBT*, September, 4, 1991, 13, for additional negative responses.

158. *The Fundamentalist*, May–June, 2003, 2; *Baptist Bible Tribune*, November, 2004, 6-8.

159. *National Liberty Journal*, April, 2005, 19, 21. Randy Ray, "A Great Awakening," in Neal Weaver and James Combs, eds., *Our Biblical Baptist Heritage,* (Shreveport: Eagle Publishers, 2004), 206-13.

160. For an account of the World Baptist Fellowship from a Southern Baptist point of view, see Wilburn S. Taylor, "World Baptist Fellowship," *Quarterly Review*, XIX/2, (April–June, 1959), 35-39.

161. For Norris's relationship to the SBC, see E. G. Toulouse, "A Case Study in Schism: J. Frank Norris and the Southern Baptist Convention," *Foundations*, XXIV/1 (January–March, 1981), 32-53, and Bobby D. Compton, "J. Frank Norris and Southern Baptists," *Review and Expositor,* LXXIX/1, (Winter, 1992), 63-84.

162. Taylor, 38. Patsy S. Ledbetter, *Crusade for the Faith: The Protestant Fundamentalist Movement in Texas,* (Ph.D. dissertation, North Texas State University, 1975), 208-209.

163. *The Fundamentalist,* November 4, 1932, 1,3; November 11, 1932, 3; and January 27, 1933, 1.

164. *The Fundamentalist*, January 28, 1938, 1; January 21, 1944, 1; January 9, 1948, 1, 3, 7; January 2, 1950, 3; and November 17, 1950, 1, 3. See Billy Vick Bartlett, *A History of Baptist Separatism,* (Springfield, MO: Roark & Son, 1972), 25-30, for the early years of the World Baptist Fellowship but with an incorrect date of its founding. Also see an informal account of the beginnings of the WBF by Harvey H. Spring in *World Baptist Fellowship: Minutes, By-Laws, and Doctrinal Statement,* (Fort Worth: World Baptist Fellowship, 1952).

165. Bible Baptist Seminary, *Twentieth Anniversary* (booklet).

166. D. G. Reid, "J. Frank Norris," *Dictionary of Christianity in America*, 828, and Taylor, 38-39.

167. On the separation from the viewpoint of the BBFI, see Billy Vick Bartlett, *A History of Baptist Separatism*. For early accounts of the BBFI, see articles in the volume, *What God Hath Wrought!,* II, (Springfield, MO: Baptist Bible Fellowship, 1957), and Marjorie Moore Armstrong, "Baptist Bible Fellowship," *Quarterly Review,* XIX/2, (April–June, 1959), 31-34.

168. For a biography of Vick, see Mike Randall, *G. B. Vick* (Springfield, MO: Baptist Bible College, 1993).

169. Randall, 24, 118-19.

170. Bartlett, 64-68.

171. *What God Hath Wrought!,* 4-5, 25ff.

172. *Baptist Bible Tribune*, January 15, 1996, 9.

173. *Mission Handbook,* 2004–2006, 90.

174. Randall, 102. Norman W. Cox, "Baptist Bodies in the United States," *Quarterly Review,* XIX/2, (April–June, 1959), 7.

175. *Baptist Bible Tribune,* September 4, 1991, 15. For information on the large Sunday schools among Independent Baptists, see the surveys in *Christian*

Life, beginning in 1968 and into the '70s, and books by Elmer L. Towns, *The Ten Largest Sunday Schools and What Makes Them Grow,* (Grand Rapids: Baker Book House, 1969), and *America's Fastest Growing Churches,* (Nashville: Impact Books, 1972).

176. *Baptist Bible Tribune,* January 15, 1996, 29.

177. *Baptist Bible Tribune,* September 4, 1991, 13.

178. *Baptists Bible Tribune,* January 25, 1974, 4.

179. For problems of independent churches, see Elmer L. Towns, "The Perils and Impact of Independent Churches," *Christianity Today,* January 1, 1982, 32-33. See Fenlason, a northern fundamentalist, in his work, *An Insider Looks Back,* 72, and Albert W. Wardin, Jr., *Baptists in Oregon,* (Portland: Judson Baptist College, 1969), 565-67, for critiques of BBFI work in the West for lack of persistence and failure to adapt to Western culture.

180. For Falwell's career, see Jerry Falwell and Elmer Towns, *Church Aflame,* (Nashville: Impact Books, 1971); *Christianity Today,* December 9, 1956, 62-67; and Susan Friend Harding: *The Book of Jerry Falwell: Fundamentalist Language and Politics,* (Princeton: Princeton University Press, 2000). For information on the Liberty Baptist Fellowship, see *National Liberty Journal,* February, 2007, 2.

181. For the ministry of Hyles, see John N. Vaughn, *The World's Twenty Largest Churches,* (Grand Rapids: Baker Book House, 1984), 101-108.

182. Telephone conversation with Duke Hergatt, Halfmoon, New York, March, 2004.

183. See Mr. and Mrs. Earl K. Oldham, *USS-WBF: Sail On,* ([Grand Prairie, Texas]: Authors, c. 1992), 338-46, for an account of the separation from the viewpoint of adherents of the WBF.

184. Raymond W. Barber, *J. Frank Norris: "A Man Among Men,"* (Fort Worth: Author, 1986), 17.

185. *Baptist Bible Tribune,* April 15, 1998, 5.

186. For the ministry of the Highland Park Baptist Church, see "Highland Park Baptist Church," in John N. Vaughn, *The World's Twenty Largest Churches,* (Grand Rapids: Baker Book House, 1984), 109-16.

187. For Roberson's relations to Southern Baptists and the formation of the Southwide Baptist Fellowship, see Kenneth C. Hubbard, *Anti-Conventionism in the Southern Baptist Convention, 1940–1962,* (Th.D. dissertation, Southwestern Baptist Theological Seminary, 1968), 143, 203, 252-54; William R. Glass, "From Southern Baptist to Fundamentalist: The Case of I. W. Rogers and The Faith, 1943-57," *American Baptist Quarterly,* XIV/3 (September, 1995), 250-54; "The South Carolina Baptist Fellowship" and "Southwide Baptist Fellowship," *Encyclopedia of American Religions,* I, 380-81; "Southwide Baptist Fellowship (SBF)," in George W. Dollar, *A History of Fundamentalism,* (Greenville, SC: Bob Jones University Press, 1973), 242-44; and "The History of Southwide Baptist Fellowship," in Southwide Baptist Fellowship *Directories*.

188. *Dollar,* 243.

189. For the origins of BIMI, see the pamphlet, Tom Freeney, *Beginning of Miracles,* c. 1976.

190. *Mission Handbook,* 2004–2006, 91-92.

Chapter 7

191. For material on Landmarkism, see High Wamble, "Landmarkism: Doctrinaire Ecclesiology Among Baptists," *Church History,* XXXIII/4, (December, 1964), 429-47; Harold S. Smith, *A Critical Analysis of the Theology of J. R. Graves,* (Th.D. dissertation, Southern Baptist Theological Seminary, 1966); and James E. Tull, *A Study of Southern Baptist Landmarkism in the Light of Historical Baptist Ecclesiology,* (Ph.D. dissertation, Columbia University, 1960, and New York: Arno Press, 1980).

192. For histories of the American Baptist Association and its antecedents, see Conrad N. Glover and Austin T. Powers, *The American Baptist Association, 1924–1974,* (Texarkana, Texas: Bogard Press, 1979), and Robert Ashcraft, ed., *History of the American Baptist Association,* (Texarkana, Texas: Baptist Sunday School Committee of the American Baptist Association, 2000). For an account of the ABA by a Southern Baptist and minimizing the differences between the ABA and SBC, see Erwin L. McDonald, "American Baptist Association," *Quarterly Review,* XIX/2, (April–June, 1959), 10-18).

193. For the career of Bogard, see L. D. Foreman and Alta Payne, *The Life and Works of Benjamin Marcus Bogard,* (Little Rock: Authors, 1965–1966), two volumes.

194. *Religious Bodies: 1926,* II, 224-25.

195. *Yearbook of American Churches,* 1949, 12.

196. For the division from the view of the ABA, see A. J. Kirkland, *Why Association Baptists Divided and Other Vital Issues,* (Henderson, TX: Author, 1961), and Ashcraft, 297-322.

197. *Religious Congregations and Membership in the United States,* 2000, 1, 38. Robert L. Vaughn, "American Baptist Association: A Survey of Its Churches and Associations," (ms.), 25.

198. For a history of the BMA, see John W. Duggar, *The Baptist Missionary Association,* (Texarkana, Texas: Baptist Publishing House, 1988). For the division from the viewpoint of the BMA, see *The Lakeland Review,* (Little Rock: Baptist Publications Committee

of the North American Baptist Association, 1950), and Duggar, 31-65. For a conciliatory Southern Baptist view of the BMA, see Don Hook, "North American Baptist Association," *Quarterly Review*, XIX/2, (April–June, 1959), 19-23.

199. See the booklet from the BMA, *Fifty Days of Prayer and Giving, 2005,* for the mission work of the BMA.

200 *Religious Congregations and Membership in the United States*, 2000, 1, 38. Vaughn, "American Baptist Association," 25.

201. *Religious Congregations and Membership in the United States,* 2000, 3, 24, 28.

202. Robert L. Vaughn, "Listing of Unaffiliated Independent Landmark Baptist Churches," (ms.), 2001.

Chapter 8

203. *Mission Handbook,* 2004–2006, 167.

204. *Mission Handbook,* 2004–2006, 164.

205. Keith Kenemer at Randall House Publications, Nashville, provided the author in 2005 much helpful information on the members of the National Convention of Free Will Baptists.

Chapter 9

206. For a discussion of common characteristics of Old-Time Baptists, see Clifford A. Grammich, Jr., *Local Baptists, Local Politics,* (Knoxville: University of Tennessee Press, 1999), 93-111.

207. See Appendix C, 449.

208. "United Baptists Today," (www.unitedbaptists.org) lists forty-four associations including: the National Association but excluding Cumberland River Association. "United Baptists Today" also lists Ellijay, Jasper, and Pleasant Valley Associations, which do not carry the name "United Baptist," and King's River Regular United Association that this volume includes with Old Missionary Baptists.

Chapter 10

209. A very helpful study of Primitive, Old Regular, and Regular Baptists in Appalachia is the work by Howard Dorgan, *Giving Glory to God in Appalachia,* (Knoxville: University of Tennessee Press, 1987), in which he also includes: Missionary, Free Will, and Union Baptists (whom he now considers Regular Baptists).

210. See Julietta Haynes, *The History of the Primitive Baptists, (*Ph.D. dissertation, University of Texas, 1959), 244-57, on the controversy between Old Line and Predestinarian Primitive Baptists.

Chapter 11

(No endnotes)

Chapter 12

211. For the currrent spread of Calvinism among Baptists and other evangelicals, see Collin Hansen, "Young, Restless, Reformed," *Christianity Today*, September, 2006, 32-38.

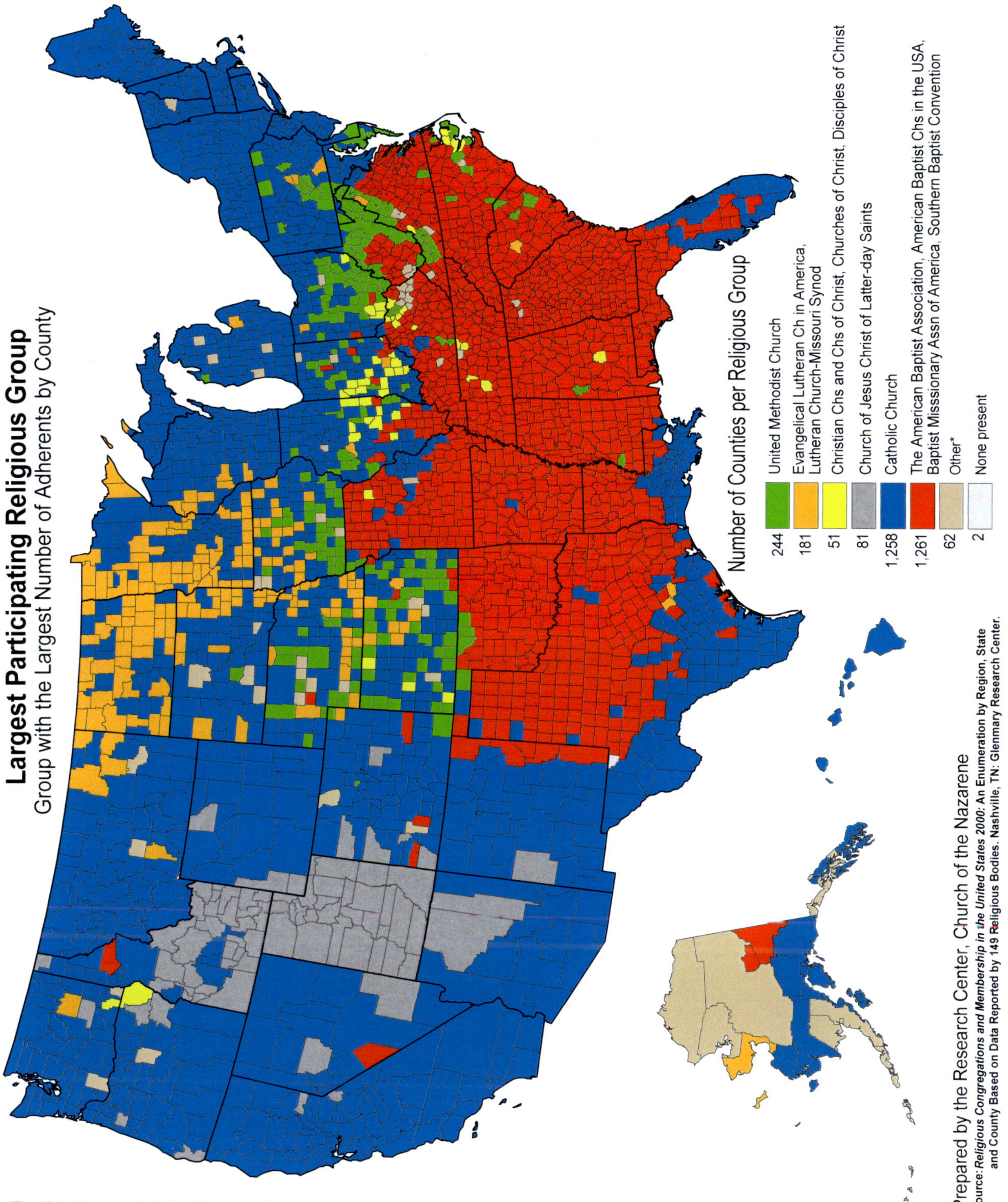

*The "Other" category includes 30 groups with less than 10 counties each.

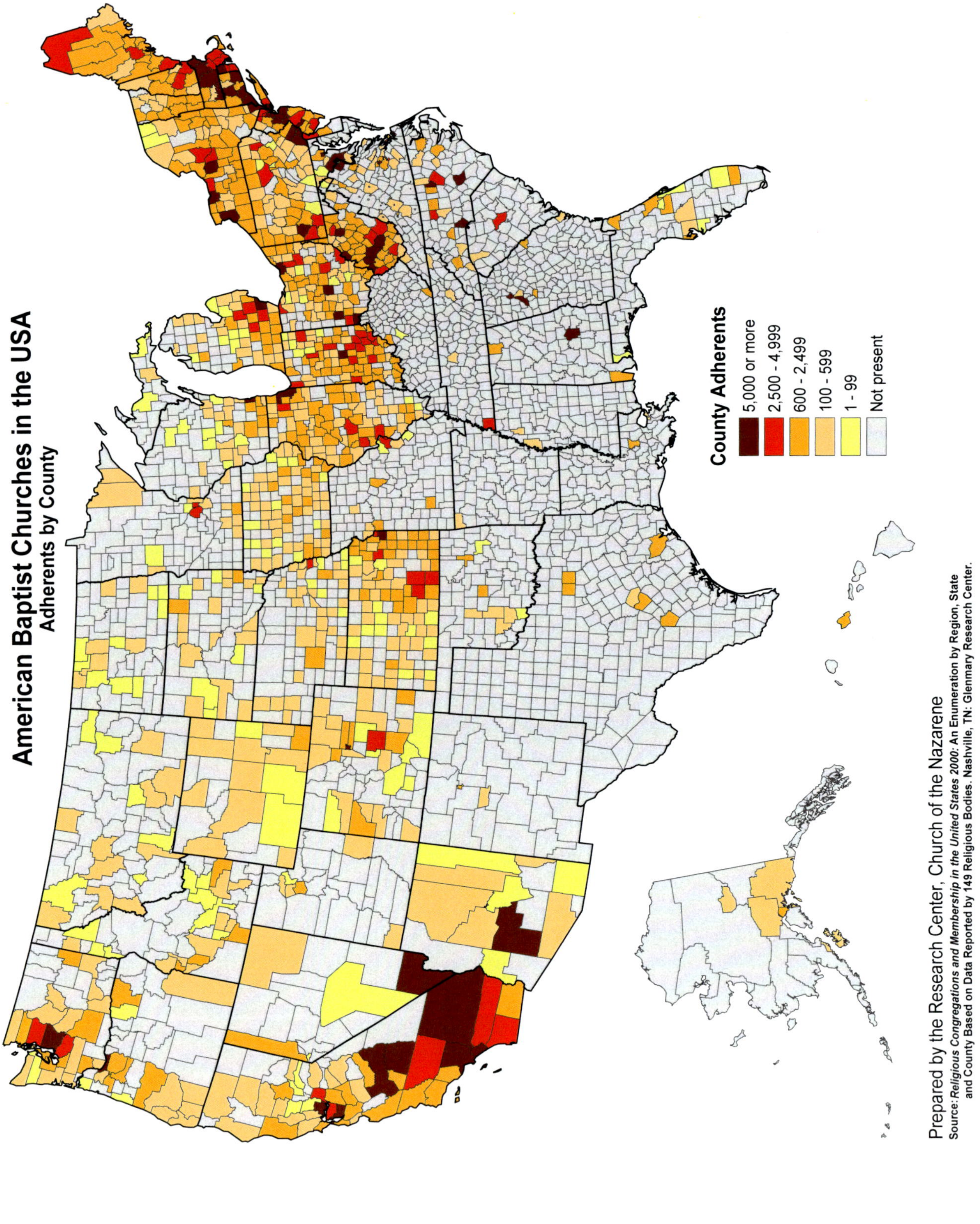
American Baptist Churches in the USA
Adherents by County
County Adherents
5,000 or more
2,500 - 4,999
600 - 2,499
100 - 599
1 - 99
Not present
Prepared by the Research Center, Church of the Nazarene
Source: Religious Congregations and Membership in the United States 2000: An Enumeration by Region, State and County Based on Data Reported by 149 Religious Bodies. Nashville, TN: Glenmary Research Center.

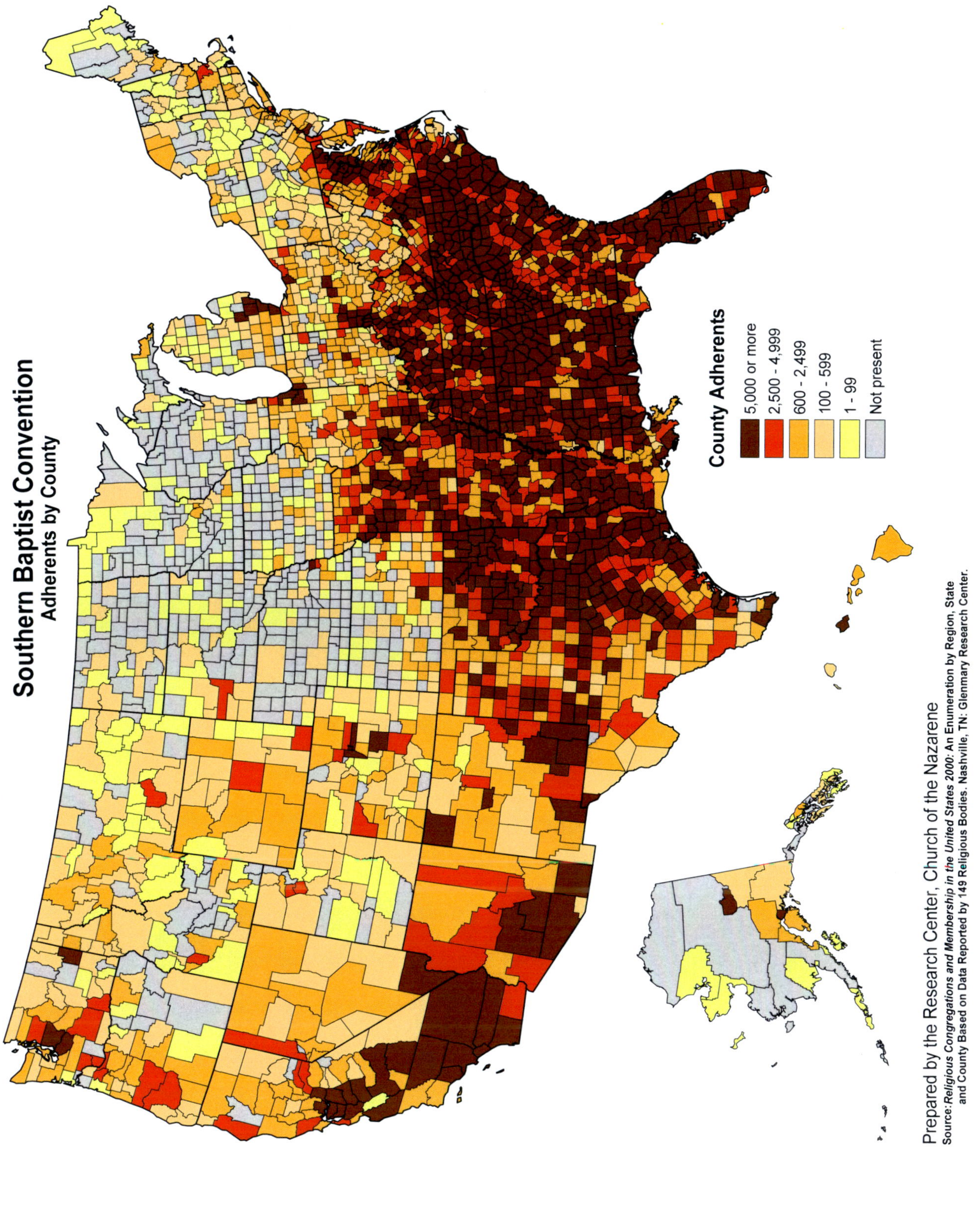
Southern Baptist Convention
Adherents by County
County Adherents
5,000 or more
2,500 - 4,999
600 - 2,499
100 - 599
1 - 99
Not present
Prepared by the Research Center, Church of the Nazarene
Source: Religious Congregations and Membership in the United States 2000: An Enumeration by Region, State
and County Based on Data Reported by 149 Religious Bodies. Nashville, TN: Glenmary Research Center.

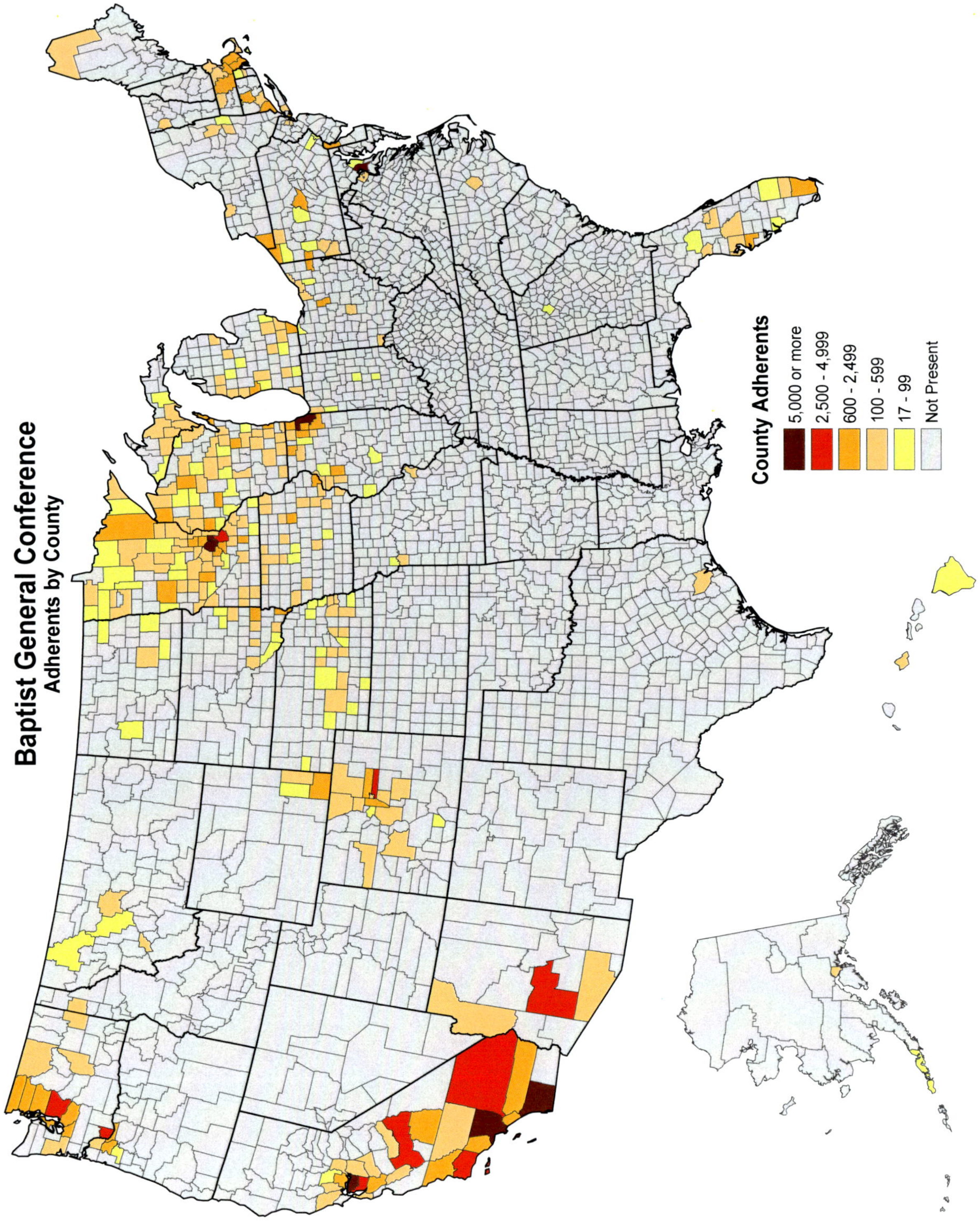

Prepared by the Research Center, Church of the Nazarene

Source: ***Religious Congregations and Membership in the United States 2000:*** **An Enumeration by Region, State and County Based on Data Reported by 149 Religious Bodies. Nashville, TN: Glenmary Research Center.**

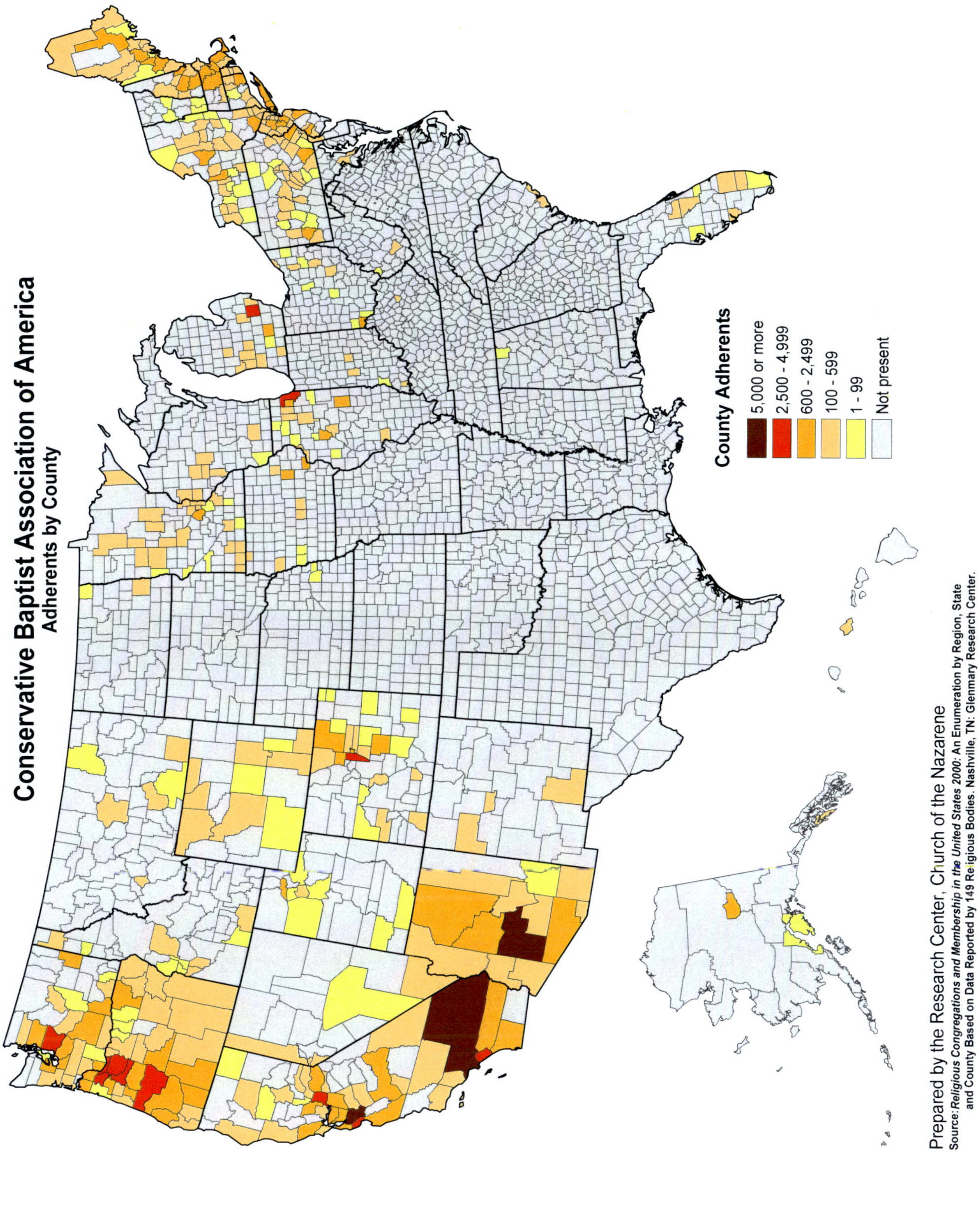
Conservative Baptist Association of America
Adherents by County
County Adherents
5,000 or more
2,500 - 4,999
600 - 2,499
100 - 599
1 - 99
Not present
Prepared by the Research Center, Church of the Nazarene
Source: Religious Congregations and Membership in the United States 2000: An Enumeration by Region, State and County Based on Data Reported by 149 Religious Bodies. Nashville, TN: Glenmary Research Center.

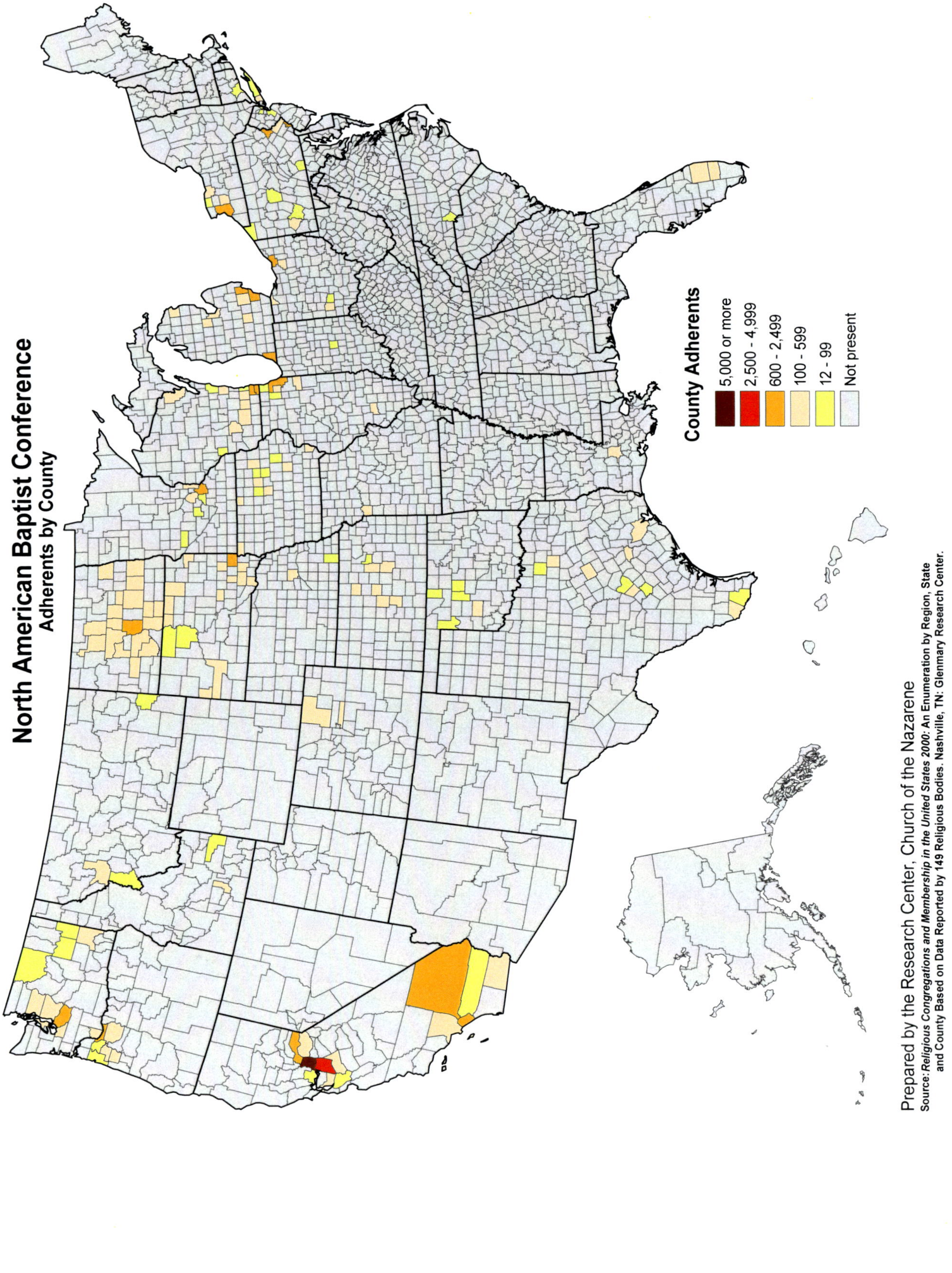
North American Baptist Conference
Adherents by County
County Adherents
5,000 or more
2,500 - 4,999
600 - 2,499
100 - 599
12 - 99
Not present
Prepared by the Research Center, Church of the Nazarene
Source: Religious Congregations and Membership in the United States 2000: An Enumeration by Region, State and County Based on Data Reported by 149 Religious Bodies. Nashville, TN: Glenmary Research Center.

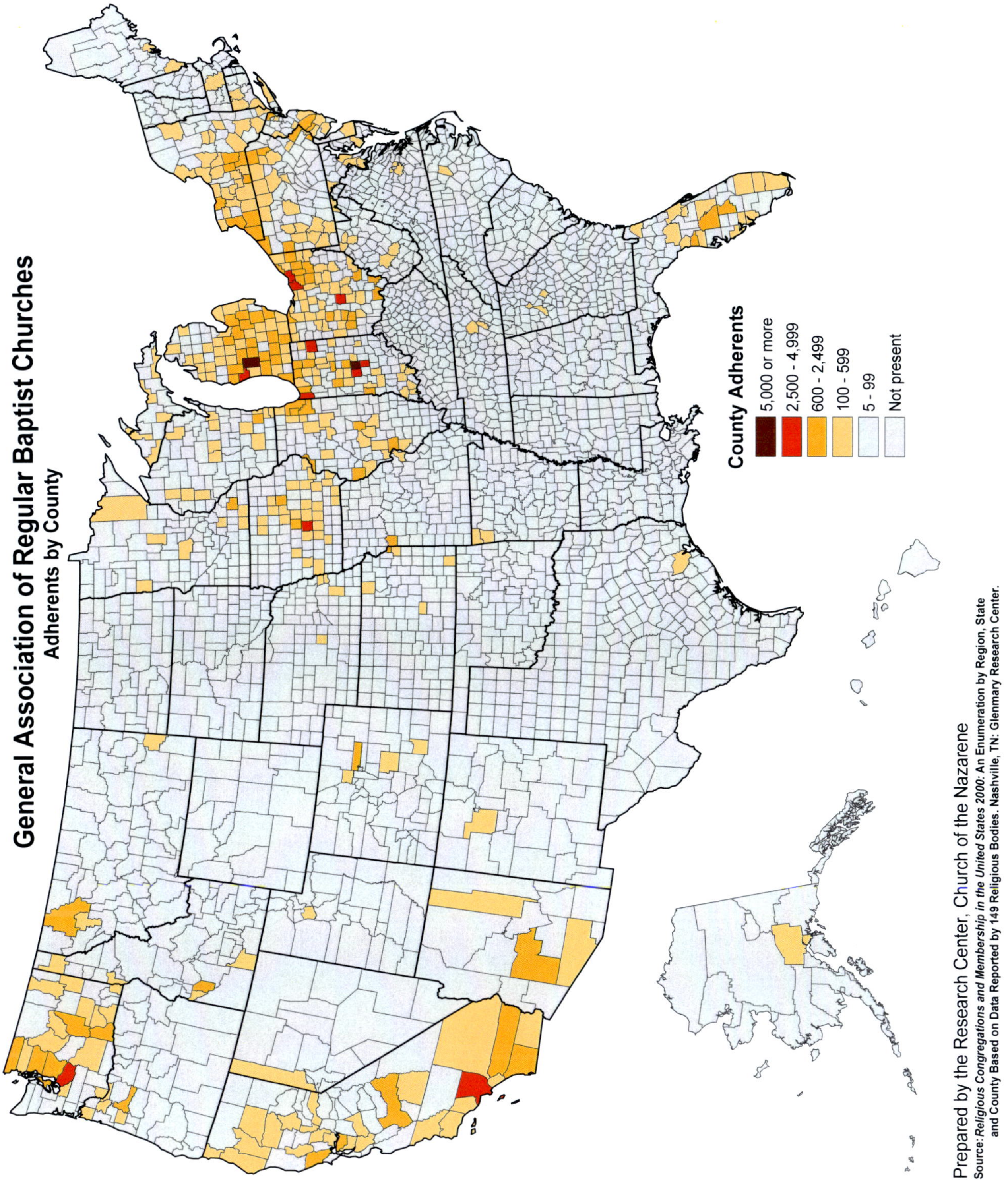
General Association of Regular Baptist Churches
Adherents by County
County Adherents
5,000 or more
2,500 - 4,999
600 - 2,499
100 - 599
5 - 99
Not present
Prepared by the Research Center, Church of the Nazarene
Source: Religious Congregations and Membership in the United States 2000: An Enumeration by Region, State
and County Based on Data Reported by 149 Religious Bodies. Nashville, TN: Glenmary Research Center.

New Testament Association of Independent Baptist Churches and other Fundamental Baptist Associations/Fellowships
Adherents by County

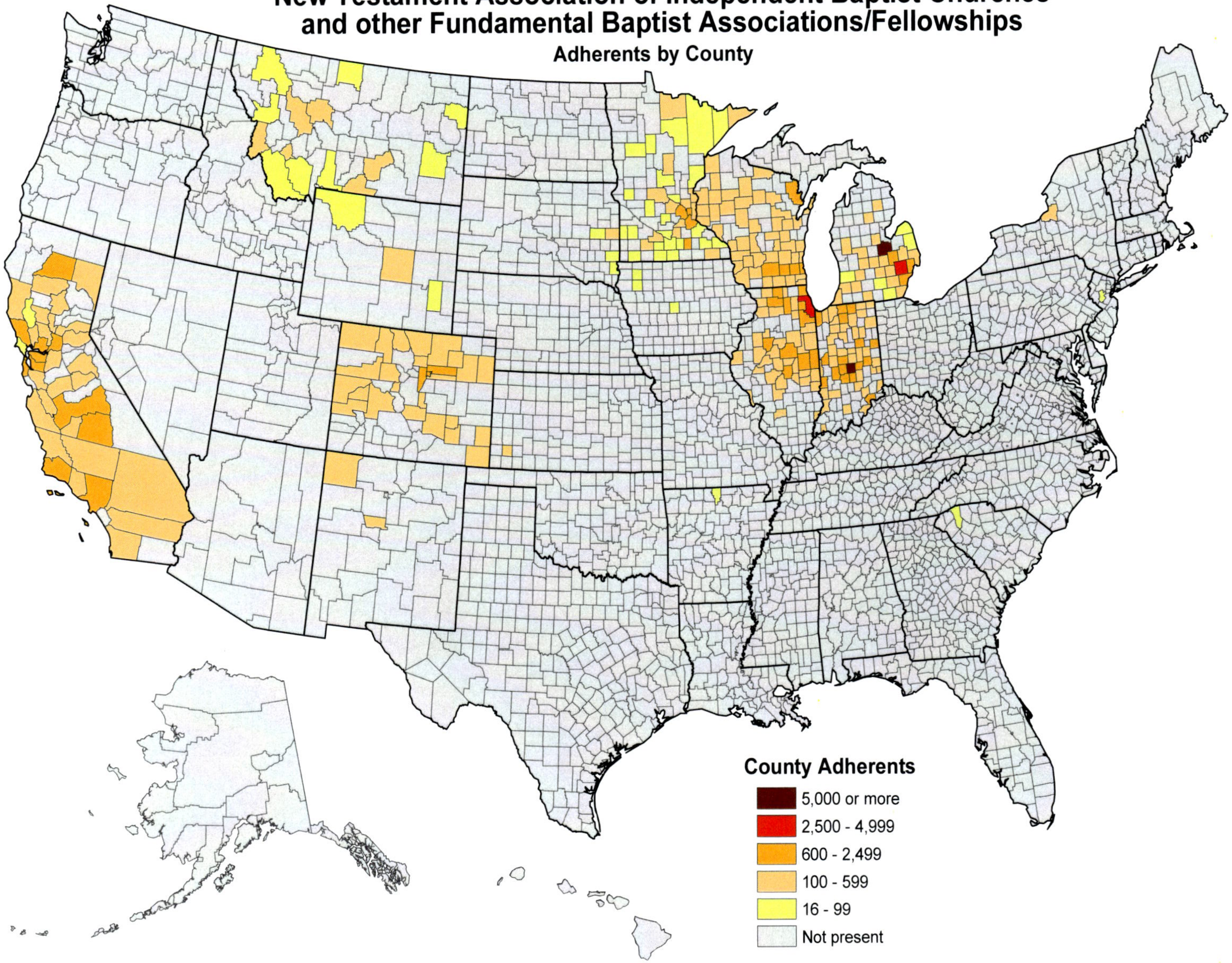

Prepared by the Research Center, Church of the Nazarene
Source: *Religious Congregations and Membership in the United States 2000:* An Enumeration by Region, State and County Based on Data Reported by 149 Religious Bodies. Nashville, TN: Glenmary Research Center.

Baptist Bible Fellowship International

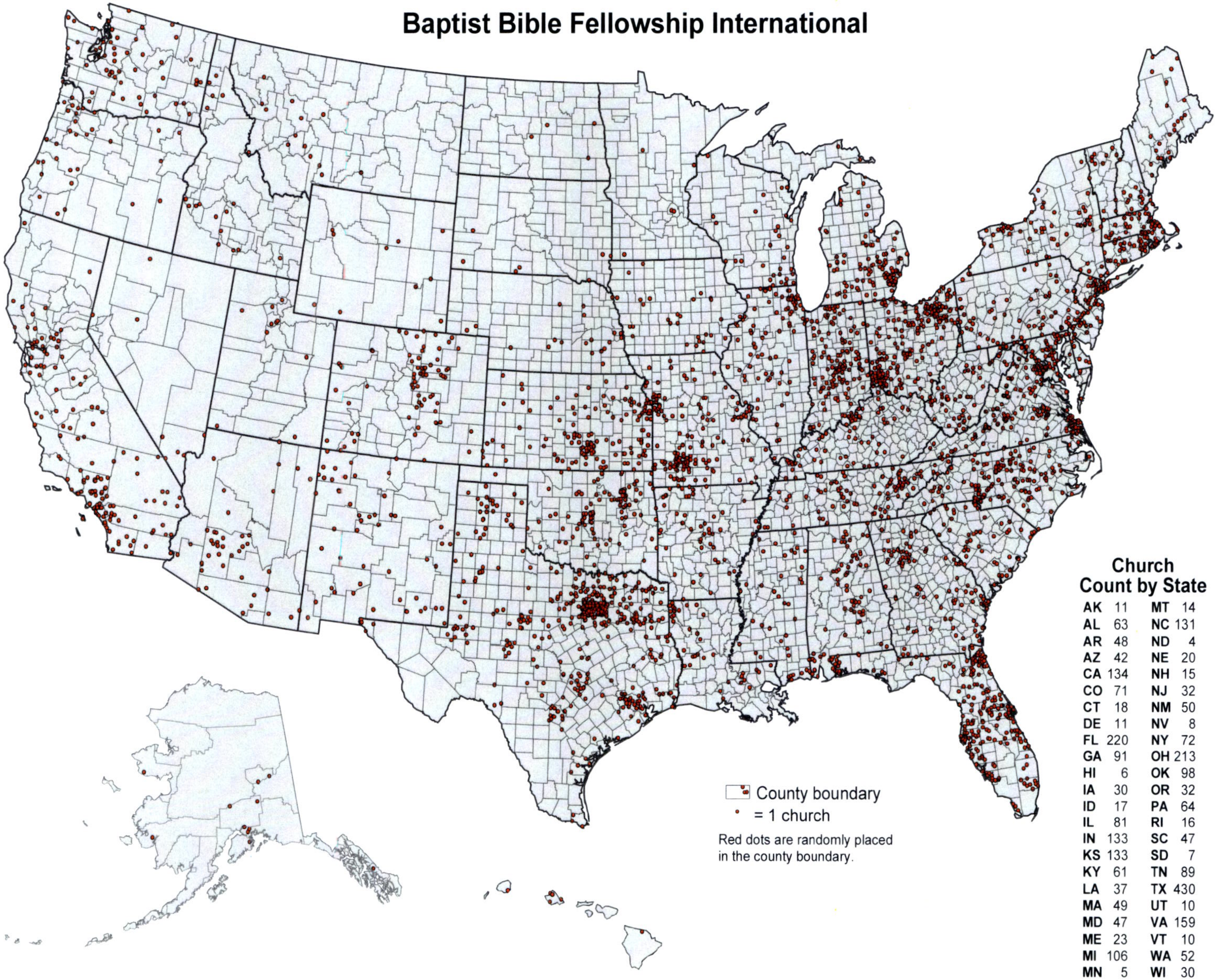

County boundary
= 1 church

Red dots are randomly placed in the county boundary.

Church Count by State

AK	11	**MT**	14
AL	63	**NC**	131
AR	48	**ND**	4
AZ	42	**NE**	20
CA	134	**NH**	15
CO	71	**NJ**	32
CT	18	**NM**	50
DE	11	**NV**	8
FL	220	**NY**	72
GA	91	**OH**	213
HI	6	**OK**	98
IA	30	**OR**	32
ID	17	**PA**	64
IL	81	**RI**	16
IN	133	**SC**	47
KS	133	**SD**	7
KY	61	**TN**	89
LA	37	**TX**	430
MA	49	**UT**	10
MD	47	**VA**	159
ME	23	**VT**	10
MI	106	**WA**	52
MN	5	**WI**	30
MO	149	**WV**	51
MS	39	**WY**	10

Prepared by the Research Center, Church of the Nazarene
Source: 1999-2000 Baptist Bible Fellowship International directory

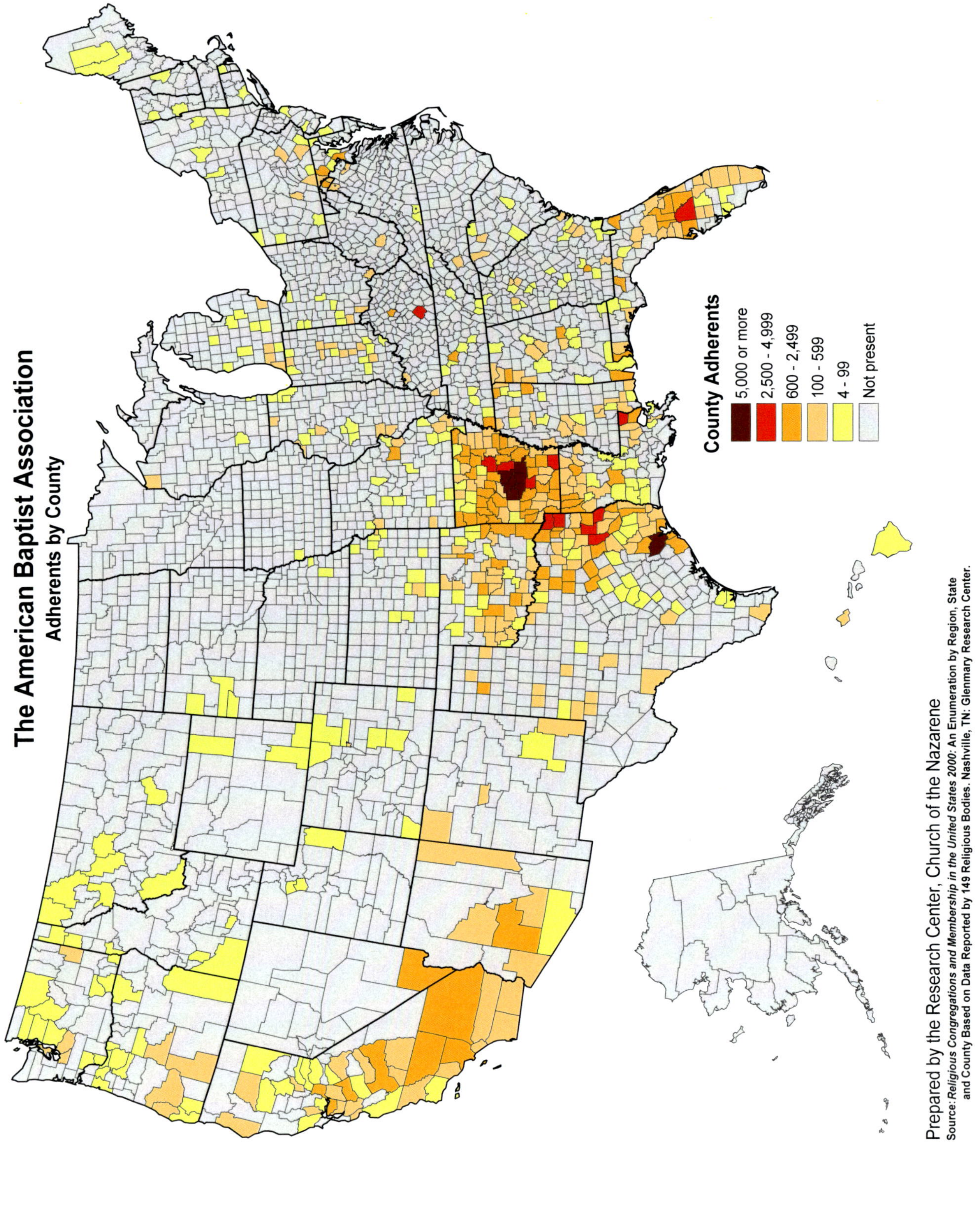
The American Baptist Association
Adherents by County
County Adherents
5,000 or more
2,500 - 4,999
600 - 2,499
100 - 599
4 - 99
Not present
Prepared by the Research Center, Church of the Nazarene
Source: Religious Congregations and Membership in the United States 2000: An Enumeration by Region, State
and County Based on Data Reported by 149 Religious Bodies. Nashville, TN: Glenmary Research Center.

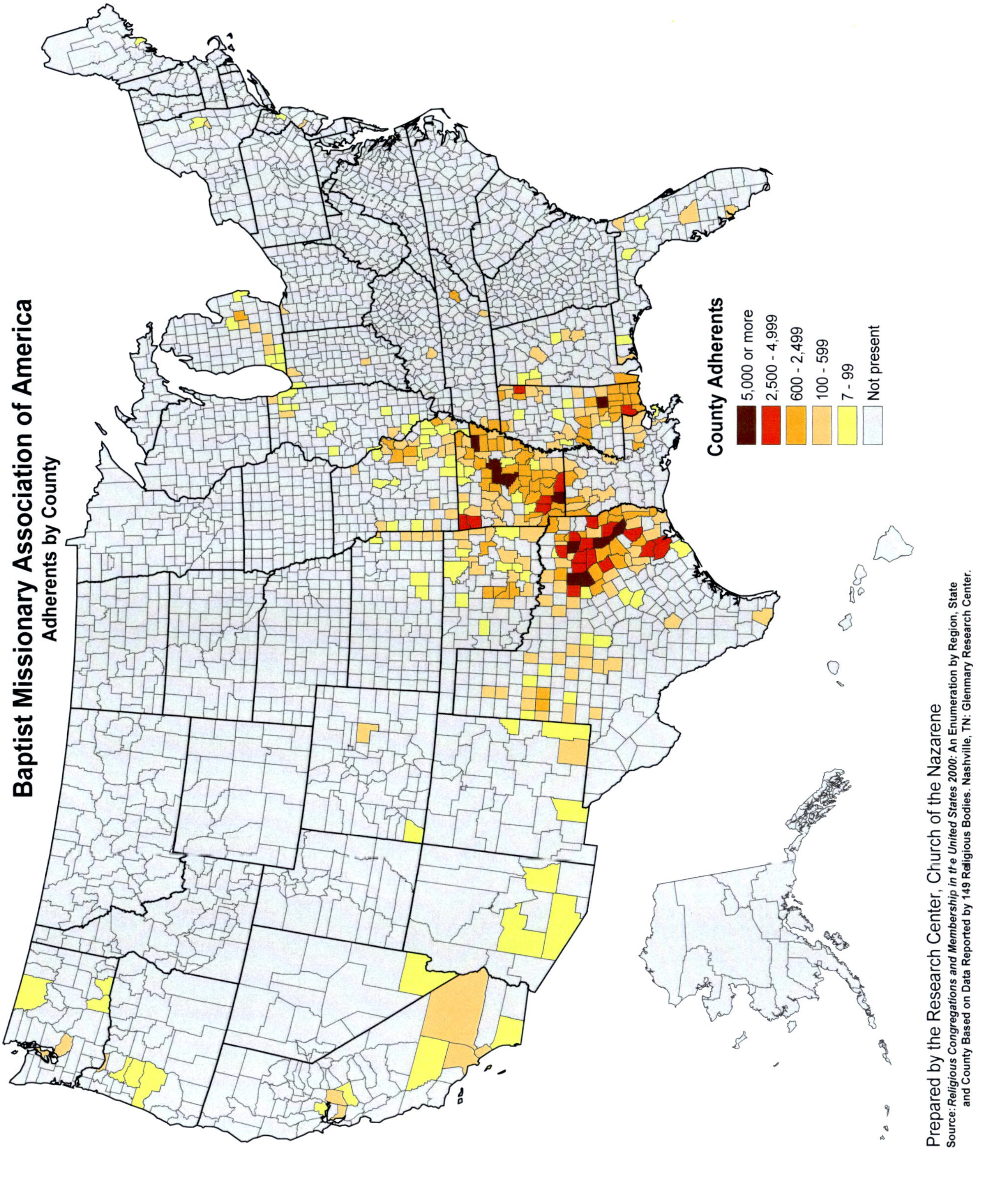
Baptist Missionary Association of America
Adherents by County
County Adherents
5,000 or more
2,500 - 4,999
600 - 2,499
100 - 599
7 - 99
Not present
Prepared by the Research Center, Church of the Nazarene
Source: Religious Congregations and Membership in the United States 2000: An Enumeration by Region, State and County Based on Data Reported by 149 Religious Bodies. Nashville, TN: Glenmary Research Center.

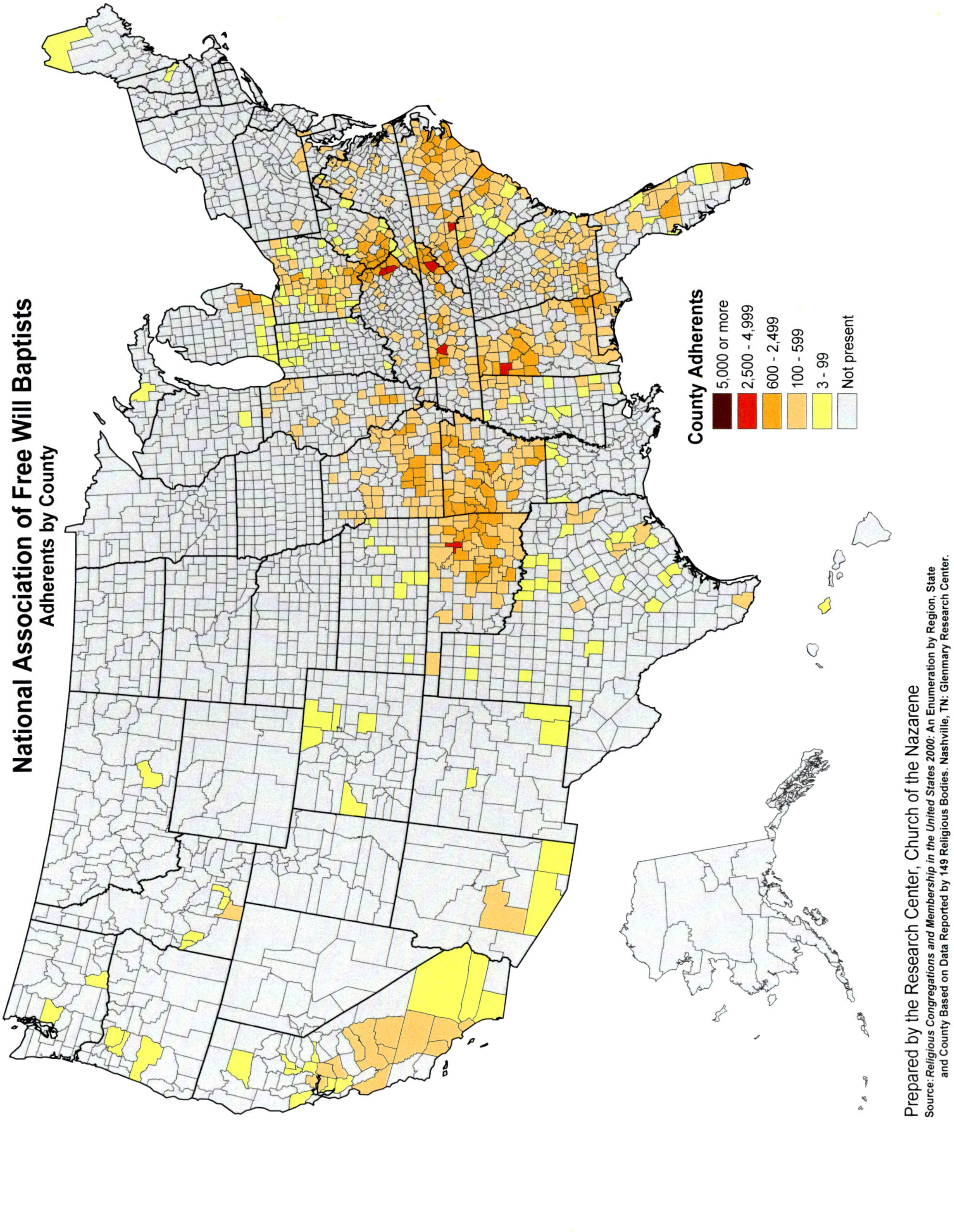
National Association of Free Will Baptists
Adherents by County
County Adherents
5,000 or more
2,500 - 4,999
600 - 2,499
100 - 599
3 - 99
Not present
Prepared by the Research Center, Church of the Nazarene
Source: *Religious Congregations and Membership in the United States 2000*: An Enumeration by Region, State and County Based on Data Reported by 149 Religious Bodies. Nashville, TN: Glenmary Research Center.

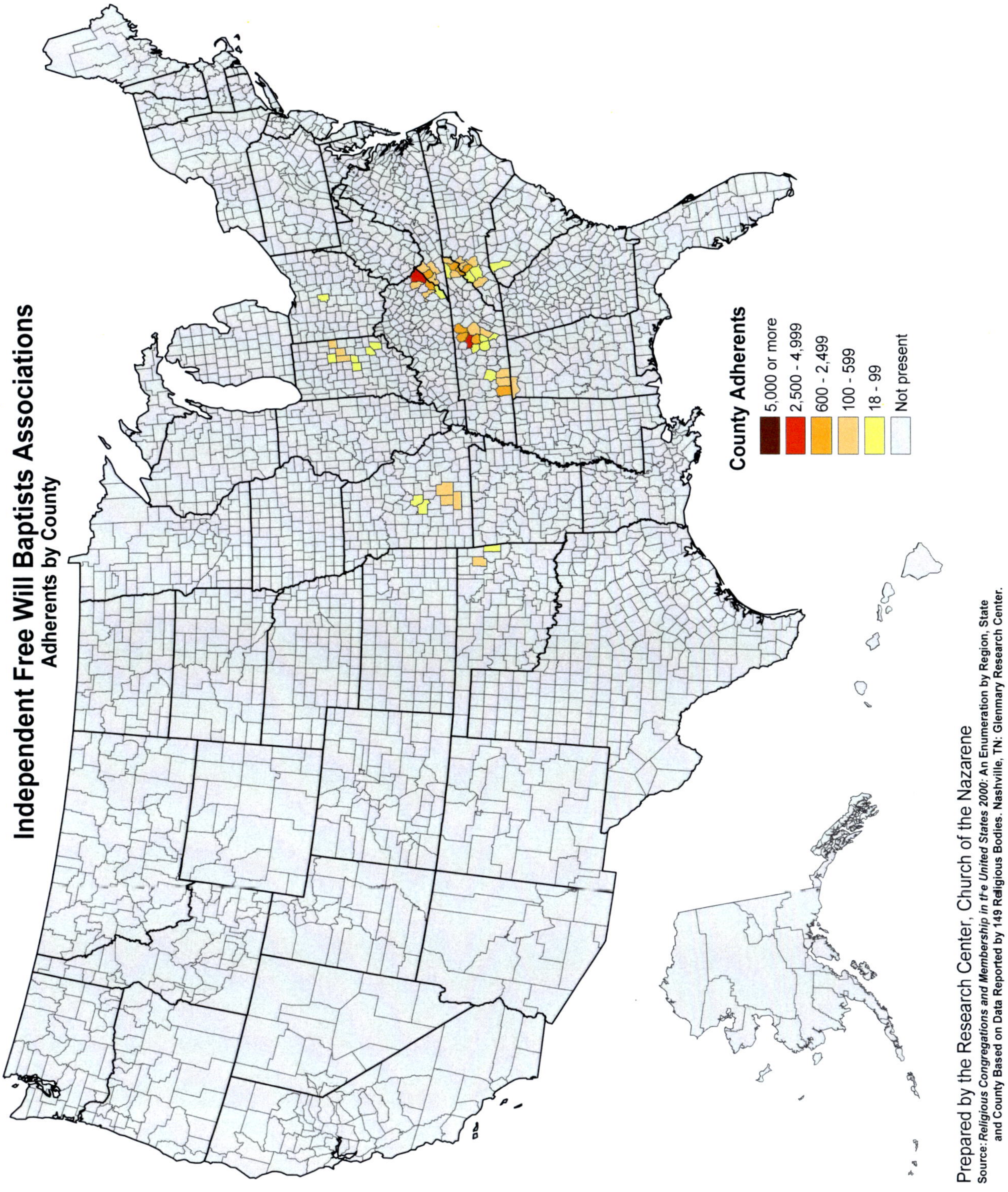
Independent Free Will Baptists Associations
Adherents by County
County Adherents
5,000 or more
2,500 - 4,999
600 - 2,499
100 - 599
18 - 99
Not present
Prepared by the Research Center, Church of the Nazarene
Source: Religious Congregations and Membership in the United States 2000: An Enumeration by Region, State and County Based on Data Reported by 149 Religious Bodies. Nashville, TN: Glenmary Research Center.

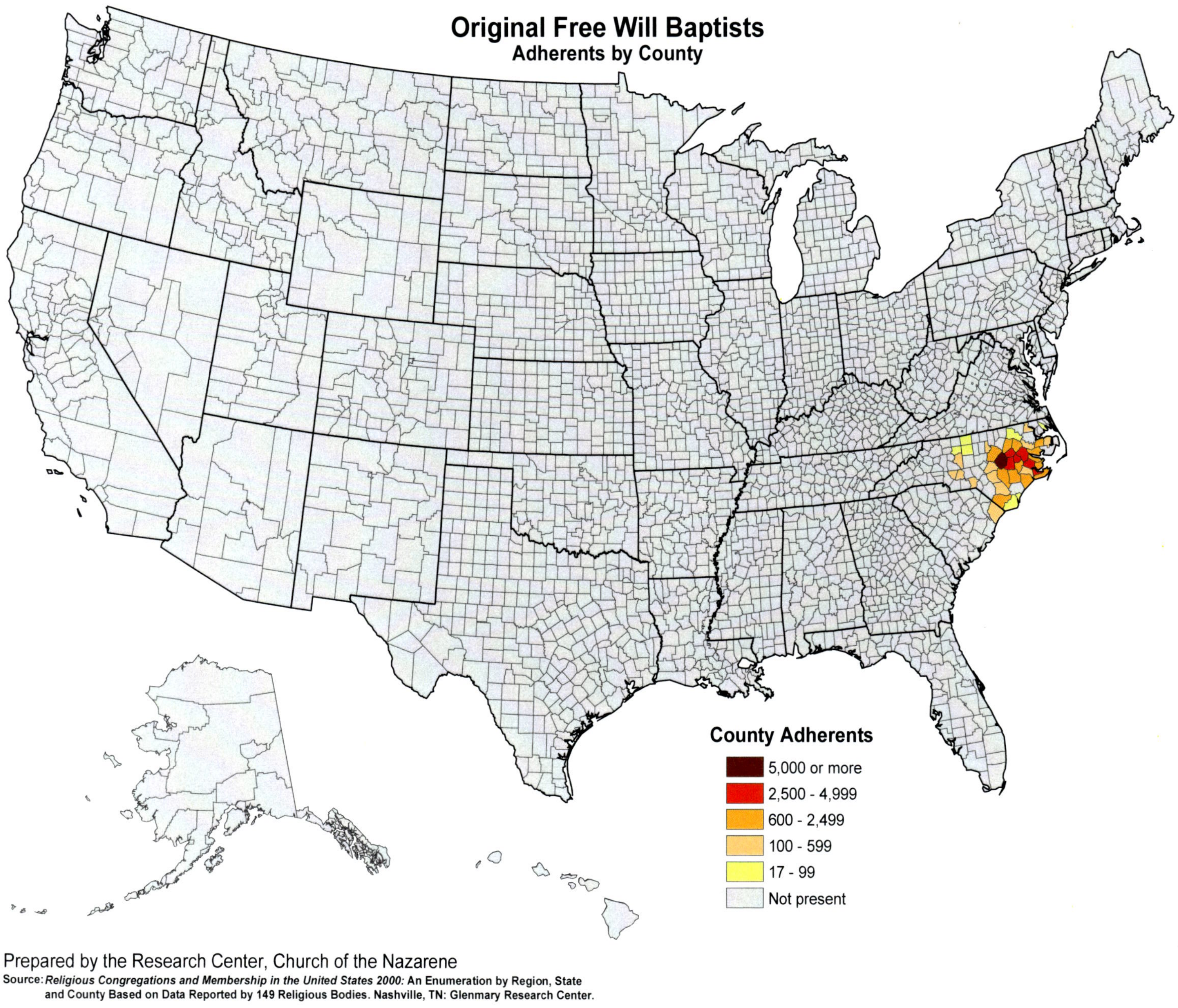
Original Free Will Baptists
Adherents by County
County Adherents
5,000 or more
2,500 - 4,999
600 - 2,499
100 - 599
17 - 99
Not present
Prepared by the Research Center, Church of the Nazarene
Source: *Religious Congregations and Membership in the United States 2000:* An Enumeration by Region, State and County Based on Data Reported by 149 Religious Bodies. Nashville, TN: Glenmary Research Center.

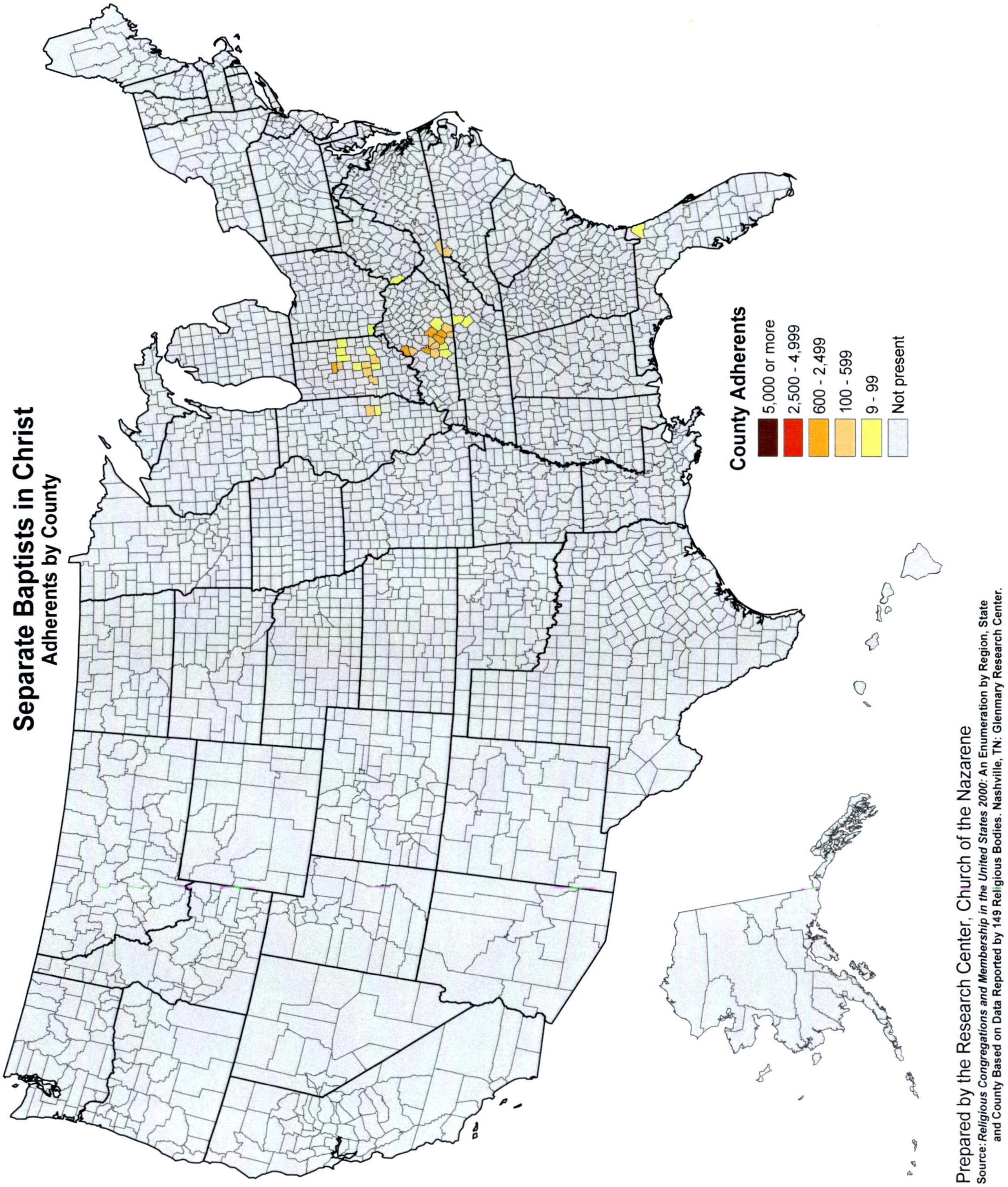
Separate Baptists in Christ
Adherents by County
County Adherents
5,000 or more
2,500 - 4,999
600 - 2,499
100 - 599
9 - 99
Not present
Prepared by the Research Center, Church of the Nazarene
Source: Religious Congregations and Membership in the United States 2000: An Enumeration by Region, State
and County Based on Data Reported by 149 Religious Bodies. Nashville, TN: Glenmary Research Center.

Primitive Baptist Churches—Old Line

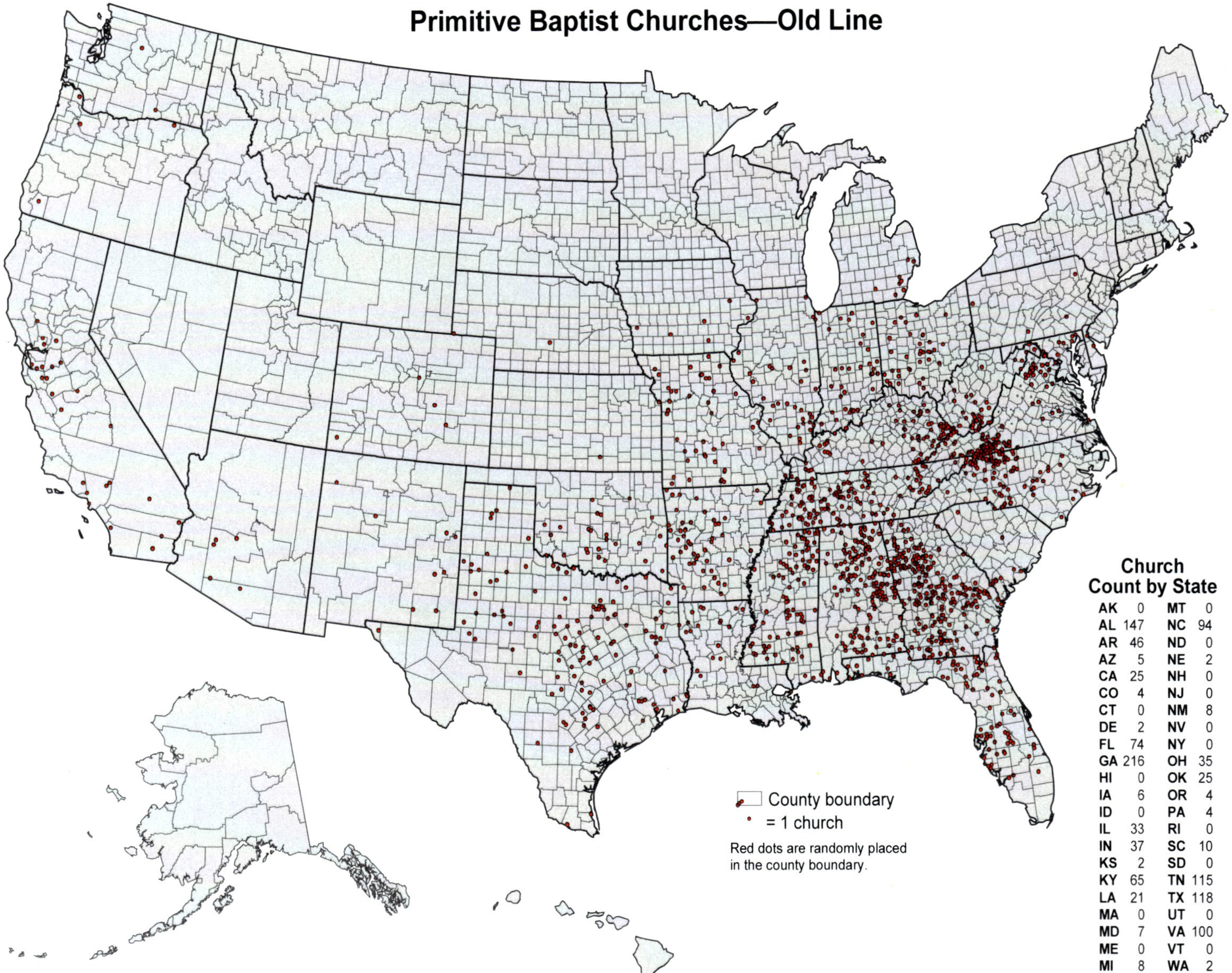

Church Count by State

AK	0	MT	0
AL	147	NC	94
AR	46	ND	0
AZ	5	NE	2
CA	25	NH	0
CO	4	NJ	0
CT	0	NM	8
DE	2	NV	0
FL	74	NY	0
GA	216	OH	35
HI	0	OK	25
IA	6	OR	4
ID	0	PA	4
IL	33	RI	0
IN	37	SC	10
KS	2	SD	0
KY	65	TN	115
LA	21	TX	118
MA	0	UT	0
MD	7	VA	100
ME	0	VT	0
MI	8	WA	2
MN	0	WI	0
MO	43	WV	36
MS	87	WY	0

Prepared by the Research Center, Church of the Nazarene

Source: ***Religious Congregations and Membership in the United States 2000:*** **An Enumeration by Region, State and County Based on Data Reported by 149 Religious Bodies. Nashville, TN: Glenmary Research Center.**